THE BEST OF MILT DUNNELL

Over 40 Years of Great Sportswriting

Edited by Robert Brehl

Foreword by Angelo Dundee

DOUBLEDAY CANADA LIMITED

CANADIAN CATALOGUING IN PUBLICATION DATA
Dunnell, Milt
The best of Milt Dunnell:
over 40 years of great sportswriting
ISBN 0-385-25433-4

1. Sports — Canada — History. 2. Athletes —
Canada. I. Brehl, Robert. II. Title.
GV585.D8 1993   796'.0971'09   C93-094461-5

Jacket and text design by Tania Craan
Printed on acid-free paper
Printed and bound in the USA

Published in Canada by
Doubleday Canada Limited
105 Bond Street
Toronto, Ontario
M5B 1Y3

To Cobi, Rita and Mary

CONTENTS

HOCKEY

FOOTBALL

MILT AT LARGE

HORSERACING

BOXING

BASEBALL

Foreword
by Angelo Dundee

For more than 30 years I've been getting Milt Dunnell to send me newspaper clippings whenever he wrote about any of my fighters. He's sent lots of clippings. I've had thousands of fighters and Milt has written about plenty of them.

Of course, he's written a helluva lot more about one of my fighters — Muhammad Ali — than any of the others. But I'll get to talking about Muhammad's relationship with Milt in a minute.

I wanted those columns because I wanted to know what Milt was thinking, what he was saying. Believe me, I wasn't the only one in the fight field who wanted to know what Milt was writing in *The Toronto Star*.

Let's face it, Milt was — and is — respected all over the boxing world, the entire sports world. Anybody who was anybody in the pugilist profession knew Milt Dunnell.

Milt and I first met back in the 1950s when I had a couple of fighters doing the route around Canada. I made a point of meeting Milt because he was the sports editor of the biggest newspaper in the country. And in this profession, you need people talking about your fighters. The worst thing is silence. If nobody mentions your fighter, you're in dead city.

Almost right away I knew there was something special about Milt. He fit into the boxing scene like a fist into a glove. He never interrupted the work going on inside a gym. He'd just go about his work. He was so smooth that you'd never feel like he was interviewing you, you were just having a chat.

I could tell, right from the start, that Milt knew a lot about boxing. No wonder. I found out later he had spent a lot of time over the years talking with the likes of Jack Dempsey, Gene Tunney, Joe Louis, Rocky Marciano, Sugar Ray Robinson and plenty of other world champions. I used to get my fighters to talk to him, not only for the publicity but also so they might learn a thing or two.

One fighter who loved talking to Milt was Muhammad Ali. Muhammad liked talking to almost anybody, but he really liked Milt. The champ enjoyed Milt's sense of humor and his knowledge of the "sweet science."

I remember a game Muhammad used to play sometimes when newspapermen would gather around in the gym and begin firing questions. The odd time the champ would turn it around or make like he was asking the questions. "Well, I don't know about that one," Muhammad would say. "Why don't you ask Milt Dunnell."

Sure, it was a game. But the champ thought a lot of Milt.

We had plenty of laughs up in Canada during our visits to fight George Chuvalo in '66 and '72. I remember having breakfast one morning with Milt before the fight in Vancouver in 1972. A whole crew ended up joining us at the hotel coffee shop — my brother, Chris, New York promoters Murray and Bob Goodman, local promoter Murray Pezim and Irving Ungerman, a guy who made a ton of dough in the chicken business and then saw the light and became a fight manager. I've always had a high regard for Ungerman; we're probably as good friends as enemies can be in this game.

But Ungerman kept yakking about how we were gonna pull something on him during the fight. He insisted the gloves weren't regulation so there was this big show when the gloves were weighed. He even accused Muhammad of holding Chuvalo in the first fight. This from a guy whose fighter threw so many low blows in the Toronto fight that Muhammad damn near had shin splits.

Anyway, that morning in Vancouver, Ungerman was going on about Muhammad obviously having a weight problem, from what he'd been reading in the papers. It was all B.S. because Ungerman is a great guy but he squawks a lot. So I made up some excuse about a mistake in converting Muhammad's weight from kilograms to pounds.

Now, at the best of times, when Ungerman and I get together

it can be confusing, this time especially. But Milt sorted through, somehow, and came up with a pretty funny column the next day about the kibitzing that goes on whenever two or more boxing folk are in the same room.

Years after Muhammad retired, he spotted Milt in an airport and went over to talk with him. I understand Milt was a bit surprised the champ recognized him. But Dunnell is not one you're likely to forget, even if you happen to be the greatest fighter who ever lived.

What makes Milt such a great sportswriter is that he sees past the game and into the people involved. He breaks down the intricate, and often complex, individuals of sport.

Milt is in the same league with great sportswriters like the late Red Smith. I know it and Muhammad knows it. People in Canada have been spoiled having Milt all to themselves for all these years.

It's a special delight for me to add my two cents to this book. Milt started writing his columns in 1949, one year after I got into this business. And for most of that time he's been like family to me. We've been all over the world together, from Manila to Zaire. And he's been writing about my life's love — boxing — better than anyone else I've ever read.

No doubt, Milt is one of the smartest newspapermen who ever took a sniff of resin, and from what I've read in his other columns, he knows a thing or two about rawhide, pigskin, horseflesh and hockey pucks, too.

Angelo Dundee

Acknowledgments

I would like to thank several people whose aid has been instrumental in helping me pull together this book. First and foremost, Milt Dunnell, both for writing so well for so long and for trusting me with the project; my father, Jack Brehl, for teaching me about writing and introducing me to Milt's column in the late 1960s; Carol Lindsay, Sonja Noble, Joanne Lima and the rest of *The Star*'s library staff for their invaluable help; Mike Pieri and Bob Crew of *The Star*'s special projects team for giving me a terrific opportunity; Domenic Battaglia in *The Star*'s dark room for help with the old photos; Paul Brehl, Steve Douglas, Todd Ladner and Eric Ladner for their terrific ideas and encouragement from the start; Gay Leno, perhaps Milt's greatest fan, for pictures and ideas; Susan Folkins, Maggie Reeves of Doubleday Canada and Tania Craan for making the book look so good; and lastly, my wife, Cobi, for temporarily becoming a sports widow but still providing indispensable help to me during this project. Thank you all.

Introduction

The keys on Milt Dunnell's typewriter are stamped with the memories of Canadian sports fans. For almost 45 years, Milt has been there, watching virtually every important sports event and then delighting readers of *The Toronto Star* with his observations. All told, he has written more than 11,000 columns and ten million words. Nearing age 88, Milt is still going strong, writing three columns a week.

He's seen it all: from Bobby Thomson's 1951 shot heard 'round the world to Devon White's marvelous catch in the first truly international World Series in 1992; from Rocket Richard and Gordie Howe leading their clubs into some of the great Stanley Cup battles of the 1950s to Wayne Gretzky playing maestro on the Edmonton Oilers of the mid-80s; from the fierce rivalry between Bud Grant's Blue Bombers and Jim Trimble's Tiger-Cats to Alouette Chuck Hunsinger and Argo Leon McQuay wearing Grey Cup goat's horns; from Northern Dancer's thrilling win in the Kentucky Derby to Secretariat's romp home to the Triple Crown at Belmont; from Rocky Marciano hanging them up at a perfect 49–0 to the rise and fall of the greatest of them all, Muhammad Ali.

Milt's career has taken him all across Europe and North America and to Russia, the Philippines, Australia and Africa. He has been at 42 consecutive Kentucky Derbys and more than 35 Stanley Cups, World Series and Grey Cups.

Besides longevity, Milt has a style, both in writing and in life, that makes him stand out. Speak with any of the famous people who know Milt — Sparky Anderson, Bobby Hull and Jack Kent Cooke and others — and most will use the word integrity. In fact, John Bassett, who owned the Argos, part of the Leafs and *The Toronto Telegram*, used to scoop his own sports

*Milt Dunnell and sons, Milt Jr. (*left*) and Mike, try to land a big one in 1949, just before Milt is named sports editor of* The Toronto Star. (PHOTO BY ALEX GRAY, COURTESY THE TORONTO STAR)

department by telling Milt things he wouldn't tell his own reporters. Asked later why he had so often given stories to a writer with the rival newspaper, Bassett once growled, "Well, why wouldn't I? He had great integrity and he was a great pal of mine. If I had a story today, I'd call Milt."

Milt was once described as having as many friends among the stable boys at Woodbine as he has in the box seats. This natural charm rubs off in his writing. His forte is giving a common man's touch to star-filled sports.

One of my favorite examples comes from a time when Gordie Howe and Bobby Hull ruled the NHL. Their teams, the Detroit Red Wings and Chicago Black Hawks, met in a critical playoff series and each side knew the key to victory was to shut down the other club's superstar.

Chicago's strategy was simple. Young, scrappy Eric Nesterenko was to shadow Howe, go everywhere he went: up and down the ice, in and out of corners. All the while, Nesterenko was to keep Old Elbows off the scoresheet. A daunting task. Though in his mid-30s by this time, Howe was still one tough son of a gun who could dish out the rough stuff and pop plenty of goals.

After it was over, Milt summed up the series in his daily column: "Nesterenko had more bruises than the Three Stooges." In one clear, concise sentence, sprinkled with humor, Milt cut to the essence of an entire playoff series. It was vintage Milt Dunnell, the dean of Canadian sportswriters.

What is so amazing is that he has been doing it daily in *The Toronto Star* since 1949. Here are a few more gems:

On Los Angeles committing six errors in Game Two of the 1966 World Series: "The Dodgers attack fly balls like drunks escaping from the paddy wagon."

On one of Muhammad Ali's opponents, Oscar Bonavena, who was a boxer with "all the grace, poise and finesse of a fat man in a sack race."

On Secretariat, the best racehorse Milt has ever seen: "Secretariat — the Thoroughbred of the Century in most gallop polls."

On Joe Frazier's inability to get swept into pre-fight hype the way Muhammad Ali could: "As a salesman, [Frazier] couldn't give away dynamite in Belfast."

On the lean years of the 1980s for Toronto hockey fans who continued to pack the Gardens night after night: "Leaf-loving is something like baldness. It's incurable and it gets passed along, from generation to generation."

Milt was born on 24 December 1905 in St. Marys, Ontario,

near Stratford. His career began at *The St. Marys Journal* before jumping to the big-city *Stratford Beacon Herald,* where he was sports editor when he left for *The Toronto Star* in 1942.

He took a respite from sports for a few years at *The Star* while serving in several different jobs before being named deputy sports editor in 1948 and then sports editor one year later.

Throughout the 1950s Milt wrote six columns a week, assigned stories to his staff and supervised the makeup of *The Star*'s sports pages when he wasn't traveling. It was such an incredibly heavy workload, even for Milt, that he dropped back to five columns a week in 1959. Through the 1960s he also was a regular panelist on CTV's "Sports Hot Seat" as well as a sports commentator on CHFI radio in Toronto.

In 1971, at age 65, Milt retired as editor, but continued writing five columns a week while following the big stories around the world. At the time, he tried to retire from writing, too, but he was talked out of it by *Star* Publisher Beland Honderich, whom Milt brought to the paper in 1943. Milt has attempted retirement several times and each time Honderich, now chairman of *The Star*'s parent company, Torstar, persuaded him to keep writing. In 1984, Milt actually did retire — for all of two months. But he came back, albeit cutting down to his current three columns a week.

Milt has been inducted into the Canadian Sports Hall of Fame, the Hockey Hall of Fame and the Canadian Football and Horseracing Halls of Fame. And he has received numerous civic and academic honors.

I grew up in Toronto cheering the Leafs, Argos and Blue Jays — and reading Milt Dunnell. Just as for many other sports fans, as for me Milt has always been a "must read." One frustrating thing about having four older brothers was always waiting for them to finish reading the sports section of *The Star.*

The idea for this book came about in the summer of 1992 while I was working with Mike Pieri and Bob Crew on *The Star*'s special projects team. All year, as part of the paper's centennial celebrations, *The Star* had been running flashback pages filled with old newspaper stories. One of my tasks was to dig up these old stories.

While in *The Star*'s library doing research one day, I began to see Milt's columns popping up on the microfilm. They were wonderful. It wasn't long before I started searching out his 1950s columns to read during breaks from other work.

The old microfilm was often out of focus, but the writing was sharp and clear. The columns were so good I felt they needed to be brought back to life, lifted from the reels of film in *The Star*'s morgue where only a handful of people have access to them.

Milt's vocabulary is varied (he's as likely to quote Shakespeare or Kipling as Casey Stengel) but there is one word he doesn't know: self-importance. Not one drop of self-importance runs through his veins. His reaction when I approached him about a book of his columns was typical.

Toronto mayor Art Eggleton presents Milt with the city's Award of Merit in 1991. He won the award for his work on numerous charity committees and his "great" columns over the years, the mayor said.
(PHOTO BY JEFF GOODE, COURTESY THE TORONTO STAR)

"No one would be interested," he said. I insisted plenty would be interested. A dozen friends polled informally about the idea had all said the same thing: "You mean a book of Milt's columns hasn't already been done? It should be."

Milt wasn't impressed. "Go ahead, but leave me out of it. I'm too old to get involved in something like that." He was 86 at the time. Milt also refused a share of the royalties. If the book made any money, his portion was to be forwarded to The Sportsmen's Corner of *The Star*'s Santa Claus Fund, which provides gifts and food for needy children at Christmas. Milt has collected money for the charity for 40 years.

After getting Milt's okay, I set out to collect his 11,000 columns. Some were on microfilm, others in separate microfiche files and the last eight years were stored in *The Star*'s computers. With the aid of researchers Renée Shute and Christina Yip, this harvesting took almost three months.

The next step was reading and selecting columns for a book. The most difficult part of the selection process was paring down the number of terrific columns to a manageable number. Reading through the stacks of columns was like panning for gold in a river with Hemlo as its source.

Though I am listed as "editor" of this book, that title applies to selecting columns, not editing Milt's words. His columns appear here exactly as they did in *The Star* over the past 44 years. Inevitably, the odd word or phrase may seem out of date today, but in many ways Milt's writing is ahead of its time.

Some columns were included because of the significance of the event: the Montreal riot after Rocket Richard was suspended from the 1955 playoffs; Northern Dancer's Derby; the Thrilla in Manila; the Blue Jays' opening day in 1977 and their World Series in 1992. Other columns were selected because they were just plain interesting: the Leafs reneging on their sale of Frank Mahovlich for one million dollars in 1962; Harold Ballard's vow to leave everything to charity when he died and Casey Stengel being fired after managing the Yankees to ten pennants in twelve years.

From Underwood typewriter to laptop computer, from the Polo Grounds to the SkyDome, Milt's writing has withstood the test of time and improved with age by giving us a look back at some of the great sporting people and events of almost half a century.

This book is a compilation of some of those magical moments and a tribute to a man who never fails to answer the bell.

Robert Brehl

HOCKEY

The Rangers couldn't use Howe

Gordie Howe was a special athlete, as witnessed by his skills in the batter's box. The story about the Red Wings jacket is legendary in hockey circles. This column appeared on 31 January 1951.

TORONTO — Jack Adams was watching the annual roundup of potential Red Wing pucksters and wondering how he was going to separate the sheep from the goats. He was startled out of his pondering by a big kid who shifted his stick from the right to the left, in order to get a better shot at the net.

"Who's the big switch-shooter?" Adams called to his little coach, Tommy Ivan. Tommy didn't know.

"What's your name, son?" Ivan asked the kid. "Name's Howe," the lad replied, "but um no relations to that guy." He pointed his stick in the direction of Syd Howe, a veteran of the Detroit club.

That was Adams' introduction to Gordon Howe, the then budding ice beauty out of Floral, Saskatchewan, via Saskatoon. Although he was impressed with the big homespun youngster, Adams would have laughed at the suggestion he'd be calling Howe his player of any era, within a comparatively few years. But that's how it's worked out. Adams argues that his big, likeable winger must be ranked with any of the best: Apps, Schmidt, Conacher, Cook or Morenz. And, of course, Adams has seen them all — and not from a seat in the grays.

It developed that young Howe had been around. At least, he

figured he had traveled a bit. The Rangers, he revealed, had taken a look at his hockey talents during a Winnipeg hockey school. But they didn't look long enough, according to the story young Howe told Adams. He said he got only about three minutes on the ice before they told him to pack. Back he went to Saskatoon, where the late Fred Pinkney, a scout for Detroit, spotted him eventually. That's how he landed at a Red Wings school.

Detroit sponsored Galt juniors at the time, and Adams decided he'd send his young switch-shooter there. He found Howe a reasonable kid when they talked money, but there was one stipulation Howe made: the Detroit club must provide him with one of those gaudy windbreakers with the crossed flags on each sleeve. Adams said he thought that could be arranged. But those were war years. Materials were scarce, and Adams forgot that part of the deal. He was reminded of it the following year, when he attempted to sign Gordie for the Omaha club of the

Detroit Red Wings famed Production Line, here in 1947, consisted of a young Gordie Howe (left), Sid Abel (center) and Ted Lindsay. (PHOTO BY ALEXANDER STUDIO, COURTESY THE TORONTO STAR)

United States league. He couldn't seem to get the kid excited over the prospect of turning pro.

"What's the trouble, don't you like your contract?" Adams finally asked. "Money's okay," Howe replied, "but what about that windbreaker from last year's contract?"

Late last season, when the Detroit Production Line was running one-two-three in the National league scoring derby, we mentioned to Howe that he stood a pretty good chance of shading his two mates, Ted Lindsay and Sid Abel.

"Shucks, that couldn't happen to me," Howe protested. "Looks like one of our line will win it, but it would have to be Sid or Ted."

As it turned out, Howe was right. Lindsay was first and Howe was third. But he shared in the boodle, by reason of a private agreement which the three Red Wings had made. If any pair of them were one-two in league scoring, the three grand in league and club prizes would be split three ways. By being third, Howe was the gunner who got in free. This season, he's looking like a shoo-in for the scoring title. It's up to Lindsay or Abel to make the runner-up slot. Then the three-way divvy will work again. If Howe should win it, with a "foreigner" like Max Bentley or Milt Schmidt finishing second, Howe would have to buy Lindsay and Abel $100 suits.

Adams tells this story to show that Howe generally is right: Lou Boudreau, the former manager of the Cleveland ball club, is a great friend of the Red Wings. He spends a lot of time with the Wings when he's in Detroit, and they visit him at the Detroit ball park. One day, after watching a game, Howe suggested he could hit big league pitching. Immediately, he became the victim of much needling by his hockey mates. Some of them told Boudreau, who went along with the gag.

"Lou came down to the rink and told Gordie he wanted to take him up on his offer to hit big league pitching," Adams recalled. "Gordie said it was all right with him, so away we go to the ball park. Lou dug up a uniform for Gordie. The rest of us sat in the stands to see the fun."

The pitcher Boudreau selected was Sam Zoldak. According

to Adams, his first three or four pitches were fouled off by Howe. Gordie lined the next two to the outfield. Like a good artist, he knew when to quit. Having proved his point, he tossed away the bat.

A legend between two little incidents

The respect and admiration Milt held for the late Lionel Conacher, who died suddenly after a softball game on Parliament Hill, comes through on 27 May 1954. Rarely over the years has Milt used the word "we" — and never the word "I" — because it places him inside a column, instead of being a distant observer. But in this tribute to the Big Train, Milt becomes part of the story and even mentions his hometown of St. Marys, Ontario.

TORONTO — The first time we saw Lionel Conacher, he was leaning on the handle of a field lacrosse stick on the velvety old flats between the river and the mill race at St. Marys. A ruckus had arisen between a couple of the local beloved Alerts and a corresponding number of villains from the visiting Toronto seniors. The Alerts were intermediates, and it was good for their ego, not to mention the sale of tickets, when they could knock off one of the Toronto top-drawer clubs in the traditional holiday exhibitions. Oftimes, it was necessary to knock on a few noggins, in addition. This was in process while Conacher watched with detached interest. It wasn't his fight, so he kept out of it. His attitude was misunderstood by the town tough guy, who hurdled the single strand of rope surrounding the field and challenged Conacher with a "Hey, you yellow —." It took a few minutes for the tough guy's buddies to drum up courage to lug away the carcass of their idol. Conacher had flattened him with one punch. Thirty minutes later, he managed to mumble: "The dirty so-and-so kicked me." Bill Lavelle, a reinstated pro who played for the home side, overheard the remark. He told the fallen muscle man: "You're lucky this guy didn't get sore. He's Lionel Conacher."

The last time we saw Conacher, he was sitting in a steamy dressing-room of the Montreal Forum on a stormy night last winter. Stripped to the waist, he brooded, with chin on his chest, because the Ontario clan of the National Hockey League Old Timers had lost a charity game to the Quebec division. He was disconsolate, too, because he hadn't been able to score, although he had spent much more time on the ice than his admirers considered advisable. In between those first and last times we saw him, a legend in the Canadian way of life had been woven. Looking back on that dressing-room scene, it's easier to understand the legend. It didn't matter that he had been acclaimed, almost by unanimous vote, as Canada's athlete of the first half-century, that he had gathered considerable personal wealth, that his fellow-Canadians had elected him to Parliament. All he knew at the moment was that his side had lost. The fact he was over 50 years of age, and that his amazing legs had lost their piston-like drive, in his book was no excuse for failure.

A benevolent Providence had endowed Conacher with physical blessings such as are bestowed on few humans. But it was pride which powered the Big Train, an international symbol of greatness in athletics. This was demonstrated on many occasions — but never more strikingly than in professional hockey. The Big Train was waived from the big league. No club was interested. The word was out that he had developed a fondness for whiskey.

Milt has as much respect for the great Lionel Conacher as any athlete he's seen. Pictured here in 1933 with the Chicago Black Hawks, the team Conacher led to the Stanley Cup that year, the Big Train also played football, baseball and lacrosse, and was named Canada's greatest athlete in the first 50 years of this century. (COURTESY THE TORONTO STAR)

His answer is in the record books. The sidetracked Big Train roared back to captain two successive Stanley Cup winners in two different cities — something that never had been done before and probably never will be done again. He became known as a rigid tee-totaller. Tommy Gorman, who was his manager on those championship teams, recalled that amazing comeback while mourning Conacher's passing, early this morning.

"I had bought both Conacher and Roy Worters from the old Pittsburgh club in 1928, when I was managing the New York

Americans," Gorman explained. "When I went to Mexico to manage a race-track, Lionel succeeded me as manager of the Americans. Later, he went to Montreal Maroons. That's where he was when I came back from Mexico to take over the Chicago Black Hawks. I got him for Chicago by arranging a deal in which I gave up Teddy Graham.

"Lionel did all the work for me that season — it was 1933–34 — when we won the Stanley Cup with the Black Hawks. His knees were shot. We had to tape and double-tape them. The very next season, I switched to Maroons, and I told Major McLaughlin, who owned the Hawks, I wanted Lionel to go with me. McLaughlin wouldn't hear of it. But Lionel told him he would shoot the puck into his own net if Chicago didn't make a deal for him. The result was one of hockey's biggest swaps, involving three clubs. Howie Morenz, Lorne Chabot, Marty Burke, Roger Jenkins, Leroy Goldworthy and Nels Crutchfield all figured in it. I wound up with Conacher — and the Stanley Cup again. Lionel won it for me."

Harold Cotton, now commissioner in search of talent for the Boston Bruins, likes to tell how Conacher amazed US football coaches when the Big Train and Cotton sought book learning and football berths at a school in Pittsburgh. The Yanks agreed that Conacher could be a stick-out in their game, just as he was on Canadian gridirons. It was that way in every sport the Big Train tackled. Ron McAllister, the mike man and biographer, told one story which illustrated Conacher's football prowess. At a banquet in Montreal, he said, a veteran coach was asked to pick an all-Canadian football squad. He said: "Give me Lionel Conacher and Joe Wright, Sr., when both were in their prime. Throw in ten Boy Scouts to hold their coats and make the team legal."

The big fellow had color to go with his ability. Often the combination is lacking. That was the quality which impressed Conn Smythe, himself a showman extraordinaire. Conacher, he had noted, always did things in the grand manner. It was a throw-back to his earliest days in sport, when he would dash from a lacrosse field to a baseball diamond — changing uniforms as he roared across town in a taxi. He'd wind up the day by playing hockey.

Gorman remembered a day in Chicago when Conacher was guest star at a sports forum in a huge department store. A spectator asked: "Was Jack Dempsey a good boxer?" Conacher replied: "He must have been; he went three rounds with Conacher." The spectator figured he was being ribbed. But it was true. Lionel had fought the Mauler in an exhibition. On the subject of the Big Train, the truth always will be better than fiction.

It couldn't happen? It could — in Montreal

It took guts for Clarence Campbell to suspend Rocket Richard for the entire 1955 playoffs. Richard had injured a Bruin with his stick and punched out a linesman. Montreal lost the 1955 final in seven games to Detroit. The next year, the Canadiens began a string of five straight Stanley Cups. Had they had Richard in 1955, surely it would have been six in a row. This column ran 18 March 1955.

TORONTO — Memo to Montreal: How close to cowtown can a big city get? We send a staffer, one Jim (Shakey) Hunt, to cover the impeachment of Rocket Richard. And we assure Hunt, who has homing pigeon instincts, that it's a job which will take a few hours. Then he can swing his way back via TCA. But so many supposedly sane Montreal citizens threaten to kill Clarence Campbell, the National Hockey League president, for doing something he should have done months ago — namely, heave Monsieur Rocket out on his ear — that we're forced to tell Hunt he had better stick around for the game with Detroit last night. Civilized people couldn't possibly carry out the threats which were made against Campbell. But then civilized folks don't make that kind of threat. So you never can tell. Just in case there are that many kooks in Montreal, we also ship out rough-and-ready Frank Teskey, a reporter-photographer, to team up with Hunt. It's a routine assignment, lads. Nice chance to see the two best teams in the NHL. You both can take the night train home. Riot? Attempts to harm Campbell? Shucks, you know how those things turn out. It probably will be the tamest and dullest game of the year.

So, Hunt calls about 10:00 p.m. Game has been forfeited to the Red Wings because the Montreal authorities fear someone will get killed. Our man is still in the Forum. Can't get out. Neither can the Red Wings. Nor a good number of the fans. Hoodlums outside are knocking the glass out of the building. The league president has been punched and pelted. Never saw such disgraceful goings-on in his life, our reporter says. Before he went wrong and switched to the sports beat, he used to cover strikes, riots and things like that. It was nice and peaceful, compared to this.

Then Teskey calls. Still choking from tear gas. That routine assignment was as uneventful as a world war. He still can't believe it happened. But he saw it with his own eyes and got a snootful of gas up his own nose.

This will be called a dark day for hockey, and the day hockey got a black eye. Those are phrases which seem to pop from the typewriters on occasions such as this. Actually, it's neither. It's no more the fault of hockey when a mob of morons goes on the rampage than it was the fault of soccer when those knuckleheads in South America tried to shoot the referee. The Montreal Canadiens are one of the finest organizations in

Blood streams down the face of Maurice "Rocket" Richard as he exchanges handshakes with Boston goalie Sugar Jim Henry after Montreal won the 1953 Stanley Cup. It was against the same Boston team that Rocket's violent play earned him a suspension from the 1955 playoffs, which touched off the infamous Montreal riot.
(COURTESY THE TORONTO STAR)

professional sport. Their product is the best in the business, and they attempt to dispense it in a setting that's big league. They suffer more than anyone else if the roughneck element barges in and breaks up their show. And we'd like to wager there were very few regular Forum customers involved in last night's rowdyism. Hunt mentioned that a bunch of demonstrators had crashed the gate. The ones who assembled outside the Forum obviously were hoodlums, rather than fans. A fan doesn't bum around outside the rink if he has a ticket that will take him inside. So, it's Montreal that gets the black eye — not the club nor the game.

It's easy to say that Campbell should have stayed home from last night's contest, in view of the tension which had built up over the Richard case. The Habs, themselves, felt it would relieve the pressure if Campbell didn't attend. Actually, the fanatics of Montreal left him no choice. He had to be at the Forum in order to retain his self-respect. There was no reason to expect he could look for courtesy from the Montreal crowd. But he was entitled to police protection against assault. He didn't get that, either, despite the fact every paper and every radio station in Canada had carried reports of the threats on his life.

By this time the league must be convinced its head office should be moved from Montreal. The town is too small — in its thinking, that is. Only hick towns do the things that happened in Montreal last night.

P.S. to Hunt and Teskey: Gas masks shipped for Saturday night's game.

He can't read
the calendar

Like an alkaline battery, Gordie Howe lasted a long
time and just kept getting better and better. This
column ran 10 May 1963.

TORONTO — Away back in the early part of the Fat Fifties,
Jack Adams, who was running the Red Wings, used to say:
"You don't have to tell me Howe is great. But you haven't seen
anything yet. Wait until Howe is 30."

Adams was just like all shinny men — impatient. He couldn't
wait for a boy to mature properly. What Adams must have
meant was: "Wait until Howe is 40." This big switch-shooter,
Gordie Howe, is a slow developer. He's 35 already — and you
can't even be sure he has reached his potential. Wait until he's
50. He'll be holding the Hart trophy in his hamlike hands —
sure as CCM makes hockey skates.

Howe won the Hart for the sixth time today, as has been
mentioned in dispatches. As if you didn't know, the Hart is the
Oscar of the puck-shooting profession. It means you're the top
man on the totem pole. The symbol fits Howe perfectly. He's
also the Atlas who carries the world of the Detroit Red Wings
on his back. If he ever shrugs his shoulders and throws off the
burden, the Detroit Olympia will be in danger of becoming a
discount market.

There's a touch of irony in the fact that Howe has the Hart
— and the scoring title — and the all-star right wing berth this
spring. In 1958, when Rocket Richard nudged him off the first

string all-stars, Adams used the Rocket's advanced years as a needle with which to jab Gordie.

"I'm disappointed you didn't make the first all-stars at right wing," Adams heckled, "especially when I see a man there who is 35 years of age. If I didn't win it myself, I'd hate to admit it was a 35-year-old who beat me out."

Now, at an equivalent age, Howe wins just about every award except the door prize. Before the frost is on the pumpkin next fall, he's almost sure to rub the Rocket's most treasured record out of the log book. Richard scored 544 goals, in regular league play, during his fabulous career. The guessing was that the mark would stand until some genius introduces the 100-game schedule. Howe is up to 540 goals. All he needs is a new season to become the all-time champion shooter.

Why does Howe hit a six-year peak — his best since 1957 — when other veterans are hanging on by their toenails? There are several reasons, but two will do: One, Howe is more relaxed — almost casual — than any other top-flight pro. Pressure is something he puts on his stick. For him, there is no other kind. Two, Howe is powerfully built and has such an effortless glide that he hasn't burned out his motor. He's like Charley Gehringer used to be when he played second base for the Tigers. They used to say Gehringer made the job look so easy that people forgot he was on the ball club.

Although Howe has been hurt badly — almost got killed in his famous 1950 crash with Teeder Kennedy — he's as durable as the Caledon Hills. He went 382 consecutive games before he missed a league match. That was in the fall of 1954, when he suffered a shoulder injury at Maple Leaf Gardens. The brain concussion and fractured jaw which resulted from the Kennedy collision actually did not break his service streak, because that accident occurred in the playoffs.

Emotionally, Howe is the ideal type for his profession. He's completely incapable of self-pity. Shortly after Sid Abel took over as coach of the Wings, he fined every member of the club $100 after the team turned in a shabby performance.

Howe should have been hot over the injustice inflicted by his buddy, Old Bootnose. After all the great games he had played over the years, surely Howe was entitled to one bad one. He couldn't dredge up a tear for himself. His reaction was that he sorrowed for Old Bootnose, whose clowns had disgraced him.

Another time, when the Leafs and the Red Wings were engaging in one of their old-fashioned playoff tong wars, Adams deliberately put the blast on Howe, Ted Lindsay and Marty Pavelich. The general tone of Jack's criticism was that several of his stars seemed to be more immersed in their personal business affairs than they were in the playoffs.

The volatile Lindsay almost exploded with indignation. Which was understandable. Howe accepted it for what it really was: An attempt by Adams to stir up his troops. Howe vented his resentment on the Leafs. That was all Adams wanted.

Although he's the toughest *hombre* in the rinks — he also has been accused of being one of the better hatchet hands — Howe carries no grudges, builds up no feuds. He claims his motto is to live and let live. Nor does he plague himself with personal goals and targets — barring one. He wants to play twenty seasons of big league hockey. That means three more. Only lightning can stop him.

Best shot came from a needle

Milt captured the emotion on 24 April 1964 of Bobby Baun's famed "drugstore goal" in overtime against the Red Wings.

DETROIT — The pen, of course, is mightier than the sword. So is the needle. After the Torontos and the Detroits had duelled to the verge of complete exhaustion last night, it took a few cc's of a local anesthetic to turn the tide of battle in favor of the sweaty horde from Hogtown on the Humber.

The name of the magic fluid shall remain unmentioned — for fear somebody tries it on a racehorse and it shows up in the saliva test. In that event, the stewards would hold up the purse and suspend the trainer.

Injected into Bobby Baun's ankle, the stuff practically changed the course of history. Instead of being the first big league shinny club in fifteen years to get rubbed out by a fourth-place team in the final scramble for Lord Stanley's tinware, the Leafs could be the first since the invention of the puck to win the old cuspidor for three-year spans in two different eras.

Maybe that sounds like being the first left-handed Eskimo to get his right hand frozen twice on Baffin Island. However, it is much better than getting kicked in the face with a stiff boot — and that's what was happening to the Leafs when the needle was jabbed into Baun's ankle.

Things started getting rough for our heroes about 15:56 of the second period. It was at that point that Gordie Howe dumped the puck into the Leaf net while our Mr. Tim Horton lay flat on his back just inside the Leaf blue line.

This was a greater outbreak of intrigue than the uprising in Zanzibar. Parker MacDonald of the Wings rapped Horton briskly with his stick behind the knees as he moved over to meet the challenge from Howe. Tim went down like a keg of nails falling off a hardware truck.

With the whole right side of the Toronto defence thus torn open, Howe had no trouble in scoring the goal which gave the Wings a 3–2 margin. Horton appealed in vain for justice to prevail — but justice was blind.

"While I was in the air I looked over and saw that (referee) Buffey was watching," Horton related later. "Naturally, I expected a penalty on the play. I can fall on my rump often enough, without getting help from Parker MacDonald."

Billy Harris, revelling in his parole from custody on the end of the Leaf bench, tied the score again at 17:48 of the period. When the teams left the ice for a siesta, the Leafs were in a most favorable position. Albert Langlois of the Wings still had one minute and 45 seconds to serve in a penalty.

But strange are the moods and fatigues that affect athletes. When the warriors returned to the ice, you had to look twice to see whether the Leafs had brought their skates with them. They were dying in their tracks. Aside from Bob Pulford, Baun and possibly one or two others, the seats of their pantaloons were dragging.

When Baun was hauled off on a stretcher at 13:14, the only thing that remained to be decided was whether services for the Leafs should be public or private. Word reached the press box that Baun's right ankle was sprained or broken. In five minutes, he was back.

This led to a rumor that Jim Murray, the Leaf doctor, had hacked a leg off Eddie Shack and changed Baun's flat tire. As it turned out, Baun's ankle merely had been frozen. It's just possible the puck was given an injection, too. When Baun fired it from the Detroit blue line, after only one minute and 43 seconds of overtime, the old biscuit did some strange things.

One witness was Mr. William Gadsby, who is described as an

old resident. Mr. Gadsby said the thing was spinning like a drunk in a revolving door. As it neared him, Mr. Gadsby said, the infernal thing dived at him. He fled, but it skipped off the handle of his shillelagh. Next thing he knew, it had hopped past Terry Sawchuk and was high in the net.

Mr. Sawchuk was interviewed, too — but everything he said was unprintable. This will become known to posterity as the drugstore goal. Now, if the Leafs can just transplant a new ankle on Baun before Saturday night, they may be guests at a champagne party. Now that his own ankle has thawed out, it probably won't be good enough.

Conn Smythe nixed Norris deal

One of the most astonishing hockey stories of the 1960s was Harold Ballard selling Frank Mahovlich for one million dollars in 1962. The deal was ultimately nixed and more information came out when Chicago owner Jim Norris died in February 1966.

TORONTO — A whim of fate decreed that Frank Mahovlich should score his 250th goal as a Leaf, a few hours after funeral services for the man who almost spent a million bucks to make him a Black Hawk.

Not more than three or four persons actually knew the real story of what happened between the Leafs and Jim Norris, the night he bought the Big M for more money than ever was paid for one athlete. Because the main participants had been into the grape, following a shinny dinner, it was logical to shrug off the whole affair as an alcoholic publicity stunt.

It wasn't that. But for Conn Smythe, who built the Gardens and organized the Leafs, the Big M would have become a Black Hawk and the new Gardens group would have pocketed a million dollars.

The deal was made by Harold Ballard, representing the Gardens, and Norris. Both had been fortified by the gargle. Conn Smythe first heard of it after midnight when he received a call at home from Bruce Norris, Jim's brother.

Bruce was concerned on a couple of counts. One, he felt Jim was being taken; and two, as owner of the Detroit Red Wings,

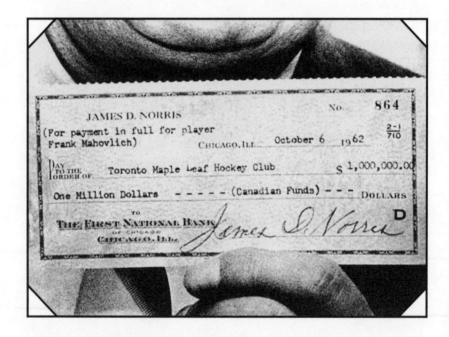

Chicago Black Hawks owner Jim Norris was prepared to follow through on the alcohol-induced purchase of the Big M from Toronto for an unheard of one million in 1962, as this check delivered to Maple Leaf Gardens proves. But the Leafs backed out of the deal struck with then Vice-President Harold Ballard. (COURTESY THE TORONTO STAR)

he didn't want to see the Black Hawks get Mahovlich to go along with Bobby Hull. That would have given Hawks more firepower on the left side than a battery of anti-tank guns.

"Find Stafford (Smythe) and have him call me," the elder Smythe instructed. An hour later, Bruce Norris called again. He hadn't been able to locate Smythe's son. Meanwhile, the story of the sale had gone out to every newspaper and radio station on the continent. *The Chicago Tribune* gave it front page, top headline billing.

It was 3:00 a.m. when Staff Smythe finally contacted his father, who asked whether it was true that Mahovlich had been sold to the Hawks. Staff confirmed the deal — and proceeded to get a lecture from his old man. Conn Smythe, a long-time friend of Norris, made two shattering points: No player was worth a million dollars, so they had taken advantage of the whiskey to make a sale. If the Leafs were lucky enough to have a player for whom that kind of money was offered, he belonged in Toronto — not in Chicago.

Stafford Smythe readily agreed with his father's arguments. He informed Ballard the deal would have to be washed out. Norris, meanwhile, had gone to bed, believing he had bought a hockey player.

In the cold light of dawn, he might not have been as enthusiastic about it as he was during the previous night's conviviality. However, he was committed, coast to coast. He knew nothing of the intervention by Conn Smythe and Bruce Norris.

So he made out his check for a million bucks and sent his general manager, Tommy Ivan, to the Gardens with it. Stafford Smythe rejected the check, with the blunt explanation to one sports writer: "We never rolled a drunk yet and we don't have to start now."

Almost a week later, sportscaster Joe Morgan announced the deal would go through after all. Morgan had discovered that Gardens directors had asked Staff Smythe to determine whether Jim Norris still wanted to get rid of his million dollars.

If he did, they were in favor of proceeding. It was pointed out that a million dollars was equal to almost a total season's take for hockey. After a respectable drying-out period, the alcoholic content of the negotiations was negligible.

Morgan assumed Norris still would buy. That was the only respect in which he was mistaken. King Clancy, who was sent to Chicago to inquire whether the market place had been closed, returned with word that it was no dice. Norris was off the hook. He was in no mood to get on again.

Conn Smythe came in for some mumbled criticisms from a few Gardens directors. Their beef was that the Little Pistol had received a good price for his Gardens stock. Having sold out, he shouldn't try to dictate Gardens policy. However, they agreed it was difficult to disagree with his logic.

Mahovlich also received a frantic call from his father. The elder Mahovlich said: "You've been sold to Chicago for a million dollars. Make sure somebody pays for moving your furniture."

Leaf deal is no deal

At eighteen, Bobby Orr already had many seasoned hockey men gushing. This column appeared 20 February 1967. Unfortunately, the prediction on the final line did not come to fruition.

TORONTO — Leighton (Unhappy) Emms, whose Boston Bruins seem determined to clutter up the NHL cellar from which he booted them last year, in his first season as a big league general manager, sounded both caustic and resigned.

"The only way to make a deal with the Toronto Maple

Leafs," Emms sniffed, "is to give up Gilles Marotte or Bobby Orr for two unidentified juniors. That's their idea of a trade. I've got news for them and everything else. Neither of those players leaves Boston."

Admittedly, Emms has some livestock that would be leaving if he could find a destination for it — at terms which he considered fitting and proper. With that lofty purpose in mind, he had been trailing the Toronto club for weeks. Since the Leafs were losing ten in a row at the time, more thoughtful observers wondered why he would want any of them. He had enough losing players of his own.

"At one stage, they (the Leafs) told us there were only three untouchables on the club," Hap recalled, by way of explaining why he had pursued the Leafs like a hungry bailiff.

He didn't identify the three, but it would be easy to guess they were Frank Mahovlich, Dave Keon and Ron Ellis. All the others were supposed to be sitting on the sales lot, like beat-up jalopies.

"But when we tried to talk trade," Emms lamented, "the names of Orr and Marotte came up immediately. I have come to the conclusion that it just isn't possible to make a deal with Toronto."

Stafford Smythe, chancellor of the exchequer at Maple Leaf Gardens, confirmed and refuted what Emms had said — in a single sentence. Asked what he thought would be a fair exchange for Orr, Smythe said bluntly: "Our whole hockey club."

This was after Orr, the 18-year-old from Parry Sound by way of Oshawa, had packed all the attributes of Eddie Shore (the player, not the executive), King Clancy (the player, not the coach) and Doug Harvey (the player, not the businessman) into a single game of shinny.

So Smythe, like everyone else in the Gardens, was in a mood to over-value Orr, if that's possible. Orr did everything but carry the Bruins on his back. They still got defeated.

Hap Emms is right, of course. If he ever traded Orr — even for the whole Leaf cadre, as Smythe suggested — it would be necessary to hang Emms by the neck on the Boston Commons. This would be a sorry spectacle, because any man guilty of dealing away Orr obviously would be off his rocker — therefore not responsible for his actions.

There's no guessing how good this guy may get. He does so many things like an experienced pro that it's easy to forget he's a novice. As Allan Stanley, who is old enough to be his father, said: "He skates, he shoots, he makes the plays. There doesn't seem to be anything he can't do now."

Bobby's coach, Harry Sinden, is somewhat resentful that the kid was not elected to the first all-star team at the halfway mark of the schedule. He was picked for the second squad. Which was quick recognition for a rookie.

"If he isn't on the first team at the end of the season you're going to hear some screaming from Boston," Sinden promised. "Orr has played 35 to 40 games for us that were every bit as good as the one you saw tonight. When he's off his game, he's merely great. When he's on his game, he's super."

Orr was omitted from the perfectos who played the Montreal Canadiens in the all-star game at Montreal last month. The reason given was that he played junior hockey last season. It was unthinkable to have him among the superbas. And it also was unthinkable to leave him at home in favor of chaps who couldn't carry his school books.

It's inconsequential because Orr is destined to win just about every prize in the catalog before he's through with hockey. He will start with the Calder (rookie) trophy this season. That's strictly no contest. The NHL should give it to him now. It would provide an excuse for a "night" in Boston.

Ron Stewart, a man who mixes humor with hockey had a cheering thought for Boston fans, who haven't had a super-star since Milt Schmidt was in full flower.

"Just think," Stewart said, discussing Orr, "this guy has another 25 years to go."

The sentimental side of Punch

The Leafs' "Over the Hill Gang" had one last fling with glory during the Original Six era's swan song. It was May 1967, and expansion would overrun and dilute hockey for several years to come. Milt captured the moment with an interesting look at Punch Imlach and his gang. It was Toronto's last Stanley Cup to date.

TORONTO — Punch Imlach, the Peerless Leader of the Leafs, is said to have ice water for blood and a paving stone for a heart. In other words, Punch supposedly is as warm and kindly and considerate — according to the charts — as a Moscow cop's handcuffs.

That being the case, he was out of character last night. With all the marbles in the ring, Punch revealed himself as a sentimental creampuff. Before the game, he made a speech in which he said some of his warriors would be playing their last game as members of the club.

"Some of you have been with me for nine years," he went on. It would be nice to say there wasn't a dry eye in the room but it wouldn't be quite right. Several of the serfs fingered their whip scars and waited suspiciously for what would come next.

"It has been said that I stuck with the old men so long we couldn't possibly win the Stanley Cup. For some of you it's a farewell. Go out there and put that puck down their (the Canadiens') throats."

Imlach then pointed at a somewhat startled Johnny Bower,

the elder statesman of shinny, and told him he was to dress in full regalia and sit on the bench.

Johnny, who confesses to being 42 — but never under oath — would have squatted on the time clock in a bikini if Imlach had asked — and especially if it would improve his chances of collecting the winners' end of the loot.

But Bower had spent the last five days ducking doctors who sought to punch needles through his leathery hide as treatment for a muscle which popped during the pre-game warmup last Thursday night. There was no chance he could go in goal if Terry Sawchuk got hurt.

"You won't be asked to play, but be there," Imlach roared. Al Smith, a third goalie who is too young (21) to be considered seriously by the Leafs for about fifteen years yet, was dressed and stashed away in the television room.

Thereupon, one of the elders — a member of the probable departing patriarchs — skated out and robbed the Habs of everything but their underwear. The Canadiens are not discouraged easily. Otherwise Terry Sawchuk would have broken their hearts before the game was fifteen minutes old. He did almost as many impossible things as he did in Chicago the day the Leafs ambushed the Black Hawks — and as he did in Montreal last Saturday afternoon.

This was the same Sawchuk who couldn't stop a porcupine with a pike pole last Thursday night. Frustrated fans had applauded derisively when he cleared a loose puck from the side of the cage. It was the kind of encouragement Dick Stuart, the Old Stonefingers of baseball, used to receive when he picked up a gum wrapper that was blowing across the infield.

"I got mad," Sawchuk admitted last night. "I got mad at myself."

That was when the Montreal Canadiens commenced their slide into oblivion, although they didn't realize it at the time. They thought they were lucky getting rid of Bower, who had allowed only two goals out of 94 shots which the Habs fired at him in two games.

After last night's crushing defeat, the Habs were saying: "First Bower — then Sawchuk. But we might have expected it. They're

The great storyteller, King Clancy, Maple Leafs
vice-president of anything, spreads his blarney with
Milt Dunnell in Boston, April 1972.
(PHOTO BY FRANK LENNON, COURTESY THE TORONTO STAR)

both old pros. And look at Gump (Worsley) in our net. He hadn't played a full game since March 12. Yet he was great."

Thus, the Stanley Cup carnival just ended may become known as the mardi gras of the condemned. Some of the outstanding performers were men who will be marked for exile to the six new expansion clubs — strictly on the basis of age.

Who was better than Sawchuk — just for openers? He put the Leafs into the final round by killing off Chicago. Then he bailed out the good guys with two key wins after Bower got hurt. He's 37.

Bower is 40-plus. Red Kelly, Allan Stanley, Marcel Pronovost and George Armstrong all are getting extremely long in the tooth. Kelly definitely played his final game as a Leaf. It was his best since the playoffs began.

"There will be something within a day or two," the old redhead promised last night when he was asked about his future plans. It has been practically an accepted thing that Kelly would be named coach at Los Angeles, although no official approach has been made to the Leafs.

Sawchuk denies a story that he would ask to be returned to Detroit. Stanley has no retirement thoughts and no coaching plans. He would like to be back. Sawchuk probably feels the same way. Armstrong, too.

Imlach, though, left them all wondering with this Old Boys' reunion stunt. They probably are wishing he hadn't gone soft and sentimental. Why couldn't he have been his snarly, chilly, impatient, normal self?

From net to Nader: Dryden's program

There has always been much more to Ken Dryden than just hockey. He became the first — and likely only — player to win the Conn Smythe Trophy as the play-offs MVP before he won the Calder as rookie-of-the-year in the next season. He was the reason heavily favored Boston went down and he also played a major part in defeating Bobby Hull and the Black Hawks in the final. This column ran 12 May 1971.

MONTREAL — It was inevitable that the man who discovered the flaws in Boston's relentless shinny machine should line up with Ralph Nader, the man who was the first to say that Detroit's tailpipes were porous.

In a way, Ken Dryden, the learned goaler from Cornell, was even more effective than Nader might have been in similar circumstances. What if the big automobile builders did have to recall a few thousand cars? When Dryden dealt with the Bruins, he left them stone cold dead on the Boston Common.

Now, he has been invited to join the Nader organization when he takes his summer retreat from the Montreal Canadiens, the McGill law school and the million or more fans who want his autograph.

"It's going to depend on whether I can get a working visa," Dryden reported while cooling out after the Habs had put something that approximated a death chill on the Chicago Black Hawks.

Normally, in a hockey club's dressing room, the post-game conversation concerns the phenomenon that a referee, who has been blessed with perfect eye-sight, should become completely myopic the moment he steps on ice.

Another standard topic is whether home ice actually is a factor for professionals who spend at least 50 per cent of their time in foreign buildings. Al MacNeil who coaches the Habs doesn't pretend to know for sure. He puts the question on a personal preference basis: "If I had the privilege of saying whether the extra game of the series should be at home or away, I'm sure it wouldn't be in Chicago."

In Dryden's corner of the cluttered diggings, the discussion dealt with the welfare of the war veteran who returns from the rice paddies of Indo-China and is turned loose in a society that is plagued by inflation, unemployment and pollution.

"That's the program on which I would be working for Nader," Dryden revealed. "It's a fascinating subject. From what I am able to see, the military leaves them pretty much alone. If I get that working visa, I will be looking into it."

Dryden, who has derricked his law books pending a decision in the case of the Habs versus the Hawks for Lord Stanley's old hardware, has given little thought to his future.

He almost certainly could spend the next twelve to fifteen years tending goal at a handsome stipend. It's most unusual for a young fellow to launch his big league career in the Stanley Cup circus.

That's roughly what Dryden did. He had played half-a-dozen games for the Habs during the season. Any respectable bookmaker would have quoted you at least fifteen to one that he wouldn't be tending store when the Habs took on Boston.

But that is what happened. If the Habs should be successful in regaining the Stanley Cup, it wouldn't be surprising if Dryden emerged with (a) the Dodge car offered by *Sport Magazine*; (b) the Conn Smythe Trophy as the most valuable man in the playoffs; and (c) a more lucrative contract.

That wouldn't be bad for a man who brushed off the Canadiens, in favor of Canada's national team, when he first came out of Cornell. It wasn't until the Nationals went belly-up that the Canadiens finally collared him. Sam Pollock, shrewd managing director of the Habs, should see that a fresh rose is placed each day on the last resting place of the Nationals.

"It wasn't that I was against pro hockey," Dryden is careful to explain. "What I wanted most was the opportunity to study law. The best chance seemed to be if I played for the national team.

"After the Nationals folded, the Canadiens made it possible for me to continue my studies while I played pro hockey. That removed the objection. Now, I'm in the position where the area I know most about is hockey."

The Boston Bruins will endorse that opinion. If there were any dissenters among the Black Hawks, they were converted rather quickly.

In the interest of accuracy, though, it should be said the Black Hawks have been something less than impressive while blowing their two-game cushion at the Forum.

They lost their momentum, their poise and their cool along with their commanding margin. Worse still, coach Billy Reay seems to have run out of good luck charms.

In the first game at Chicago, he unveiled towering Rick Foley. Just about everything Rick did was right. He helped turn the tide in favor of the Chicagos.

It didn't work here. Foley put a perfect pass on Yvan Cournoyer's stick for Montreal's fourth goal last night. The last time Rick had looked, Yvan was in the penalty box. He stepped out, just in time to pick a plum.

Cournoyer must have suspected Christmas came early. His second goal resulted from Pete Mahovlich's interception of a pass from Stan Mikita to Bobby Hull, while the Hawks were a man short.

Hull has been showing the results of those extra man-hours spent on the ice. He has looked weary. That's something Dryden will have to investigate, after he gets to know the Nader system.

Bucks and Bobby are old friends

Bobby Hull was 33 when he signed a World Hockey Association contract in June 1972 worth an unprecedented three million dollars over ten years. By leaving the NHL, Hull was ruled ineligible to play for Canada against the Russians later that year. The country was hopping mad over that one and even the prime minister got involved, but to no avail.

WINNIPEG — Just because Bobby Hull picked up a certified check for one million dollars, plus assurance of another two million dollars where that came from, people get the idea that Hull and prosperity always have been as inseparable as cheese and crackers.

Nothing could be farther from the truth. Hull was an ancient thirteen before he discovered that some hockey players receive their reward in peanuts, while others are paid in peaches.

Bobby had been playing in the midget division, when along came a man and asked how he would like to take part in the bantam all-star game. There would be a new pair of gloves, a hockey stick and a set of shoulder pads in it for him.

"I'd had my eye on a pair of white gloves," Hull remembers. "All of a sudden, I had found a way to get them. Who needed money? The next year, though, when I went to Hespeler for Junior B hockey, I actually got five dollars a week, over and above my living expenses.

"I used to take a girl friend to the movies twice a week. We always stopped at a candy store on the way home. Come Saturday night, I still had a few cents in my pocket."

With this background of affluence, Hull didn't even sound an "ooh" or "ah" when he accepted the World Hockey Association's little token of its confidence in his ability to make it respectable.

He had flown down to St. Paul, Minnesota, in a Transair plane charted by Ben Hatskin, along with an assortment of sports writers, broadcasters, photographers and television technicians, such as had not been assembled in one spot since Muhammad Ali signed to fight Joe Frazier.

Hatskin is the Winnipeger who had been more or less dismissed by the nobles of the National Hockey League as a dreamy stubblebender from the Prairie. Now, he has replaced the stockyards as the source of Chicago's most disagreeable odor.

By persuading Hull to go over the wall, Ben has knocked NHL barons back on the heels of their alligator brogans. He also has assured Chicago Black Hawk partisans of countless dreary evenings in their smoke-polluted stadium. The Hawks, without Hull, will look like Bonanza without horses.

A Chicago hockey writer, who caught up to the caravan at St. Paul, capsuled the agonies of Hawk fans in a single sentence when he wailed: "Only the Black Hawks could give up Bobby Hull and Phil Esposito."

Bobby Hull and his family arrive in Winnipeg after signing the largest sports contract ever with the World Hockey Association in June 1972. Milt says Hull was hockey's greatest salesman of his era, perhaps any era.
(COURTESY THE TORONTO STAR)

Hull is the top goal-getter of all time among players now active. Esposito has been the most productive shooter in the last three seasons. Fortunately, Bobby Orr, the camp's new whiz kid, went to the Bruins. So the Hawks didn't have to get rid of him.

The contract which Hull signed at St. Paul was contained in twelve pages. It set out the terms of agreement between him and World Hockey Association properties. A second contract, signed with the Winnipeg Jets, required 25 pages.

"I'm not anxious to stir up an argument with the Canadian tax people," Harvey Wineberg, a tax expert from Chicago, was saying in a corner of the salon at the posh Minnesota Club, where the transaction was recorded for posterity, "but Canada is not entitled to taxes on this payment."

There's a stipulation in US tax law, at the moment, which limits the bite of the revenue officers to 50 per cent of an athlete's earnings in a single year. That stipulation ends December 31, according to some authorities. It might not be renewed. They give that as one reason why Ali and Frazier should have their rematch in 1972, while they still know the extent of the shakedown.

"If the league (WHA) should fold tomorrow, Hull emerges with two million," Wineberg added. "I want to say the terms on which we settled are the terms on which we started to negotiate. We didn't ask them to come up and they didn't ask us to come down. Ben Hatskin is a wonderful person with whom to do business."

While Pops Hull displayed a blowup of his million-dollar check for the television crews, his sons, Bobby, eleven, and Brett, eight, got into a hassle over a rubber band. Which proves all things are relative.

On the return flight to Winnipeg, while host Hatskin sprang for champagne and steak, Bobby Hull initialed each page of his new contract. On some pages, he initialed specific paragraphs.

His attractive wife, Joanne, enthused over plans to open an antique shop in Winnipeg. Bobby had promised her that as one of the conditions of the deal. Because she is not Harvey Wineberg's client, perhaps, it wasn't included in the contract.

"Whoever would have expected anything like this?" Bobby asked, as he surveyed the crowded plane and the stewardesses passing out bubbly. "I'll tell you what I really had in mind. My intention was to sign one more contract with Chicago for five years. When that ended, I figured I'd be through."

There is no doubt Hull would have signed, a year ago, for what the Hawks finally offered him — a million for five years. They didn't do it then because they didn't have to do it. By the time they realized his discussions with Ben Hatskin were not about the price of wheat, Hull had the smell of fresh new money in his nostrils.

On arrival back at Winnipeg, the question arose: What does a chap do with a certified check for one million dollars? If he leaves it in his hip pocket, he's liable to forget and it will go to the cleaners.

From the airport, a call was made to John Bradstock, an engaging type who manages the Toronto Dominion Bank at Notre Dame and Portage. A new customer wanted to open an account. John promised he wouldn't lock up until the client arrived.

His eyes popped when he saw the numbers on the deposit slip. He didn't even have a thermos jug or a sugar bowl which banks sometimes give to let newcomers know they appreciate the business.

Canada loses its home series — amid a thunder of boos

One of the lowest points for both Canadian hockey fans and players occurred in Vancouver and Milt recorded it on 9 September 1972. Milt had been in Moscow with the organizing committee in July but did not return in September. Some of the younger writers covered the series there.

VANCOUVER — The march on Moscow commences in a thunder of boos, with Team Canada's bright banners in disarray and coach Harry Sinden's all-stars in a lather of rage over the ridicule heaped upon them by those they hoped most to please — the Canadian fans.

Anatoli Tarasov, Russia's father of hockey, shows his fondness for Milt with a bear hug in 1967. While covering Olympics and World Championships, Milt had witnessed the emergence of the Russian hockey machine from its infancy to its dominance. As early as the mid-1950s, Milt warned readers one day soon Russian hockey would be on par with the best Canada could offer.

(COURTESY MILT DUNNELL PHOTO COLLECTION)

Team Canada is generally conceded to be the greatest array of hockey talent ever assembled in this country. It was touted as the biggest cinch since Mackenzie King.

Yet in four games on Canadian ice, the Canadians managed to win only once over the tightly disciplined Nationals of the Soviet Union. One match, the third, ended in a draw.

Last night, as the last air escaped from the punctured balloon of a national ego, it had the angry sound of disappointment, disillusionment and — excuse the word — almost contempt.

Many of the 18,000 partisans who jammed the beautiful home of the Vancouver Canucks of the National Hockey League hooted the Good Guys, whom they had hoped to send on their way to Europe with a resounding victory over the comrades.

Bill Goldsworthy, whose two penalties helped the Soviets to practically sew up their 5–3 win before the first period was half gone, was a special target of fan abuse.

Boris Petrovich Mikhailov, the Soviet team's 165-pound forward, whipped two goals past Canada's goalie, Ken Dryden, while Goldsworthy did penance. They were almost identical goals, with the same Russians, Vladimir Petrov and Vladimir Lutchenko, drawing assists.

After the second goal, the customers gave Goldsworthy the old razzoo in brass. Their displeasure spread to other members of the team. Ken Dryden, most valuable player in the Stanley Cup series of 1971 when Montreal eliminated Boston and Chicago, was jeered when he made routine saves.

Frank Mahovlich must have figured he was in Toronto where the freight-payers used to be on his back. The Big M was hooted for sitting on Vladislav Tretiak, the Soviet goalie, who has been the outstanding individual player in the series to date.

But the entire team got the same treatment when it skated out for the third period. At that stage, the score was only 3–1 but the Canadians were playing so badly the air was heavy with defeat.

If that signalled the end of a love affair, the players were prepared to have it that way. They accused the fans of being fair-weather friends in no uncertain terms — many of them unprintable in a family gazette.

Phil Esposito, one of the few Canadians who played up to his potential in this disappointing game, took the first shots at the team's critics when he appeared on television to accept a ring as the most valuable Canadian player.

"I've cooled out since then," Esposito admitted while he was surrounded by autograph seekers after the game. "What I said still goes, though. We have 35 guys here who came from all over the country to play in this series — not because of the money that goes to the pension fund but because we love Canada.

"Hell, half the press said we should win eight games. Most of our guys never had seen the Russian team. Whoever scouted the Russians (Johnny McLellan and Bob Davidson of the Leafs) should go out of the scouting business. They said we should have no trouble. Is it our fault if they were wrong?"

Big Phil was asked what might have happened if the press and the scouts had not predicted certain victory. Being a truthful, practical type, Phil grinned and said, "Probably we'd still have lost."

Goldsworthy's comments were largely censorable. The censor could allow this sentence, though: "I'm ashamed to be a Canadian." He added that he was looking forward to the four games in Moscow where the fans would probably be more charitable to the big league all-stars.

Players such as Ken Dryden, Rod Seiling and Ron Ellis — none of them blowtops — agreed the ridicule had hurt. Ellis gave assurance that the players would back up Big Phil in everything he had said.

Dryden, as usual, made the most astute analysis when he suggested: "The people were trying too hard — just as we were in that first game (a 7–3 defeat). A big party was to take place. Suddenly, there was no party."

Although he voiced confidence — "You don't write off a team that's one game down in the Stanley Cup" — Sinden is on the same turnpike that Napoleon took some years back, and the results for Napoleon were disastrous.

Sinden's cause is even more precarious. Napoleon was a winner when he took off. Sinden's troops are shell-shocked at the loading ramp.

There was reason to believe the Canadians would improve greatly after the comrades clobbered them 7–3 in the opening heat. They did improve — whipping the Soviets 4–1 at Toronto. In the third game, at Winnipeg, they were not quite as good and settled for a tie after twice blowing a two-goal lead.

Last night, they hit bottom — their worst effort of the four games. The irony of their ineptitude was that the Russians were ready to be taken. Except for Tretiak, their slender bridegroom goaler, they didn't play up to their previous high standards.

Bobby Hull, whose ineligibility to play for Team Canada because he had defected to the World Hockey Association caused a nation-wide rumpus, concurred in that appraisal. He was especially disappointed in Valary Kharlamov, who he noted, "played on a dime all night."

Fans are fickle and not inclined to waste time on theorizing when they are disappointed — as they had a right to be last night. When they get a chance to reflect, though, they might decide that the toppling of NHL hockey from its pedestal did not happen last night — or last week — or last month.

It has been taking place for years, simply because techniques and tactics haven't changed much since the days of Lester Patrick and Art Ross. The Russians knew they were not the best, and so they had to try harder.

In Canadian hockey, things are never going to be quite the same again.

Strictly, by coincidence, the first hockey men encountered after the debacle were Walter Bush, president of the Minnesota North Stars, and Jacques Plante, the Leafs' evergreen goalie.

Said Bush: "The Russians play the way we have forgotten to play. The Minnesota Vikings (football) start work at 11:00 a.m. and quit at 4:00 p.m. Our salaries are getting pretty high. We're going to start spending more time at work."

Plante, who had no knowledge of what Bush had said, asked: "Who says one hour per day is enough for a workout? Who says we should take off three months a year?"

Bobby Orr's odds called one-in-ten

It is sad that such a great career was shortened by injury. This piece ran 26 April 1977.

TORONTO — The world's finest hockey player, during the past ten years — and possibly for all years — will not put his left foot to the ground for the next four months. During all that time, he will be on crutches.

For at least twelve months, he will not even think of returning to hockey. At least, his doctors hope he will not even think of returning to hockey. However, they do know Robert Gordon Orr. Where hockey is involved, his own welfare always has been secondary. That has been his undoing.

By the time the 1978–79 season rolls around, Bobby Orr, winner of every major award available to a man of his profession — including the Lou Marsh Memorial Trophy as Canada's athlete of the year — will be 30.

That's not the age of decrepitude for a team athlete which it once was considered to be. In Orr's case, there is a more damaging time factor. By the season of 1978–79, Orr will have played almost no meaningful NHL hockey for three years.

The records will show he competed in ten games for the Boston Bruins in 1975–76 before being sidelined by aggravation of an old left knee injury.

During the past season, he participated in twenty games for the Chicago Black Hawks, after signing a reputed three million dollar contract as a free agent. Even those skimpy work sheets are misleading.

Orr was playing on one leg, tortured by pain, unable to

exploit the talents which had dazzled friends, foes and fans alike since he came out of Parry Sound to play for the Oshawa Generals.

Bill Wirtz, president of the Black Hawks, had chortled: "Orr can play for me on one knee." In a way, that was an expression of the Bobby Orr legend. His friend and former Boston team-mate, Phil Esposito, was guilty of the same misconception.

After Espo had been traded away to the New York Rangers, he urged his new employers to barter for Orr, despite Bobby's well-known knee problems. Said Espo: "Bobby Orr can play on one leg better than most people can play on two legs."

Orr had done so many unbelievable things on ice it was understandable that mere mortals forgot he depended on bone and muscle and brain — the same as less talented humans.

Even with the crew cut and an unfamiliar number 19
during his rookie season of 1966–67, it is easy to spot the
great Bobby Orr. Milt writes that Orr could do things as
a raw rookie which veterans just couldn't fathom.
(PHOTO BY JEFF GOODE, COURTESY THE TORONTO STAR)

Dr. John Palmer, noted surgeon and famous sports physician, who conducted the latest surgery on Orr's battered knee last week in collaboration with Dr. John Kostuik of Toronto General Hospital, is much more realistic in his assessment of what an athlete can do on a gimpy knee.

He says frankly: "Putting Bobby back on ice as a big league hockey player was not a major part of the decision in this operation, although I'm sure Bobby is hoping for that one-in-ten chance that he will be able to play again.

"This was a pretty major operation on the knee. We opened it up quite widely to remove bone chips and loose articular cartilage. Bobby understands that he must not even think about hockey for the coming season.

"He has agreed to one whole year of treatment for that knee. What we want is free movement and muscle development. As I said, Bobby will not be able to bear weight on that knee in the next four months. He will, however, be using a cycle."

If the Bobby Orr saga actually has ended, the finale came in the Canada Cup tournament last fall — rather than in the painful diminishing shifts he spent on the ice as a Black Hawk.

Orr wasn't the Bobby Orr of 1974-75 in the Canada Cup. The season of '74-75 was one of his finest — despite a series of knee operations, which he hoped had ended his miseries.

He scored 46 goals and had 89 assists for the Boston Bruins that season. His 135 points made him the leading scorer in the league, earning him the Art Ross trophy. As usual, he won the Norris trophy, for the eighth consecutive season, as the league's outstanding rearguard.

That was the real Bobby Orr. The Bobby Orr of the Canada Cup was maybe 25 per cent below the standards of that Bobby Orr. He was just back from another knee operation. He still was the outstanding player among the stars of the world's leading hockey countries.

Even if he never plays hockey again — and nobody is ready to write finish to the legend — that probably will be his fondest hockey memory.

A testimonial
without a fee

Brian Spencer was a mixed-up young man who would later spend a great deal of time in jail before he was shot to death by a drug dealer. This haunting column appeared 28 December 1977.

TORONTO — The Leafs take a personal interest in their players' welfare. . . . The Leafs are in the player's corner when he's in trouble. . . . You don't get any better treatment anywhere than you get at the Maple Leaf Gardens.

Sounds like a letter from Stan Obodiac, the prolific publicist for the Gardens — or excerpts from a speech that Harold Ballard made at the annual meeting of Gardens shareholders.

Or it could be King Clancy quoting the party line to a couple of Swedes — Anders Hedberg and Ulf Nilsson — whom the Leafs hope to lure away from Winnipeg.

All it proves is that the most effective propaganda is the kind that isn't manufactured. Brian (Spinner) Spencer was saying such things, when he returned to the Gardens with the Pittsburgh Penguins.

The Spinner never was advertised as a sentimental sort — quite the opposite. He was a kid from the British Columbia bush country who was quick with his fists and adept with an elbow.

A Buffalo motorist and his wife sued the Spinner for a total of $196,000 while he was playing for Punch Imlach and the

Sabres. Spencer was accused of putting the slug on the guy, following a traffic accident. Since the Spinner settled out of court, it's reasonable to presume the plaintiff had at least one scar to offer as evidence.

"I came to hockey rough-cut," the Spinner admits, "— 3,000 or 4,000 miles out of the woods, with a meat pack on my back. Don't forget, I was eighteen before I got out of the bush.

"I wasn't really ready for the big league. I look at a kid like that (Trevor) Johansen of the Leafs. He has such poise — such confidence. How I wish I'd had some of that when I came to Toronto."

The Spinner always wanted to play for the Leafs. He realized that dream because his father sent him to a hockey school that was operated by NHL-er Red Berenson.

Red suspected there was talent beneath the unpolished exterior of this rugged kid from the back woods. Berenson took him to his parents' home in Regina and got him a trial with the Swift Current junior Broncos. He was a fifth draft choice of the Leafs in 1969.

They let him go in the 1972 expansion draft to the New York Islanders. He wasn't sore — realizing he was not helping the Leafs much and it was unlikely they would protect him.

"I never could forget how the Leafs treated me when my father was killed," Spencer says. "I know a lot of people didn't like Stafford Smythe. He put a plane at my disposal so I could get to the funeral (at Fort St. James, British Columbia) and he had Jim Gregory (the Leafs' GM) and Guy Trottier go along with me. King Clancy and Punch did everything they could to ease the pain."

His father's death was a pathetic case of a man's pride in a son depriving him of reason. Annoyed because the nearest television station to Fort St. James was carrying a Vancouver game, when a Leaf game was available, he grabbed his rifle and drove to the station, where he demanded a switch.

In the ensuing drama, he was shot and killed by police. The real irony came a few nights later. The Leafs were playing at home and the game was visible in Fort St. James. Spinner Spencer was the first star. He scored three goals.

"I like the Pittsburgh club," the Spinner advises, "but I couldn't understand the trade (from Buffalo). Punch actually gave me away because Ron Schock (obtained by Buffalo) is not with the team. I was one of the Sabres' most popular players.

"I have written to Punch, asking him why I was traded — only because it's something I might prevent happening again. Punch hasn't answered my letter, I hope he does."

Punch, you owe this young man a letter. He thinks you're tops. Don't disillusion him.

But first of all Sittler must win in self-analysis

Milt provides a nice recap of Darryl Sittler's perplexing last two years playing at Maple Leaf Gardens. Less than two weeks after this column appeared on 8 January 1982, Sittler was traded to Philadelphia for Rich Costello, a second-round draft pick, and a minor league player as future considerations.

TORONTO — The following is in response to a request from a reader (he's only the publisher) to try to make some sense out of the Darryl Sittler sit-out at Maple Leaf Gardens. Since little of the gripping (some might say monotonous) Sittler soaper ever has made sense, this mission is like fishing for tuna in Lake Ontario.

There happens to be one peg, though, on which hangs a

presumption. If Sittler is being ridiculous, selfish, unreasonable and unthinking now, it's his turn. He definitely has endured much of the same in the last couple of years of unhappy employment.

That doesn't mean Sittler is being awarded a bar to go along with the "C" that decorates his chest — not until he wins one fall in a wrestling match with his own conscience.

When he sheared that same symbolic "C" off his shirt, in December 1979, and announced his temporary resignation of the captaincy, he issued a hand-written statement, which read, in part:

"I'm spending more and more time on player-management problems and I don't feel I am accomplishing enough for my teammates. All I want is to give all my energy and all my ability to my team as a player."

He will have to settle, with himself, the question of whether he followed that credo, when he failed to make the team's two-game road trip, at a time when coach Mike Nykoluk lacked sufficient bodies to fill the uniforms.

Even allowing himself medical exemption because of battle weariness and mental depression, Sittler still has to satisfy Sittler that the depression is greater than it was after the Leafs blew the opening game of the playoffs 9–2 last April. He continued to play after that.

At $195,000 per season is the depression more unbearable for him than it is for the $195 per week subscriber in the grays who has been waiting a decade for the promised turnabout?

If Sittler can square with himself in that bit of introspection, he owes no apologies to anyone because those who know the young man are aware he's a tough self-disciplinarian.

His attitude toward Team Canada last summer is all one needs to dispel the charges of selfishness, arrogance and greed which his critics whisper about him.

Having spent most of his holidays getting himself ready for Team Canada's training camp, he wasn't even invited. Try to name a dozen players in the whole league who wouldn't have told the coaches where to head when they suddenly learned one of their selections was unavailable. Would Sittler accept a delayed invitation?

He would — much to the disgust of his employer Harold Ballard, who felt Sittler should have been invited in the first place. In camp, he worked as hard as any of the candidates — maybe harder. At cutdown time, he didn't make the team. He departed without a bleat or a beef. One team executive (not Eagleson) confided: "I never was a great Sittler fan but I am now."

It must be kept in mind that the knock-down Sittler syndrome is not something that has been around as long as Banana Joe and King Clancy. As recently as the autumn of 1976, club owner Harold Ballard was presenting the Sittlers with an expensive silver tea service, in recognition of the six goals and four assists Sittler scored against the Boston Bruins, at the Gardens. His ten points smashed an old NHL record, shared by Rocket Richard and Bert Olmstead.

In April 1976, Sittler had scored five goals against the Philadelphia Flyers, in a playoff game, to tie another of the Rocket's old records. Almost four years were to pass before Ballard, who had presented the tea hardware, was to describe Sittler as "a cancer" within the hockey club.

What went wrong?

In July 1979, Punch Imlach returned to the Gardens after an absence of ten years. When Punch became general manager and coach of the new Buffalo Sabres, in January 1970, he described himself as "one tough SOB." Who would know better? The NHL Guide Book for 1980–81 identified Punch as director of hockey operations, general manager and coach of the Leafs, who had fired him in 1969.

One of his unpleasant discoveries, on his return, was that Sittler had a no-trade addendum to his standard contract. The terms had been dictated by Sittler's agent, lawyer Al Eagleson, an old Imlach foe.

It was the kind of deal which Imlach never would have made. Ballard granted it in return for a long-term contract. Once before, in 1973, Ballard had to battle John Bassett, Jr. for Sittler's signature. He wasn't anxious to go through it again. Sittler's reason for a multi-year contract was that he wanted to be in Toronto.

Since Sittler is being accused of being money-hungry now, the 1973 scramble for his services is worth recalling. Bassett, who had brought the World Hockey Association Toros to Toronto, thought he had a deal with Eagleson. Sittler was to get one million over five years. Negotiations were called off when Eagleson tried for something like $250,000 in fringe perks.

If Sittler could have had $200,000 a year in 1973 — and is getting $195,000 (compared to Borje Salming's $325,000) now, that money hungry label scarcely sticks.

After demanding since 1979 (Imlach's return) that Sittler surrender his no-trade privilege, the Leafs now have his surrender (with reservations).

So why haven't they traded him? They've depreciated him by telling prospective buyers what a bad influence he is. Now, they can't understand why they can't get a Wayne Gretzky for him.

Note to publisher: See, none of it makes sense.

Peter Puck glad Skalbania silent on Gretzky deal

With friends like Peter Pocklington, beleaguered Nelson Skalbania didn't need any enemies. Peter Puck scooped up the world's greatest hockey player for free, as Milt revealed on 18 January 1982.

TORONTO — It was pure coincidence that Peter Pocklington should be in Toronto sharing the white light of hype and sports publicity, at the very moment Peter's old buddy, Nelson Skalbania, was getting zapped for $1.1 million in a British Columbia Supreme Court judgment.

Skalbania was being ordered to pay up for one of his numerous sports blunders — purchase of the Memphis Rogues, a soccer club of unfond memory — while Peter Puck was here, commemorating another of Skalbania's goofs — possibly his biggest.

It is going to be suggested that Skalbania's most glaring mistake was that he lured Vince Ferragamo, a quarterback of repute with the Los Angeles Rams — but a disaster with Montreal Alouettes — to his Alouette payroll for a guaranteed $450,000 (US) per season.

Sure, that does rank right up there with the Drama of Bahama among recent sports promotional turkeys. But it scarcely equals Skalbania's bestowal of the contractual rights of the world's No. 1 hockey player of the day upon his friend Pocklington.

It wasn't intended to be a gift — just turned out that way. Furthermore, please don't get the idea that Pocklington is gloating over it. He says Nelson never mentions the matter — for which he is grateful. He might add — but doesn't — that it's understandable why Nelson would prefer to forget.

"Nelson and I had been partners, for a short term, in the ownership of the (World Hockey Association) Oilers," Pocklington recalls. "When I bought him out, there was an understanding that if Edmonton ever went into the NHL, I would owe Nelson another $500,000.

"Sometime later, Nelson called me up. He was short of money. (Skalbania's Indianapolis WHA franchise was laying an egg.) Said he needed half a million dollars. I bought Gretzky's contract, along with two others, for $250,000 in cash and a note for $250,000. There was a stipulation, though, that the deal wiped out the $500,000 NHL commitment."

Since Edmonton did become one of the four WHA clubs which moved into the NHL, Pocklington actually got Gretzky's contract for nothing. Peter Puck then compounded the larceny by signing The Kid to a 21-year contract which made him an Oiler for life.

While the security feature of the contract was commendable, the financial benefits quickly became inadequate for a young man who makes a joke of the scoring records. Pocklington agrees to that.

He proposed to pay Gretzky approximately what the president of the US might expect if he were a basketball player. The necessary amendments to Gretzky's 21-year pact were being arranged, in proper legal jargon, during Pocklington's visit. So the television lights and the tape recorders and the notebooks were aimed at Pocklington almost as frequently as they were trained on Gretzky.

"I once closed a $100 million real estate deal here," Pocklington recalled. "Didn't create a ripple. I bought a packing company (Swift Canadian) that employs 5,000 persons. There were a few media people on hand for the announcement.

"That's one of the things which surprise people who come into sport from the business world — the tremendous interest. A business friend of mine was in Tokyo the night Gretzky got his 50th goal in Edmonton. He told me he saw it on Japanese television."

Pocklington insists he has not downgraded Skalbania's business acumen because of the Gretzky deal. Nelson, he appraises, is a man with a big ego (Pocklington admits he may have a bit of it himself). The difference is that Skalbania's ego sometimes warps his judgment.

Gretzky is lucky to have an employer with Pocklington's background. Peter Puck started out wheeling and dealing in used cars, while still in high school. Soon, he was Canada's youngest Ford dealer. He hit Edmonton just ahead of the oil boom. Having become filthy rich himself, he doesn't discourage it in other young men.

"Thank God, though," he adds fervently, "that there is only one for whom I must do this."

Gretzky class his trademark win or lose

The Great One has always had class as revealed by this column of 18 May 1983.

UNIONDALE, N.Y. — The watercooler smashers and the telephone yankers and the locker-room wreckers — usually identified as people who just can't stand to lose — have a chance to grow up, simply by following in the skate tracks of an old pro who won't be 23 until next January.

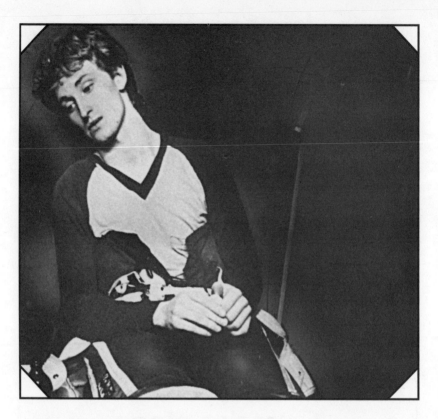

*The great Wayne Gretzky, only 20 years old, relaxes with a
beer in the Edmonton Oilers' dressing room 30 December 1981.
He has class beyond his years, Milt writes.*
(PHOTO BY DOUG GRIFFIN, COURTESY THE TORONTO STAR)

Wayne Gretzky doesn't like to lose either.

But he doesn't consider it necessary to rant and rave — like
Billy Martin in pursuit of an umpire — to prove how sincere he
is about winning.

Gretzky has won so much — and so frequently — that it
wouldn't have been surprising if he had found it difficult to
keep his cool as a loser.

He has shown the same class, when the numbers were wrong,
as he did when the Oilers were burying the Black Hawks.

It hasn't been easy. He was being asked why he hadn't been
able to get a single goal in four games of the most important
series in his career, within minutes of accepting a new four-wheel

drive Toyota wagon for having scored 71 goals and 125 assists in the regular season.

The implication was plain. Gretzky wasn't getting the big goals. The Oilers scored a record 424 goals in their 80-game schedule. There were three other Oilers — Mark Messier, Glenn Anderson and Jarl Kurri — who had more than 40 goals each.

They were not getting the big goals either.

But nobody was asking them. The pointed questions were being aimed at Gretzky. His answer was a classic: "I take the roses when things are going well. I'll take the heat when they are not going well."

Gretzky has taken more heat than he deserved. The Islanders could have told his questioners that the Oilers make their big moves only when Gretzky was on the ice.

The Isles' slap-happy (as in slashing) goaler, Billy Smith, made some of his best moves on Gretzky.

When Billy was beaten by a blistering shot, on a Gretzky breakaway, early in the second game of the series, the puck hit the crossbar. Gretzky did not moan about his luck.

He realized he was playing well because he was getting chances to score.

Some of the Oilers' other big shooters could not offer themselves the same consolation. For that, the Islanders have to be given a lot of credit. Butch Goring, who escaped from the Los Angeles Kings to join the real monarchs of North American hockey, probably put it best when he said the way to beat the Oilers is to make them do things they don't want to do.

They don't want to do their shooting from the angles. Their shooting ground is the slot. The Isles closed it for the duration. One interviewer asked Gretzky whether he thought the Oilers had choked. Obviously, he took Gretzky's temperament into consideration.

Can you picture a Reggie Jackson or a Dieter Brock fielding that question?

But, as Gretzky said himself, the heat grows with the roses.

He gets the big bucks to handle both. Most of the money guys forget that. Gretzky doesn't.

Ballard to leave Gardens to charity

This famed "scoop" appeared 2 January 1988, only a day before Ballard was rushed to a Miami hospital while on holidays. Ballard did leave the bulk of his estate to charity, but, as of three years after his death in 1990, the charitable organizations are still waiting to see the money due to court wranglings and other webs woven by those close to the scene.

TORONTO — Samuel Butler, a master of satire, wrote that great actions are not always true sons of great and mighty resolutions. Harold E. Ballard, who came along much later, although he is creeping up on 85, agrees, without conceding anything to Samuel Butler — or anyone else, for that matter.

It's just that Ballard believes in keeping things in their proper environment. When he sat down, therefore, to record his New Year resolutions, he chose not the solitude of his private study but the little gymnasium, across the corridor from the dressing room of the Toronto Maple Leafs.

There's a sign on the door of the gym that warns you'd better keep out unless you're somebody who is well up in the pecking order at Maple Leaf Gardens. Ballard is the man who signs the checks, as he has mentioned a few times. That assures his place in the pecking order.

So, sitting on one of the many rigs that keep his hockey players fit, if not necessarily fearsome, Ballard looked the new 1988 right in the eye — just as he did the two Gardens employees he fired early on Christmas morning.

"Found one of them on the floor when I made my early tour of the Gardens," Ballard snorted. "He had cut his head. The other one was asleep on his desk, in one of the most sensitive areas of the operations room. Fell down when he tried to get up. Both dead drunk.

"Nobody's gonna believe this but these are the first people I ever fired. No, I didn't fire Punch Imlach, despite anything you've read. I told Punch I was transferring him to a desk job. Punch said he had been hired to manage the hockey club and refused the change. That ended it."

Now, about those New Year resolutions:

"I'm giving up tryin' to be the most miserable old bastard in the country. That's the image I've tried to create. I've failed. Everywhere I go, people ask for my autograph. My mail and the messages I get indicate the whole damn thing has been a total failure. I'm more popular than I ever was."

Persistence might still pay off, you hasten to assure him. After all, isn't there a town garbage dump, somewhere out west, named in his honor?

"When you've been around as long as I have — since the first shovel of dirt was turned for this building, and prior to that at Mutual Street (arena), you learn to appreciate the people you've encountered through sport. Appreciation of them is a New Year resolution. Ten years from now, I . . . "

Ten years from now? Didn't he mention he will be 85 in July? Does he foresee another decade at the Gardens?

"Damn right. And we'll have the Stanley Cup long before that time. Believe me. People keep asking me who's gonna take over here, when I'm gone. You just asked if I'm bringin' in (son) Bill to prepare him for the job.

"To begin with, I'm not goin' anywhere except maybe to Hartford or Chicago when we play there. Bill never will move in to run the Gardens and the hockey club. Bill has his own business (he's big in a rock concert production). The worst thing that could happen would be for my three kids (daughter, Mary Elizabeth, sons Bill and Harold) to take over. It just wouldn't work.

"They have fought among themselves ever since they were

kids. My daughter is the worst. Bill sometimes asks when I intend to move on. He's kidding but sometimes he sounds serious."

As if summoned by radar or mental telepathy, who should stick his head through the gym door but Bill Ballard?

"Just been talking about you," Ballard the elder advised. "I said you never would be movin' into Maple Leaf Gardens. Of course, I've told you that before."

"Humph, I wouldn't want to move into this building. I'd have a new one."

Let's get this straight, Harold. For more than 50 years, you dreamt — some might even say schemed — of being the big boss of Maple Leaf Gardens and owner of the NHL franchise regarded as one of the best in pro sport.

In 1961, you talked a bank manager into a two million dollar loan, so you and your buddies, Stafford Smythe and then publisher John Bassett, could buy the stock held by Conn Smythe, who rounded up the original bankrollers of the building.

Almost a decade later, you went into hock at the bank again for six million dollars, so you and Stafford Smythe could buy Bassett's stock, in keeping with an agreement that, when any of the partners wanted out, the others had first shot at the shares.

After Stafford died, in October 1971, while awaiting trial on tax and fraud charges (which cost Ballard a valuable year in Millhaven), you went to the bank once more, for almost eight million dollars, to purchase the Smythe stock.

Now that you own as much as an estimated 83 per cent of Gardens stock, you don't want to see it remain in the Ballard family? Is one of the current directors (food markets king) Steve Stavro, for instance, ready to take over?

A big league hockey franchise isn't exactly a tinker toy. *Fortune* magazine, in a 1986 survey of sports franchises, put the Leafs in the $31 million to $35 million bracket, exclusive of real estate. At today's market price on the Toronto Stock Exchange, Ballard's holdings (almost three million shares) are worth close to $90 million.

"One of the good things I have had out of sport has been my

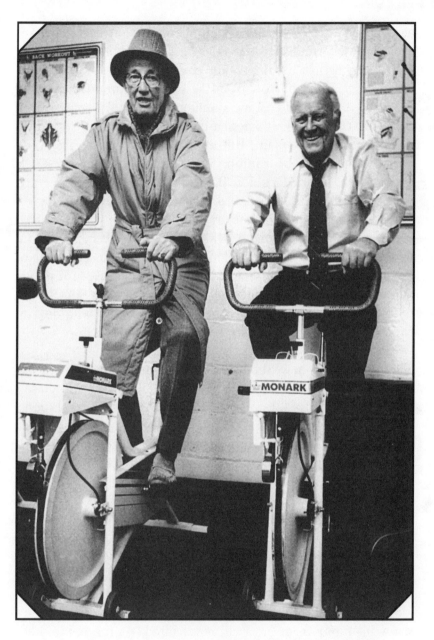

Two spry gentlemen work out in the gym of Maple Leaf Gardens in December 1987. At the time, Harold Ballard gave Milt the scoop that he was leaving the Gardens to charity, not to his squabbling children.
(PHOTO BY BORIS SPREMO, COURTESY THE TORONTO STAR)

association with Steve Stavro. But, no, I'm not sure Stavro is even remotely interested. He is not a big shareholder.

"The bank has no important equity. I have paid off those loans. Sure, I still borrow from the bank, as a matter of doing business. A new roof cost me a million and a half. The new floor came in at a million. It's gonna cost me a million for improvements in the power plant. But the bank won't be taking over."

Then, who will be running Maple Leaf Gardens and the hockey club, when Harold E. Ballard goes elsewhere than Hartford or Chicago or his beloved hideaway on Georgian Bay?

"The Gardens and the hockey club will be run by a trust that represents charities, some of which already are very important to me. It will be up to each charity to name a trustee. Some of them might even be present Gardens directors. I'm not gonna name the charities now but you can bet the Cancer Society will be one of them. My parents died of cancer. My wife died of cancer. Lawyers are working on the arrangements."

There's nothing new about Ballard's interest in charities. He was about to write a cheque for $25,000 to an associate's charity when he took time to ponder his New Year resolutions. It is completely uncharacteristic, however, to hear Ballard propose that anything should be run by a committee. The Gardens and the hockey team have been a one-man show. He always has insisted on making the final decisions.

It isn't difficult to guess there will be concern (as in consternation) within the National Hockey League over the prospect of a group of charities — sweet as charity may be — operating one of its top franchises. Charities have been known to quarrel among themselves. Is the league aware of his proposal?

"If you're asking whether I ran to (John) Ziegler (NHL president) and asked his permission, the answer is NO. He wouldn't know his fanny from . . . well, never mind. As far as the other owners are concerned, they're so damn greedy that I wouldn't give them the satisfaction. What I do with my own team surely is my own business."

There is another person who might have more than a

passing interest in Ballard's startling resolution. He is not married to Yolanda MacMillan but she has been a regular companion for several years. The courts have been considerate of such companions.

"I'm aware of that, but who is to say I don't have an agreement with her? I am not gonna marry Yolanda. She is 25 years younger than I am and probably wouldn't marry an old coot like me — but she brings me a lot of pleasure.

"She is cheerful, considerate, mouthy. But all women are mouthy. Family hates her, of course."

"She is probably the closest person to me now. I don't think my kids have any affection for me. I don't need their affection. They have their own lives to live. I never want to be in the position where my kids are saying they have to do something for dear old dad."

Resuming his pursuit of resolutions, Ballard conceded there might come a day when he would be more tolerant of the Russians, whose hockey teams have been barred from his building, much to the annoyance of Hockey Canada, the NHL and most of the local media.

No, his mellowing is not the result of *glasnost* nor of the red carpet treatment Mikhail Gorbachev received in Washington. The influence is money. Ballard foresees a European division of the NHL — teams in Prague, Moscow, Stockholm, Leningrad, Helsinki, with the European winner playing the North American victor for the Stanley Cup. The financial windfall is mind-boggling.

"Then, we'd have a real world championship," he argued. "The Stanley Cup is only half a world championship. If it came to a series between the Leafs and Moscow, I guess I'd have to let them into the building."

Does he expect it to happen before charity takes over the Maple Leafs and the most storied sports building in the country?

"Damn right I do. When I go, it's gonna be throat trouble. They're gonna have to hang me."

FOOTBALL

Karpuk-can't-think club hereby disbands

It was one of the most bizarre occurrences on a football field, 3 November 1951 in Toronto. As a result, The Canadian Rugby Union (CRU), which governed football then, changed the rules. Now in the CFL, the rules award an automatic touchdown if someone tries a similar stunt. Karpuk's Ottawa Rough Riders went on to win the Grey Cup in 1951.

TORONTO — Pete Karpuk, who became the Fred Merkle of Canadian football, has had his revenge. He was labeled and libeled as a donkey who didn't know the rules of the game he played. Now, he's going to make them rewrite the book. Merkle was the rookie who forgot to touch second base. He cost the Giants a pennant, and although it happened more than 40 years ago, his name has been another way of saying "boner" down to this day.

Karpuk's error of omission was of more recent date. Pete was the unhappy Rough Rider who neglected to pick up the ball in the 1948 Grey Cup game, because there was a horn on the play. What Pete forgot was that the referee's whistle — not the umpire's horn — governs the game. His lapse set up a Calgary touchdown, and since the Stampeders went on to win, 12–7, the significance of the Karpuk crock wasn't underplayed.

Saturday afternoon, almost three years later, Pete was sitting on the Ottawa bench at Varsity stadium when he saw Ulysses Curtis, the Ole Crazy-Legs of the Argos, grab a pass that was intended for Ottawa's Howie Turner. This was the turn of the tide in the kind of game only Hollywood could dream up. If you saw this one, quit worrying about those Grey Cup tickets. The Grey Cup has to be an anti-climax.

But let's get back to Karpuk. And get the picture. It's fourth quarter. Ottawa is leading, 18–12. If the Argos lose, they are out. And it looks as if they're going to lose — until the ball lands in Curtis' paws like a plum dropping down a well. Ulysses takes a look as he opens the throttle and starts up the field, from about his own 40-yard line. Not a Rough Rider between him and the Ottawa goal stripe. There are a couple but they're out of the line of Uly's vision — far over to the right. Knowing the way this lad can give with the speed, scarcely a soul in the 21,000 present concedes a red-shirt a chance to halt Curtis in his flight.

There's only one Rider who remembers how it can be done. That's Karpuk, who recalls the instructions of Wally Masters, who coached the Riders for a number of years. According to Karpuk — and other former Ottawans who now play for the Argos back up his statements — Masters told them: "If a player from the other side gets in the clear, nail him from the bench. It isn't covered in the rules."

That's how come No. 76 suddenly appeared in front of Curtis. Even at that, Pete made a poor tackle. But he got a piece of Curtis, and slowed him up so he was downed at the 25.

What followed was enough to make the law-makers of football sneak away and take a hefty drag of the gas pipe. The Argos obviously had been robbed of a touchdown, at a moment when they were in dire need of one, and the usually placid Frank Clair, coach of the Scullers, was on the field screaming for justice. The stripe-shirted officials went into a huddle.

It suddenly occurred to all and sundry that the revised and reclassified rules don't provide for jay-walkers from the bench. When the crowd sensed that the Argos wouldn't be awarded a touchdown, snowballs started zooming down from the stands. They exploded among players and whistle-blowers, like popcorn bouncing on a hot pan. Referee Seymour Wilson, Dr. M. D. Kinsella, the stately Argo executive, and Nat Turofsky, the camera jockey, were among the victims of direct hits, as witnessed from the safety of the press coop.

Billy Foulds, dean of the rules committee, got into the pow-wow. Kibitzers horned into the argument. Jimmy McCaffery, manager of the Ottawas, and Clem Crowe, his coach, were in and out. And all the while the snowballs were flying. Which poses another problem for the CRU. What's the point of paying twelve grand for a tarpaulin to keep snow off the field if you don't buy a net to intercept snowballs?

Ottawa finally was penalized, under the rule which provides for one team having too many men on the field. This is a ten-yard penalty, plus the loss, for three minutes, of one man for each extra man who got into the game. There's another clause in the book which says the referee shall adjudicate upon disputes or cases unprovided for by the rules. This would have seemed like just the spot for such authority. If the rule means what it says, Seymour Wilson could have ruled a touchdown.

The league was lucky enough to get out of the mess because the Argos went on from there to win. But if Saturday's handling of the Karpuk incident is the official interpretation for Canadian football, you can look for a new specialist in our game. This will be a guy whose job it is to sit on the end of the bench and make sure no break-away ball-carrier gets free passage to the goal-line. A coach will be foolish if he doesn't play it that way, because, obviously, he has everything to gain and not much to lose.

The brass had better get their heads together and come up with a communique. Karpuk, the man who didn't know the rules, has hit them with their own book.

Slight mix-up in a public hanging

Chuck Hunsinger's blunder in November 1954 led to the greatest upset in Grey Cup history. The mighty Montreal Alouettes from the East were favored by three touchdowns. Going into the game, Western teams had won only five Grey Cups in the previous 27 years, their last in 1948. After Edmonton's 26–25 win, Hunsinger would wear the Grey Cup horns as Mr. Miscue until an Argo named McQuay came along.

TORONTO — Steve Owen, the long-time New York Giants' football coach, may have wrapped up the neatest package of comment, after the condemned man suddenly slipped the noose around the necks of the hangmen and left them dangling from the gallows at Varsity stadium. Said Mr. Owen: "For Edmonton to win it, Montreal had to lose it." Even Pop (Poison) Ivy, the Mr. Placid of the coaching profession, might not find fault with that. Mr. Placid seldom finds fault with public utterances. Maybe that's just as well. If he did, he'd be sore at more people than Senator McCarthy. There couldn't have been fewer than a million jerks, including this one, who tried to impress him with the futility of resistance at this slaughter of the innocents. During this ordeal, Ivy showed amazing patience. Beyond a mild complaint that people were slandering his league, he made no attempt to change any opinion.

After it was over, he said: "I felt we had as much chance as they did." Since he felt that way, he must have figured to capitalize on all Montreal errors, because it's one of Ivy's pet sayings that, in big games, you seldom make enough plays to win. The other fellow has to make mistakes that help you.

It follows, therefore, that Mr. Ivy couldn't disagree too strenuously with Steve Owen's summary. The Alouettes, sometimes referred to as Canada's greatest-ever football team, pulled the biggest rock since Fred Merkle by-passed second base in the dim and distant by-gones. For more than 40 years, all disastrous boners in sport became known as Merkles. For the second successive Saturday, it was a hero who wore the goat horns. A week earlier, it was little Ron Stewart who blew the ball game for Queen's. Saturday, it was Chuck Hunsinger.

Comparing Stewart and Hunsinger is like comparing Bo Peep and Lady Godiva. They scarcely belong in the same company. Just why an old pro like Hunsinger would throw away the ball, as he did Saturday, is one of those mysteries that pop up periodically in sport. As Lew Hayman, campaign-hardened general manager of the Als said after Saturday's set-back: "If we knew the answers to all these things, there wouldn't be much interest in the ball games." Hunsinger himself probably doesn't know, if he's honest about it. His story now is that he intended to toss an offside pass, which would have meant the ball was dead. The officials in charge of the game probably realized they were on the hook, as soon as they got time to consider their predicament. If the ball did go forward when Hunsinger threw it, then they pulled an even bigger rock than Hunsinger did when they permitted ambling Jackie Parker to scoop up the lemon and dangle 90 yards for a touchdown that took the Grey Cup to Alberta. So they called it a fumble. If that was a fumble, there will be hundreds of thousands of folks who will figure they're in need of glasses. They distinctly saw Hunsinger throw the ball. The only question that remained: Was it thrown forward or was it a lateral?

A reasonable assumption is that Hunsinger was a bit fuzzy upstairs. He had been rocked by Big Rollin' Prather. In his daze, he may have figured he saw a Lark, and attempted a

*Edmonton Eskimo Jackie Parker romps 90 yards
for the winning touchdown in the 1954 Grey Cup after a
famous miscue by Montreal's Chuck Hunsinger.*
(COURTESY THE TORONTO STAR)

lateral. There wasn't a redshirt on that side of the field. The main thing Parker had to overcome was his own amazement. It was the biggest steal since Woody Strode picked up a loose ball in the '48 game and galloped 40 yards, after an offside horn confused Ottawa's Pete Karpuk. Woody's play gave the Grey Cup a long lift toward Calgary. That's one thing about those Alberta teams: They don't even wait for opportunity to knock. They're on the doorstep — waiting.

Whether the officials booted one on the Hunsinger heave and whether they were whistle-happy when they cost Herb Trawick of the Alouettes a touchdown earlier in the game, doesn't matter and doesn't enter into the argument. The fact still remains that Als beat themselves by giving away the ball when they were five points on top, with five minutes to go, and they had possession at the Eskimos' ten-yard stripe. With an indictment like that against you, it takes brass to complain about the

76

officiating. And we didn't hear any beefs — not from the Montreal executive. The Als got some bad breaks. The final one cost them their very last chance of salvaging a tie. The clock was running out when Sam Etcheverry threw to Red O'Quinn at the Edmonton 35. O'Quinn was hit so hard he fumbled. The Esks recovered. A quick whistle on that play would have saved O'Quinn and might have meant a tie ball game. It was a quick whistle which cost Trawick a touchdown. But if the Als were thinking of a tie then, they weren't in that mood when they appeared on their way to an easy win, well into the fourth quarter. They were inside the Edmonton ten and lost the ball on a third-down pass, without getting even a single. That one point looked big later.

It could be the Als never recovered from their shock of the first half, when the spell-binder, Bernie Faloney, hypnotized them with his ball-handling magic. The only people in the park who knew where the ball was were Jackie Parker, Normie Kwong and Rollie Miles. They knew because they had it. The prediction had been that Faloney would be separated from his gimpy knees by Doug McNichol, who cleaned and pressed every Big Four quarterback. Big Doug seldom caught up with Faloney. Doug never had it so rough. That tough Edmonton line apparently knew about him.

Never has there been a more popular win. And that's no reflection on Hayman, Peahead Walker and that popular Montreal executive. It's just that the Esks refused to believe what they read on the odds-board, and their determination was contagious. Ivy said repeatedly: "This club never lost a game it had to win." The only persons who listened were the Eskimos. And they knew already.

The Tommy Gun versus The Rifle

Two great quarterbacks, Sam Etcheverry and Tobin Rote, hooked up 1 October 1960 and it was the Argonauts who came out on top 50–15 in record-setting fashion. Unbelievably, Rote again threw seven touchdowns against Montreal later that month. Even more incredible, Rote's record was broken two years later when Hamilton's Joe Zuger threw eight TDs in one game.

TORONTO — The students of statistics must be completely confused by Saturday's pitching duel between Tobin The Tommy Gun and Sam The Rifle. This one ended with a new champion. Texas Tobin Rote, ex-Green Bay Packer, ex-Detroit Lion, who came to Canada because he liked the climate and the 25 G's per annum which the Argonauts were happy to pay, now holds the record for touchdown passes thrown in a single Big Four football fiesta. The magic number is seven.

It was announced that the Tommy Gun had moved in to share this honor with The Rifle. Researchers issued a rebuttal. Sam The Rifle Etcheverry's high mark was six. It's true the Montreal Alouettes, for whom The Rifle explodes, did have seven TD shots in one ball game. One of them was fired, however, by Bruce Coulter who used to sit on the bench for the Larks just in case The Rifle blew a breech lock or something.

Nothing like that ever happened. Etcheverry persisted in being the healthiest character who ever stepped on a gridiron.

He must have retired for a quick shave the day Coulter got into a ball game long enough to throw a touchdown pass. That was one of the raps the critics had against former Montreal coach Peahead Walker. They said the only time Peahead ever gave The Rifle a rest was before and after a ball game — never while a ball game was in progress.

The form chart readers who didn't actually sit in on the Saturday show must have been perplexed to note that The Rifle actually completed four more passes than The Tommy Gun and wasn't too far behind in overhead yardage. Yet Rote ran off with all the cigars for throwing and the Argonauts stripped the Larks down to their last pin feather.

The answer was painfully simple to Alouettes and sundry well-wishers who had accepted a point spread ranging from nine to a dozen and bet their money on the Als to come up with a big effort. Two of The Rifle's most important shots were caught by the Argonauts. They both came in the first half and they changed the complexion of what had all the trademarks of a very dreary ball game.

That's why The Rifle appeared, on the record, to enjoy a big edge over Rote in the passing duel up to half-time while the Larks actually were getting killed, 14–1 on the scoreboard. Tobin had completed only three passes — but two of them were for touchdowns. The Rifle had completed six — but had two costly interceptions.

The big break of the game came when Menan Schriewer tipped one of The Rifle's screen shots and the ball was deflected to Bobby Oliver at Montreal's six-yard stripe. Two plays later, Argos had a touchdown when Dick Shatto accepted Rote's short throw and did a ballet routine across the goal-line.

Etcheverry might have been a trifle careless in making his pass. To suggest such a thing is to impugn the alertness of the Argonaut defence. Sam said, after the game, he thought he had thrown the screen pass high enough.

"The fact it was tipped by Schriewer proves I was wrong, I suppose," The Rifle added glumly. "There was just enough interference with the pass to deflect the ball into Oliver's hands."

Famed cartoonist Duncan Macpherson presents himself with the Milt Dunnell Award, a mock tribute to the person who loses the most bets to Milt in a given year. Renowned around The Star *as a knowledgeable bettor always searching out suckers, Milt has won plenty over the years from the late Macpherson, former* Star *publisher Beland Honderich and the late humorist Gary Lautens. Milt once took Macpherson by betting it wouldn't rain on a football field for at least 24 hours before kickoff of a big game. What Macpherson didn't know — and Milt did — was that the game was being played inside a domed stadium.* (COURTESY THE TORONTO STAR)

The Rifle was in a position to nullify the Argonaut TD when it happened again — another interception. This time, there was no deflection. Sam made a bad throw. It was a clothes line peg which Stan Wallace took at the Scullers' twelve-yard line. He got to the 26 before the Als spilled him. That was the last time the Larks looked as if they might win the ball game.

Toward the end, the Montrealers were playing by ear. Seldom have professional footballers looked more bewildered than Charlie Baillie and Dick Cohee did on Dick Shatto's third and final touchdown. Shatto picked off Tommy Gun Tobin's pass while Baillie and Cohee were attempting to decide which one of them deserved the honor of intercepting it. With the ball tucked underneath his arm, Shatto walked over the goal-line.

He was so casual about it that observers figured he must have thought he was over the stripe when he made the catch. Shatto denied that in the dressing room. He was perfectly aware he had four yards to go, he said, but he knew he had no additional Larks to beat, so why get in a tizzy?

That was Rote's sixth touchdown pass. Four seconds remained on the clock when he tossed his record setter to Ed Ochiena, the former North York Knight. The tall Texan was asked later whether he knew he had a new mark in the making.

"No. All I wanted to do was build up that score," The Tommy Gun reported.

Are naturalized Canadians citizens?

On 16 February 1965 Milt spoke out against a CFL rule he thought unfair. Later that year, the rule was changed.

TORONTO — The Canadian Football League which always has qualified as one of the cheaper outfits operating professional sport on the continent, earned new notoriety at the recent bumblings in Bytown. Now, the CFL is being recognized for its stupidity as well.

The CFL, in its usual grab for a stray dollar, has decided that naturalized citizens of Canada are a brand apart from the native-born kind. Naturalized citizens can be separated from the main body and told there are special rules which apply to them.

If you think things are rough for Negroes in Selma, Alabama, take a look at what the CFL decreed Saturday in the capital of this country. Henceforth, the CFL said, it will not permit more than three naturalized Canadians to play on any one club, if they were born in the United States.

Who are these second-class citizens? They're fellows like Bernie Faloney, and Dick Shatto, and John Barrow, and Ralph Goldston and Ernie Pitts. They're athletes who listened to CFL coaches and general managers who conned them on the many advantages of Canadian ball.

"It's true that Canadian football has no pension plan," they were told, "and the folks back home will not see you play on TV. But the business opportunities are great. Canadian football is geared to permit its players to own a business or develop a good job. You'll be farther ahead in the long run."

Faloney got himself into a business at Hamilton. Goldston settled into what he considered a permanent position teaching school. They had been around long enough to regard themselves as members of the community — just like the people who signed them had urged. Faloney had been a Ticat for seven years — Goldston for nine.

Suddenly they were traded to the Montreal Alouettes. Tough luck — but that's one of the hazards of the trade. Now they're being told: "Look, you guys are not real Canadians. Only three of your kind can be on a club. If there are more than three, the others will have to be classed as imports."

Faloney, who doesn't have to worry about making the Alouettes — if they finally come up with the kind of money which he demands — is disturbed by the implication that he isn't entitled to the privileges of citizenship just because he's a naturalized Canadian.

"To me, it smacks of discrimination," Faloney says. "How can they pick out one group of Canadians and make special rules for them? When I qualified for citizenship and was naturalized, I thought I became a Canadian. Am I wrong?"

What Faloney overlooks is that Canadian football is run by men who are less concerned by what is right than they are about what will benefit their own clubs.

Years ago, somebody got the bright idea that a boy born in the US of a Canadian parent could declare Canadian citizenship up to age 21. There was a rush to discover football players who qualified under this kink in the import rule. Gerry McDougall was one of the first to arrive. Eventually, the inevitable happened. One or two clubs became so strong through signing synthetic Canucks that all the others ganged up on them and closed the door.

Now it's the same story with naturalized Canadians. The rules in Canadian football are a matter of expediency. Any group of clubs that smells an advantage for themselves can form a bloc and have the rules changed.

John Bassett, who is chairman of the Argonaut board of management, calls the current discrimination against naturalized Canadians "pure bush, disgraceful and a retrograde step." Because he's a director of a club that has seven naturalized players, Bassett will be accused of grinding his own ax. That's how Canadian football executives always think. It wouldn't occur to any of them that he might be fearful of the effect on Canadian football as a whole.

The shame of the new legislation is that it is aimed at what Canadian football likes to describe at banquets and presentations as "fine young types who came up here to play football and remained to be citizens."

In the flag ceremonies at Ottawa, the governor-general spoke of "all our people — the founding races, as well as Canadians of all other origins."

To the second-class citizens of football, that must have been a grim joke.

A replacement for Hunsinger

Leon McQuay's famous fumble in November 1971 remains the most memorable gaffe in the history of the Grey Cup. At the time, it had been nineteen years since McQuay's Argonauts had captured the Grey Cup and it would be another twelve years before they'd once again lay claim to the mug.

VANCOUVER — Those who live by the goof must expect to die the same way. Chuck Hunsinger will be ousted from the historic Order of Grey Cup goats now and the horns will be hung on the unwrinkled brow of Argonauts' youthful Leon McQuay.

It was Hunsinger who gave up the ball, on a fluke, to Jackie Parker of the Edmonton Eskimos in 1954 and turned what had all the earmarks of a Montreal rout into an Eskimo three-year reign.

Historians have said this was a mistake which ranked with Sonny Liston's game plan to decimate Cassius Clay. Hunsinger is pre-empted now simply because more citizens saw Leon (X-Ray) McQuay spit out the football at the Stampeder ten-yard line, when all the marbles were up for grabs, than were able to witness the Hunsinger gaffe. In 1954, nobody knew television was here to stay.

This is unfair to the unflappable Mr. McQuay. He was only one of several lionized gladiators who contributed mightily to booting Earl Grey's galvanized beaker into the ashcan.

The Argonauts, for example, never would have been in the

position to smell the money at the moment of McQuay's fumble if Jim Sillye of the Stampeders had not attempted a shoestring catch of an Argonaut punt, early in the third quarter, while the cowhands had a comfortable 14–3 lead.

Who needed heroics at that stage? The Argonauts needed it. That's who. Joe Vijuk, the Boatman who overslept and missed the Argonaut plane for the trip west, demonstrated the virtue of extra rest. He grabbed the loose ball and lateraled to Roger Scales, who rumbled for the Argonauts' only touchdown of the matinee.

It wasn't the kind of thing a coach includes in his game plan. A touchdown from a guard is like getting a heifer with a bottle of milk. Sillye's bauble became just another incident in an exciting afternoon — because McQuay suffered dropsy when the clock was running out.

Leon took just about everyone off the hook. That included Jerry Keeling, the Stampeder quarterback, who hung up a fat juicy pass to the Argos' Dick Thornton to pick off, with only two minutes and twenty-six seconds remaining in the game. Keeling would have been feeling the heat today if the Stamps had lost again.

The most reasonable appraisal of the soggy afternoon's antics would be something like this: Calgary made enough mistakes to let the Argonauts win. The Boatmen blew it because of their own sins.

The Argonauts committed the unpardonable crime of making the last two boo-boos. After McQuay went skidding on his chinstrap and surrendered the ball at the Calgary ten, the Boatmen still had a slim chance to bail out. Even that was squandered when Harry Abofs kicked the ball over the sideline at the Argo 49.

That gave Calgary repossession of the ball, under one of the oldest regulations in the book. As Charles Dressen once put it: "Them Argonauts thereupon was stone cold dead."

All of which changes nothing on the scoreboard. It merely constitutes a reminder that McQuay had accessories before and after the fact of his momentous goof. Some of the culprits wore red shirts. Others wore blue.

There will be profound thinkers who may live in fear, from

Leon McQuay hangs on to the ball during one of his spectacular runs in 1971. Unfortunately for him, he will always be remembered for the one that he dropped in the Grey Cup later that fall against the Calgary Stampeders.
(PHOTO BY DOUG GRIFFIN, COURTESY THE TORONTO STAR)

now to next June, that the terrible weight of his responsibility will crush the spirit of young Mr. McQuay and possibly ruin a promising career. They can relax, Mr. McQuay does.

"When I skidded and my elbows hit the ground and the ball jumped loose," McQuay said, after he had taken a leisurely shower, "I said to myself: 'There goes the ball game'."

No one could sum up the moment in which the world stood still more succinctly than that.

It may not have occurred to McQuay that he cost the venerable Boatman, Dick Thornton, a new car, courtesy of Labatts. This goes to the most valuable player in the show. Thornton had it won if the Argonauts had been able to complete the dozen or so yards which he failed to make on his runback after intercepting Keeling's pass.

Said Thornton: "All I needed was one more block and I'd have done it myself."

These Argos are more like 1952 version

A long time coming. After 31 years and numerous superstars like Tobin Rote, Jackie Parker, Joe Theismann, Anthony Davis and Terry Metcalf unable to take the Argos to the top, the Boatmen finally found the secret to the Grey Cup. Instead of high-priced imports, the organization saw the forest for all the trees and utilized local talent on the field and in the front office. This column appeared 28 November 1983.

VANCOUVER — That really is the Grey Cup you are going to see being paraded up Bay Street. It hasn't changed much except that it was worth a lot more than the $48 which His Lordship paid for it.

But what else is new?

The last time that old beaker appeared in the hands of the Argonauts, Nate Phillips was running for mayor on a platform of penny parking.

The fact that the Boatmen have it back, after 31 years, cannot be attributed entirely to patience. They finally got around to doing the things they had forgotten. Ed Soergel made a key interception in that 1952 game, the last time the Argos won. Yesterday, under Vancouver's shining dome, Carl Brazley made the interception and recovered a fumble. He also leveled John Pankratz, on a key tackle.

Joe Barnes, an oil man from Texas, became Nobby Wirkowski, who threw those 1952 passes to Zeke O'Connor and Doug Pyzer. Their roles were being played yesterday by Terry Greer, Emanuel Tolbert and Cedric Minter, who became O'Connor for the day.

In other words: "Same old Argos."

Only this time you don't have to duck when you say it. These are the Argonauts for whom a whole generation waited in disbelief that turned to despair.

The parade of futility under big brand names must have seemed endless — Anthony Davis, Terry Metcalf, Bruce Clark, Vernon Vanoy, Forrest Gregg, John Rauch, Joe Theismann, Tobin Rote.

But yesterday, when the badly battered old craft finally slipped off the shoal where it had been stranded for those 31 years, the solution looked so simple.

Ralph Sazio chugged a few miles down the Queen E. and did what he had been doing at Hamilton. Bob O'Billovich, who has been in the league all along and knows the Canadian game, finally got the call over somebody who had been fired at Cleveland or Chattanooga.

The story of the Argonauts' emergence from what appeared like another pratfall at the door to the throne room belonged to Barnes, a man who was undecided about playing football this season. He was alleged to have an oil well that was showing promising signs in Texas.

Mr. Barnes struck oil here yesterday before more than 59,000 fans — most of whom were disappointed. After a first half, in which the Argos looked suspiciously like the Argonauts of old, ready to blow the big one, Texas Joe replaced starting quarterback Condredge Holloway and immediately took charge.

It was revealed after the game that Holloway had been ailing slightly, because of the flu.

Barnes, his replacement, never looked healthier, although the Argonauts, who were trailing, 17–7, on the scoreboard when he arrived, were slow to respond.

In an unbelievable third quarter, they outplayed the Lions completely and even started getting the breaks. But out of two interceptions and a recovered fumble they picked up only two points. Could a team that squandered so many golden chances possibly play catch-up football?

The worst culprit was Hank (Thunderfoot) Ilesic, supposedly the best booter in the business, until the Argos doubled him up this season as field-goal kicker as well as punter.

Hank simply could not find the field-goal range in that third quarter of missed opportunities. He failed from 32. He failed from 34. And he failed from 47. Give Hank credit for this, though, he made the biggest one of all, moving the 43 in the fourth quarter, thus providing the points that put the Argos in position (17–12) whereby the big play, still to come, would win the game.

After the game, Sazio revealed that Ilesic had apologized for his failures. He didn't have to apologize. His punting gave the Argos an edge most of the afternoon.

With Barnes demonstrating that the offence was back in business, the defence became practically ferocious in its tackling and its protection against the pass.

It was fitting that Marcellus Greene, a defensive back, should make the final play of the game, snuffing out the last hope of the Lions. It was a desperation pass that BC quarterback Roy Dewalt heaved from his own 25 in the hope of pulling the game out of the fire. Greene went high into the air to tip the ball away from Jacques Chapdelaine.

The winning points already were on the board — a pass from Barnes to Cedric Minter in the end zone. It was an alert play by Tolbert that made it possible. After catching a pass at the BC 45, Paul Pearson had fumbled. Tolbert recovered the ball to keep the winning drive alive.

"We finally achieved what we wanted," President Sazio enthused. He meant the Grey Cup, of course? No, he said he meant what he called "a team concept." Whatever that means, we're going to take it.

Sopinka has fond memories of CFL days

A lawyer gets promoted to the top justice team in the land — The Supreme Court of Canada. Leave it to Milt to link that news with the lively, colorful days of Canadian football in this 28 May 1988 column.

TORONTO — Unlike Whizzer White, who galloped all the way from the playing fields of the National Football League to the US Supreme Court, Toronto's John Sopinka, newest member of Canada's top bench, sees no reason to close the book on one of the most exciting chapters of his career.

Once he reached the big league of legal referees, Whizzer White preferred to forget those triumphs between the white lines. There was tougher yardage to be gained in his new robe. With due respect to a fellow jurist, the Honorable Mr. Justice Sopinka, soon-to-be, disagrees.

"It (Canadian football) put me through law school," he submits, as fitting argument for keeping green his memories of sweat and blood with the threat of penury thrown in, when he played for the Toronto Argonauts and the late lamented Montreal Alouettes. It sounds like fun now, but the economics were serious then.

"I was traded to the Alouettes in my third year of law school," he was saying, between calls of congratulation on his new post. "I needed that football money to get through school and it wasn't possible to qualify at McGill.

"I asked Bora Laskin (later appointed chief justice of the Supreme Court of Canada) for advice. He was the assistant dean of the law school at University of Toronto. I asked him if I should appeal to the dean, Caesar Wright. He advised me not to do that. Just play football, attend as many classes here as I could, use the library at McGill, and see how things turned out.

"Things turned out pretty well until the last game of the regular season. Caesar Wright was watching on TV and there I was. He immediately sent me a letter advising that I must return to the school at once or I would be required to repeat my year.

"The playoffs were coming up. The Alouettes had to play in Hamilton. I had to be back at law school and I was expected to work out with the Alouettes, getting ready for the playoff game. There was nothing I could do except tell the Alouettes' coach, Peahead Walker, the position I was in."

If you are permitted to interrupt a member of Canada's Supreme Court, it should be mentioned that Peahead Walker, out of Birmingham, Alabama, was one of the most colorful and popular characters ever to migrate northward into the permafrost. He wore his trousers at half-mast and dispensed southern football philosophy in a leisurely drawl.

When he was asked how he would employ the twelfth man in Canadian football, Peahead pondered momentarily and said: "We'll just flank him real wide and play the eleven-man game."

Years after he left Montreal, he returned to promote an exhibition game of US football. He confided to media friends: "Don't let them sell you on US football. You've got a better game." From such a personality, Sopinka was a cinch to get a sympathetic hearing.

"I told him I was more anxious to become a lawyer than I was to become a football player. He said: 'Son, you go right back there to law school. Won't be nothing new in our defence for the Hamilton game.' That didn't surprise me much because Peahead hadn't added much to the defence all year. Hamilton beat us. That was my last game of pro football."

For a lawyer in the making, Sopinka couldn't have arrived in the Canadian Football League at a more opportune time. There were almost as many lawsuits as first downs. It was known as the Harry Sonshine era. Sonshine, installed as new general manager of the Argonauts, immediately fired all the teams' American imports and started raiding NFL clubs — they sued.

The New York Giants and the Detroit Lions were special targets. Billy Shipp and Bill Albright, two of the Giants' top defensive stars, became Boatmen. Quarterback Tom Bublinski left the Lions for the Boatmen, along with tackle Gil Mains and Jungle Jim Martin. Sonshine also went to the Giants for its coach, Bill Swiacki. One assistant coach, Bill Early, came from Notre Dame.

The eastern end of what is now the CFL was then known as the Big Four or the Interprovincial Rugby Football League. Alarmed over the war which Sonshine was stirring up with the NFL and also intimidated by the talent he was assembling, the other three teams threatened to toss the Argos out of the league.

"Sonshine was helpful to me," Sopinka recalls. "The American players used to work out in the mornings. Canadian players, who had jobs, had to practice later in the afternoon. I told Sonshine I needed $1,200 to pay my way at law school. I would like to work out with the American players. He went along with that.

"There were seven big name US players who had come up from the NFL but, by the terms of the settlement with the other

When John Sopinka, a former CFLer, was promoted to
Canada's highest justice team in 1988, Duncan Macpherson
depicted the judge with a Grey Cup and Argo and
Alouette banners. After his appointment, the Supreme Court
rookie was happy to relive his CFL days with Milt.
"It [Canadian football] put me through law school," he says.

(CARTOON BY DUNCAN MACPHERSON,

COURTESY THE TORONTO STAR)

three teams, only four were going to be eligible to play. Practicing with those seven Americans was like having coaches. They taught me so much about the game.

"Sonshine had boasted that the Argonauts were the highest-priced team in Canadian football and that we had the most talent. Now, it was time to show us off. We were to do a tour of the west. The first game was in Vancouver. We lost. On to Edmonton, where they had a good team, with Jackie Parker and a lot of other fine players. We lost.

"The final game of the tour was to be in Winnipeg. By this time, the ticket sales in Toronto must have been tapering off. We couldn't afford another loss. So Swiacki decided to use Jungle Jim Martin, who wasn't one of the four players who had been declared eligible. This Martin was a handsome guy, built like a Greek god. And he could play football.

"They gave him the No. 7 sweater, which belonged to a little-known Canadian kid named Kapaski. Martin booted the kickoff into the end zone and you could hear people buzzing about how that kid Kapaski kicked the ball. Martin was a defensive end. When Kenny Ploen, the Winnipeg quarterback, came out of the split-T formation on the option, Martin knocked him cold. Kenny was carried off on a stretcher. Everyone was raving about this sensational kid, Kapaski. Where did the Argonauts find him?

"I was covering Bud Grant and, when he went out for a pass, I probably interfered with him. I'm not saying I did. Anyway, when I fell down, Bud stepped on my hand. Swiacki decided to send out what we called our Wrecking Crew to get Bud.

"The Wrecking Crew consisted of Mains, Albright and Shipp, three very tough guys. They took care of Bud, but I don't think he was seriously injured. We did win the game, by the way."

There must be days when the august gentlemen of the Supreme Court get fed up to their eyeballs with arguments on constitutionality or bickering over fishing zones and offshore drill rigs.

If you were permitted to address the Supreme Court of Canada, you might say: "On the lunch break, honorable sirs, get the rookie to tell about the day Billy Shipp broke down the door of Swiacki's office in the Argonaut clubhouse. All Billy wanted to do was kill the coach. Or get him to tell about J.C. Caroline, whom the irascible Rigs Rigsby unloaded on the Argonauts. Or get him to tell . . . let the rookie decide what to tell. You'll go back to the bench refreshed."

After a rousing game like that who needs the NFL's version?

Over the years, Milt has been one of the CFL's toughest critics when it does dumb things. But he has also been one of its staunchest supporters. The 1989 Grey Cup game — like so many others before and since — proved what Milt has been saying for years: the Canadian football product is terrific entertainment, despite the meddling of executives and politicians.

TORONTO — The committee in pursuit of a National Football League franchise for the multi-million-dollar SkyDome got a resounding message yesterday in the 77th chapter of something that started out in Rosedale Field, before a handful of the faithful, and which seems determined to survive for at least another 77.

The message went something like this: "You've got the most entertaining brand of football anywhere on the continent right now. Ask any one of the millions who saw the Hamilton Tiger-Cats and the Roughriders from the wheat belt trading *blitzkriegs* yesterday for Earl Grey's battered silverware."

It's a message that scarcely is new, of course. You are reminded that, a few years back, Peahead Walker, a gentleman from Birmingham, whose drawl and his pants at half-mast were his trademarks, was sent up to Montreal to beat the drum for an NFL exhibition game. Peahead was considered an ideal missionary because he had coached the Alouettes and had many friends within the media.

"Keep what you have now," Peahead whispered to people he could trust. "It's a more entertaining game than the American brand."

You might have thought the Tiger-Cats and the Saskatchewans were aware of the threat to the twelve-man brand of mayhem when they rolled up 506 yards of offence in the first half and put 49 points on the board — six of those points on a 75-yard touchdown pass from Saskatchewan quarterback Kent Austin to slotback Jeff Fairholme. This was on Saskatchewan's first play after the Tiger-Cats had scored on a 30-yard touchdown pass from Mike Kerrigan to Derrick McAdoo.

Harry Ornest, owner of the Argonauts, whose team had trouble crossing the street all season without getting knocked down, must have agonized in his private box when he realized his retainers had given their faithful sleeping pills when they came for excitement. Anyone who saw yesterday's show would be back for a repeat today, even if he got stuck for that $15 parking fee. And any ideal wanderer who came in by mistake must have become a convert.

With 2:51 to go in the third quarter, the numbers on the board added up to 64 — only thirteen points short of the record for both teams in a Grey Cup game, set by Edmonton and Montreal in 1965. They ran out of footballs that year because the kids picked off the converts and heaved the footballs over the fence to receivers on Bloor Street. Chalk up another plus for the SkyDome. The CFL, which is concerned about such things, didn't lose a football yesterday.

The so-called purists are going to scoff that this shootout is not real football and where was the Hamilton defence that is supposed to be as foolproof as the vault in the Bank of Tokyo? There were 54,088 wide-eyed and husky-throated clients in the seats yesterday and only the 88 complained about lack of

*Milt, with binoculars, and other writers interview Hamilton
Tiger-Cats coach Jim Trimble in 1962 after the infamous
Fog Bowl, which split the Grey Cup over two days. Some
of the greatest CFL battles pitted Trimble's club against
Bud Grant's Winnipeg Blue Bombers. The two met in
the Grey Cup every year but one between 1957 and 1962,
with Grant victorious in all but 1957.*
(COURTESY MILT DUNNELL PHOTO COLLECTION)

defence. The multitude came to see action and there wasn't a
split second when it didn't get it. The gods who dictate such
things must like Canadian football. Last year, when the
bailiffs were batting on so many doors, the CFL got a spectacular Grey Cup show in Ottawa. Yesterday, with a few
bankers still wearing their collection day faces, the CFL got
another gloom-buster.

With 1:58 left on the clock, Dave Ridgway, the league's premier
booter, sealed the Tiger-Cats' fate with a field goal from 40

yards out but the Tiger-Cats didn't know their fate had been sealed. When Steve Wiggins of the Saskatchewans was called for pass interference, the Tiger-Cats were back in business on the Saskatchewan ten. With 44 seconds to go, they tied the score, on third down at the nine-yard line, when Kerrigan found Tony Champion in the end zone.

Sure, the score is tied but don't go away. In this ball game, a lot of things can happen in 44 seconds — and they did. When Kent Austin hit Ray Elgaard with a pass on the Saskatchewan 54, the Tiger-Cats realized they might be back in trouble. But they should dodge the bullet. There were only seven seconds remaining. Today, those seven seconds seem like a lifetime to the Hamilton partisans. Those seconds cost them a Grey Cup.

Hamilton coach Al Bruno put a couple of kickers in the end zone, in case Ridgway missed with the field goal which would be coming up. Their duty would be to boot the ball out. He didn't miss. With two seconds remaining, he kicked the three points which finally broke the jinx that plagued Saskatchewan teams when they sought the old goblet in the east. Now they know that if they can win here they can win any place.

As for the Canadian Football League, it should coin a new catch phrase. Something like this: "What you've seen here is what you're gonna see next season."

MILT AT
LARGE

This little gal is in the lettuce

With super promoter Tommy Gorman by her side, Barbara Ann Scott was making an unheard-of $100,000 a year skating in 1950. This column about the Olympic gold medalist and world champion appeared 11 January 1950.

SIMCOE — You were sighing a sigh or maybe shedding a tear for Barbara Ann Scott. The poor kid became champion of the world and then goes skating in her own land instead of blazing her way across the US to Hollywood. That seemed to make everyone sad — as if there were some stigma attached to skating in Canada for Canadians. Maybe that's typical of our thinking: Canada is good enough until you get to the top. Then you should streak south and wade into Uncle Samuel's shekels.

Whether Barbara Ann is on this side of the international stripe by choice isn't going to be debated here. The point is, she's skated through 6,000 miles of Canada and she's only at the halfway mark. She seems to be having fun, and she won't have to sell any apples to get by next summer.

Tommy Gorman, the irrepressible Irisher, who put Barbara Ann on tour, swore solemnly here that he'd be willing to pay off Barbara right now at $100,000 for the season. And he'd save money by taking her percentage at the finish.

There may be a few among you who will have to struggle along on less than a hundred grand for a whole year's work. So you can appreciate that it's possible for a beautiful gal on a pair of skates to make a modest stake without playing the Chicago, Detroit, New York circuit. It should be remembered that Barbara Ann is a corporation known as the St. Lawrence Foundation. And the huge Music Corporation of America holds her contract. That gives Music Corporation a 10 per cent bite of her earnings.

Gorman got her on loan for twenty weeks and is dickering with Music Corporation now for an extension. One of the reasons he needs the extra time is to play rinks in eastern Canada which have been tied up by American ice shows. They stipulate that no other ice show can appear there within 60 days of their own performance. Another reason is that his "Skating Sensations" have been invited to play Troy, New York, and Washington, D.C. These are dates which didn't appear on the original itinerary. Also, he has an offer to take part of the show to England.

In Gorman and Barbara Ann you have the most amazing team of the moment in the Canadian sports and entertainment set-up. Gorman admits to being 44 and probably is cheating. In hockey, he's won the Stanley Cup seven times. He has the Allan Cup now. He owns a ball club, a race track and an auditorium. He needs a buck like General Motors needs a Buick. Why, then, is he hopping from coast to coast on one, two and three-night stands with an ice show, of which he started out by knowing nothing?

Tommy scarcely can answer himself, except that he talked himself into it. He boasted to Morris Schrier of Music Corporation, last summer, that he could show Barbara Ann to a million Canadians and make money. Schrier demanded to know where he'd show her. Tommy mentioned far-away places like Regina and Edmonton and Medicine Hat. Mr. Schrier hadn't heard of them. After six trips to New York, Gorman found himself heading a set-up known as National Sports Enterprises, committed to show Canadians the champion of any part of this spinning old planet where it's possible to freeze water.

As for Barbara Ann, there never was any question of her being a trooper. She's shown now that she's a super-trooper. Two performances here — Gorman even had a Monday

Prime Minister Mackenzie King admires the key to the city of Ottawa presented to skater Barbara Ann Scott in 1948. Within two years the Olympic and world champion would be earning an astronomical $100,000 a season skating at rinks from coast to coast in Canada.
(COURTESY THE TORONTO STAR)

matinee, which must be something unique in show business — brought her total to 88 since the show opened in Winnipeg, October 10. When she has an afternoon and evening show, she makes fourteen appearances on the ice, without counting encores. That means fourteen changes of costume and re-arrangement of hair-do. And she hasn't missed a minute. She skated in Vernon, British Columbia, with a temperature of 102°F, after getting nearly crushed to death by admirers who broke through police lines. She skated for weeks with a plaster over a broken rib. Her side was raw where the plaster tore the skin during her strenuous numbers. She has addressed skating clubs, launched charity drives and visited hospitals. The personal appearances have been eliminated now. Any person who examines her schedule would be ashamed to request one.

The crowds here lifted total attendance to date past the 450,000 mark. Those are Gorman's figures. Edmonton was tops, because it's the biggest rink they've played. There they did nearly $80,000 worth of business. Windsor is second, despite warnings from show men to steer clear. Gorman was told that Windsor is too close to Detroit to appreciate a homespun show. His only mistake, he mourns, was that he didn't book the rink for a week, instead of for three nights and a matinee.

By streamlining his show and traveling light, Gorman plays rinks which the big ice shows couldn't touch. He has a troupe of 60, all noses counted, and a nut of $15,000 per week. Incidentally, he has some of the comeliest kids who ever laced a skate. They're from as far west as the Rockies and as far east as Sherbrooke. He's offering good, clean entertainment, minus, of course, the elaborate trappings of the big shows, such as Ice Capades and Ice Follies. Barbara Ann is putting more showmanship and less Olympic precision into her acts. Gorman even has her doing a rhumba. That brought outcries from some of the skating clubs in western Canada. They regarded it as undignified for an Olympic champion. Gorman told them: "The Olympics are over."

Although the troupe off the ice is more like a college glee club than a professional show, there have been moments when Gorman wondered why he left his hockey club and his racetrack. One night, in the west, a couple of his musicians, at intermission, took to throwing punches in the dressing-room. One battler's cheek was opened, and a patch was slapped on so he could start the second half of the show. In the excitement, the other guy's wounds were overlooked. Two minutes after the second half began he was viewing the world through one peeper. The other one was closed for the evening.

When the show arrived in Stratford, one act was fogbound in Buffalo, one was stalled at Detroit and still another was grounded at Williamsport, New York. The weather had closed in while they were trying to get back from Christmas vacation. Gorman gave them all the same message: "You're in show business; I'll expect you tonight." They all made it. The kids from Williamsport arrived a few minutes before the show began. Two cops had brought them in a cruiser.

P.S.: You were asking about Barbara Ann's romances. Gorman reports a couple of boys are regular visitors to the show. Mom Scott tells us Barbara Ann has said there'll be no sparklers until she's through barnstorming.

Inspiring sight — and a distressing one

Three months after Roger Bannister ran the first four-minute mile, he and John Landy matched up for the dramatic "Miracle Mile" at the Empire Games in Vancouver. It was the first time two men had shattered the four-minute barrier in the same mile race. As Milt reports 9 August 1954, an almost sickening athletic occurrence befell the track just moments after the Bannister-Landy race.

VANCOUVER — More millions of eyes than ever lamped any other footrace in history saw the doctor arrive in time at the Empire stadium here Saturday. The good Doc demonstrated his Four-S treatment for the cure of that slow and draggy feeling.

It's the Doc's contention that if you combine stamina, speed, savvy and science in their proper proportions, there's no reason why you can't get from here to there in one heck of a hurry. He also revealed the true meaning of the "magic mile" of which you've been hearing so much. The miracle will be if anybody beats young Doc Bannister over a mile of cinders. We're not even sure he wouldn't be swift if he were running along the railroad tracks. Certainly the Doc looks to have treated Australia's John Landy as he would handle a case of diseased tonsils. When they become troublesome, he gets them out of there. That's how he diagnosed Landy. When the right moment came, at the head of the lane, he applied the Doc Bannister kick. It had about the same effect as a jolt from a battery has on a bangtail.

"I looked back over my shoulder and my worst fears were confirmed," the patient John Landy reported a few minutes later. By this time, the patient was doing as well as could be expected of a man with microphones jammed in his teeth and reporters draped from his shoulders. Landy was speaking of that quick peek he permitted himself, maybe 200 yards from home. He had done his utmost to leave the Doc back in his prop wash. When he saw the Doc was right on his tail, he knew it was just a matter of seconds before a medical man would be bustling past him, like the country doctor racing the stork.

Bannister's superb performance was something for the millions to see and to enjoy. Luckily, there was a much smaller audience for the chilling drama which followed almost immediately. Only the 32,000 in the stadium, plus a regional TV clientele, saw marathoner Jim Peters of England stagger into the stadium. If only one person had seen him, it was too many. This was one of the most distressing scenes ever disguised as sport. The fact that it was raw courage on display didn't make it any more acceptable to the audience. One irate man yelled, while Peters was wallowing in the dirt, that you couldn't torture a dog like that without getting hauled into court by the Humane Society. The gentleman said a mouthful.

There probably will be screams that the marathon should be banned, as a result of the Peters incident. That, of course, is pure nonsense. The marathon is one of the world's oldest forms of competition. If men want to run 26 miles, plus a few yards, they should have that privilege. It's their feet: but it isn't necessary to inflict their tortures on other people. If a professional boxer goes down three times in one round, the fight is over. Peters was down a dozen times within 120 yards after his rubbery legs carried him into the stadium. He crumpled in a heap twice on the runway. Within 100 feet, he was down four times. When he got to his feet he swayed like a drunk on a swing bridge, and his eyes stared blankly. By this time, his buddy, John Savidge, the English shot-putter, was giving invaluable assistance. John created the impression he might have more in his heave than he has in his head as he waved his hat and yelped at Peters from the edge of the track on the infield: "Get up, Jim. You gotta get up. Don't lie there, Jim." John would make a good fight manager. He could stand in the corner and howl: "Get in there an' fight, this bum can't hurt us."

Women in the crowd wept and implored some person to stop the sadism. Many fainted. Men muttered and nattered it was a revolting sight. But Peters finally dragged himself to what the crowd obviously thought was the finish line. The English trainer, Mick Mays, was waving a towel back of the stripe, as a radar to guide Peters through his mental fog. There was a roar of applause as Peters fell over the line. This time, Mays caught him. The roar turned to a groan when the reminder came over the PA system that the finish line was on the opposite side of the stadium.

It was announced later that Mays had grabbed Peters, thereby disqualifying him, on the instructions of the English team's manager. But nobody was fooled much. If they intended to halt Peters' assault on his health, why did they wait until he had crossed the line which marked the finish of all races — except the marathon? Some of the officials, at least, obviously thought Peters would win if he could reach that line. There's liable to be a hey-rube yet over the confusion surrounding the point of finish. If the English team didn't know where the race ended, whose fault was that? The Scottish runner, Jock McGhee, who entered the stadium at least fifteen minutes behind Peters, obviously knew where the race ended. He steered straight to the finish line.

Peters' plight was caused in the first place by his own bad judgment. He was more than half a mile ahead of the next runner. Instead of sparing himself then, he wanted to lengthen his lead. His own advisors completed the debacle. Instead of telling him to sit and rest when he fell, on entering the park, they goaded him to his feet immediately. Maybe he never would have made it, anyway, but at least it would have shown they were using their heads.

One English correspondent, a recognized authority on track and field, described Saturday's show as "the greatest single day of sporting events ever held." Well, anyway, it was the greatest single day of sport in the life of Toronto's Richie Ferguson, and here's a boy of whom this country can be proud. A few weeks ago, he wasn't even considered a miler. After two startling efforts here against the very best in the business, he now has to be considered among the world's top six. Maybe Fergie is unlucky in that his own performances were almost obscured by the hysteria over Bannister and Landy. Then, just about the time the packed crowd was beginning to realize what a Canadian had accomplished, Jim Peters wobbled into the snake pit. After a few minutes of that, folks couldn't even remember they had just seen Bannister and Landy crack the four-minute sound barrier in the same race. That's something which never had happened before. While Ferguson may have missed some of the raves he deserved, you can't brush off what the stopwatch says: A mile in 4:04.6. And to be fair about it, he doubtless benefited from running against the best. He had to give more. That's what he did.

Only Bannister refused to be shaken by the blistering pace of the curly-thatched Landy. But the gent who came closest was Ferguson of Canada. He was the bestest of the restest. And that included Halberg of New Zealand, who was considered the dark horse of the race.

Tip of the season — and no person bet

It took almost 21 hours and 65,000 grueling strokes for 16-year-old Marilyn Bell to become the first person to swim across Lake Ontario. She battled lamprey eels and oil slicks, but entranced a city and captivated a country. Milt filed his column 10 September 1954.

TORONTO — Don't blame Gus Ryder if all his friends are not rich. The Silver Shark of the Lakeshore Swim club let them in on a good thing. They responded by getting together and debating solemnly whether something shouldn't be done about an examination of Ryder's head. After the July swim in Atlantic City, Gus reported, in effect: "Marilyn Bell can beat anything that's not equipped with webbed feet or fins." Everybody laughed, when they could have been out breaking the books. The Dutch have a word for it: *"too soon ve get too old; too late ve get some smart."*

In fairness to the scoffer, Gus had seen more than the morning works. He saw the Bell mermaid churning such a rapid pace through 26 miles of the Atlantic ocean that he deliberately slowed her pace. Maybe he thought she would run out of gas. If he did he had changed his mind by the end of the race. After 25 miles, the Toronto school girl gave Gus a home stretch rush by stepping up her strokes to 68. She finished seventh in the whole field, but first among the females. No person can be sure how many of the first six men she might have whipped if Gus had not restrained her.

Marilyn Bell, Canada's sweetheart teen who had just become the first to swim Lake Ontario, was a media darling in 1954. (COURTESY THE TORONTO STAR)

"Bell will beat Florence Chadwick any day, at any distance," Gus whispered. That's when we all knew Gus had spent too much time in the noonday sun without a straw hat. Chadwick had swum just about every ditch except the Pacific. She was an experienced pro. Ryder's pheenom, as the ball players call the talented upstairs, was a few weeks shy of sweet seventeen.

"So what?" Gus countered. "Seventeen, for swimming, is an ideal age."

Gus should be right, if for no other reason than he seldom is wrong. George Young, the man who gave Ontario its first attack on water of the brain, was seventeen when he startled the world by crossing Catalina. His present-day successor, Cliff Lumsden, was sixteen when he cashed his first CNE marathon cheque. And years ago, a kid named Gertrude Ederle earned a ticker-tape parade down Broadway because she was the first woman to beat the English channel. Unless memory plays tricks she was nineteen at the time.

Even so, it must be remembered that Young and Lumsden were husky young giants. And Ederle was built along chunky lines. This Bell kid is frail as a humming bird by comparison with them. She doesn't look to be the all-weather, endurance type of churner. Yet she licked a lake which the old marines insisted would freeze her and then attempt to tear her apart. One answer is that this gal is all heart. Just sitting in a chair for twenty hours without a break would give most mortals a case of utter exhaustion. Never mind twenty hours of biting cold, tugging currents and ten-foot waves.

Even to look at the spectacle of a marathon swim well out in the lake is a depressing experience. Yesterday afternoon, the lake was described as "flattening out." That meant the swell, which rolled toward the east, had a curling crest of roughly four feet. In a nest of assorted boats which pitched and tossed, a lonely figure in a white bathing cap stroked endlessly. Now the restless lake lifted her into plain view of those in the accompanying craft. Next instant, she disappeared in the trough between two waves. The towers of Toronto mocked from the shoreline, which seemed tantalizingly near yet was agonizing miles away.

Nothing since the Moose river disaster, in which a party of Canadians were trapped in a mine, has so completely disrupted the workaday existence of a city and province. When the phone rang a million people gave a stock answer: "She's still in the water." Even the CNE suffered from its own smash hit. You'll hear varied estimates of the crowd which charged to the waterfront in the hope of seeing the finish. The best way to determine how many were there is to take the day's attendance. Only the men, women and children went to the lake. The Exhibition continued unnoticed and unpatronized. Fences were flattened along the lakeshore drive. Cars were trapped in the flood of humanity. And as is usual at marathon swims, most everybody saw nothing. When an ambulance roared from the vicinity of the landing float, with its sirens screaming, thousands cheered and auto horns tooted. It was a noisy salute to the city's new sweetheart — only she wasn't even in the ambulance. Despite the nation-wide interest it caused, you can't prove the swim brought any new business through the turnstiles. The trend of attendance this year has been up. Yet the cold figures show that yesterday's gate was eight thousand below the turnout on the corresponding day a year ago.

There was a party but not ours

It was the end of an incredible string of successes for Canada in Olympic hockey. From 1920 to 1952, Canadian teams lost only one game in 41 matches and outscored the competition 403 to 34. But on 6 February 1956 the Soviet Union stripped Canada of the gold with a 2–0 victory. This country has yet to win another Olympic gold medal in hockey.

CORTINA, Italy — The party was in the wrong hotel last night, and the platitudes were in the wrong tongue. Up at the isolated Tre Croci Inn on the mountain there was kissing and some cackling as the speedsters from the steppes counted the loot. And, no kidding, they have something to cackle about. The kissing is something else again. Some of those chunky Russian dolls, who looked as though they might be kissable, were left out, whereas Arkradi Cherniskov, coach of the Ruskies hockey Huskies, got himself bussed right on the lips. The kisser was chairman of an all-union committee on physical culture and sport. He probably demonstrated why our hockey has gone decadent. As long as guys like King Clancy prefer money to a kiss from Conn Smythe we can't expect to be top dogs in the league. Look at what it's done to the Leafs. It's the same story over here.

Aside from the kissing and the cakes which were handed out to the athletes, there was plenty about the clambake that Canadians could copy — just as we might find use for some of the things they do on the ice. Although they were toasting their first Olympic shinny title with world and European honors attached, no person got soused. We noticed one or two characters squeezing the empty wine jugs, but no one took the hint. There were no refills. No guest violated his diet, either. The orators took care of that. Considering the importance of the occasion, it was a nice orderly gathering with dancing in the music room when the limited supply of grog gave out. The Russians picked their hideaway carefully, just as they have made all their moves to replace the Canutskies as kingpins on skates. There was a minimum of commotion and confusion at their hotel. And the players had to hit the sack on scheduled time. It was either that or play checkers, because the hotel is too far out of town for walking. Finding taxis is like winning a sweepstake, and street cars don't seem to fit that mountain trail somehow.

But don't get the idea it was revelry that downed our Dutchies. Maybe they quaffed an occasional beer rather than see the stuff go flat. And they might have cheated one or two times on curfew to catch the late, late show. But what beat the Canutskies was the speed and passing of the red-shirted Ruskies. Two or three times they spotted good skaters like Paul Knox and Billy Colvin half a dozen strides and then collared them. Their pattern-passing is the kind your grandpaw tells you he saw in the good old days. Grandpaw never saw it. He just thinks he did. The Ruskies must have been reading his mind. They've poached just about everything they like about the Canadian game, so they might as well have the mythology, too. In the Canadian brand of hockey the Russians wouldn't be able to take the chances they take in this league. There would be too much danger of getting powdered into the dasher. That practically calls for the firing squad over here. And the Europeans may be right. There's no prettier sight in hockey than those Ruskies flicking the puck around. It would look even better if it had been done by the guys with Canada on their shirts.

The Dutchies can have regrets, but should have no remorse. This probably was their top effort. In the first period they looked as if they would repeat the performance of Penticton last March. Art Hurst gave the Russians some body-slams that must have been felt in the suburbs of Moscow. But he's about the only one who can throw the brawn around. And one wasn't enough. In the second chucker you could see the Canadians shortening stride. Effort and attitude were taking their toll. What kind of a team could beat the Ruskies a year from now in their new Moscow rink? It may require a combination of the Montreal Canadiens and Mervin the kicking mule. In other words, a team that can skate, pass and clout. The Dutchies might have done it with one or more wrecker and a take-charge guy who can put the puck in the net. Then we would have had the party at the Concordia, with no kisses, no cakes and roast veal. Why veal? You can always get veal. The country must be over-run by calves.

GRENOBLE — For twenty years Europeans have been asking visiting firemen from Canada: "And how is Barbara Ann Scott? She was such a friendly girl." They haven't forgotten how she smiled and curtsied her way through Europe in the winter of 1948.

Behind the grace and the glamor, Barbara Ann was a tough little campaigner who had as much competitive fire as a Rocky Marciano or a Rocket Richard. First she scooped up the European figure skating championship at Prague in a field of 30.

In the Olympics, at St. Moritz, she tow-roped another field of 24. Away she went to Davos and knocked off the world title for a clean sweep. Europe hasn't been quite the same for dolls in spangled scanties since that time. They find themselves compared unfavorably to the blonde beauty from Bytown.

But all reigns come to an end — and the new queen is a tomboy type from Rossland, British Columbia, whose flying skis practically burn the snow off slopes. Nancy Greene probably will make Europeans forget Barbara Ann Scott at long last.

No country could ask for a better ambassador of good will. Nancy is one of those fortunate persons who says the right thing at the right time. It seems to be instinctive. After the special slalom in which she won the silver medal and Judy Nagel, the first heat winner, fell, Nancy reminded the American press: "That's inexperience. Those American girls are good. When they gain experience they will be tough to beat."

Yesterday, after she had astounded the ski addicts of the world by barreling down the giant slalom course on Mount Belladonna in 1:51.97, Nancy was given an opportunity to excuse her tenth place finish in the downhill.

Members of the Canadian entourage had leaked the story that they had made a mistake in waxing her skis. At the international racing level that's equivalent to confessing that a sky diver was given a pillowcase instead of his chute. Skiers bog down and die when their staves are painted with the wrong wax.

Nancy refused to accept the escape hatch. She said flatly: "The French girls used practically the same wax as I used. They beat me so I don't see why I should blame the wax."

As an indication of the affection in which she is held by her rivals, Annie Famose of France spoke up and said: "I don't agree with Nancy. She couldn't have lost as much time as she lost in the downhill if the wax had been right."

Nobody doubted the wax was right yesterday. Nancy's time was so fast that some Canadians in the crowd suspected she must have missed one of the 68 gates on the course. She was almost three seconds faster than Annie Famose. In a game where time is measured in hundredths of a second, that's like winning the Queen's Plate by 40 lengths.

A reminder of what happened to the Yanks in the women's slalom flashed through everyone's mind. They had four of the top six racers on the scoreboard after the initial run. Three of the four were disqualified for missing gates.

The only reassurance was the trace of a grin at the corners of the Canadian girl's mouth. If she had missed a gate, she would have known and she wouldn't be smiling. This was for real — fantastic as it was.

The term "team player" has been misapplied so frequently that its meaning has become obscure. Individualists whose greatest concern is their own batting average or scoring record have been honored with the accolade.

Olympic hero Nancy Greene from British Columbia stands tall at a Toronto City Hall party in her honor in February 1968.
(PHOTO BY DOUG GRIFFIN, COURTESY THE TORONTO STAR)

So just say Canada's double medal winner is this type: she has been on hand for the last two hockey games to wish Canada's Nationals well. She has been there to congratulate them when they came off the ice.

Nobody has seen her score a goal or block a shot: so she can't get credit for lighting the fire under our shinny team. But something is igniting them. They couldn't have beaten Lower Slobovia the way they were playing last week. Now, with an assist from Czechoslovakia, they're back in the gold rush.

Maybe they simply decided it was going to be embarrassing if one little girl from the mountains of British Columbia took home Canada's only Olympic loot.

They'd better make sure Nancy has a seat tomorrow night, right behind the Canadian bench. Nothing succeeds like success. And Nancy scarcely knows how to lose.

The Super-Mex is super-draw

The Merry Mex, Lee Trevino, has been a breath of fresh air in golf going on 30 years. This lively column appeared 12 July 1971, in the middle of Trevino's dream season.

TORONTO — Lee Trevino, the Super-Mex, reads greens rather well, but his perusal of literature has been restricted to such vital things as scoreboards, past performances at dog-tracks and airline schedules to the next place where there's a big golf pot up for grabs.

He undoubtedly missed those immortal lines: "Golf is not a funeral, though both can be very sad affairs." Golf was getting to be a sad affair just about the time Trevino emerged from the sand dunes of Texas and commenced attracting his own version of Arnie's Army. The Trevino troopers were known as "Lee's Fleas."

Anybody who was bank-rolling a tournament had to know whether Arnold Palmer, Jack Nicklaus, Gary Player and one or two others would be doing a sponsor the honor of dropping around for a share of the loot. If they were not competing, the show qualified, almost automatically, to be labeled as a flop.

All of a sudden, it doesn't seem to matter who stays home — as long as the Magnificent Mexican appears. Barring only Palmer, he's the greatest blessing to descend on the box office since Walter Hagen attacked the British Open, in his silk shirts, custom-tailored knickers and chauffeured limousine — which he used as a dressing room because pros were barred from the clubhouse.

The gold dust tour has produced an oddity — a pro who

wants to play and whom the people want to see. There are plenty who are anxious to play — but are not worth a quarter at the gate. There are a few who sell tickets — but who do the promoter a favor when they compete.

That makes Trevino the most refreshing thing to hit big league golf since Samuel Jackson Snead bought his first straw hat. He just likes to play the game. One year, at the Masters, he did 36 practice holes during the day, nine holes on a pitch-and-putt layout before dinner and nine more on a par-3 at midnight.

After winning his second US Open on June 14 — in a playoff with Jack Nicklaus — the accepted thing for Trevino to do would have been to fly back to Texas and sign some contracts for endorsements and clambakes.

He could have skipped the Canadian Open — as Nicklaus did — and swooped over to Southport, where the British Open was being held. But Trevino remembers when he was working for $30 a week as the pro at Horizon Hills outside El Paso. He would have given ten years of his life for a chance to play in a national tournament then. He's making up for those lost opportunities.

Since June 14, he has competed in four major tournaments, winning the US, Canadian and British Opens. Jack Nicklaus is on record as having said that his goal in golf is to win at least one major championship each year.

Nicklaus, admittedly, was not including the Canadian Open in his category of major titles. He referred to the British and US Open, the American PGA and the Masters. Trevino has bagged two of them within four weeks and has the Canadian Open for a kicker.

Fortunately Trevino has no appreciation of money. He was raised by his mother and grandfather in a shack that lacked lights and indoor plumbing. The only thing that was good about it was the location. It was alongside a golf course, where the members were so affluent that the temperamental ones could afford to fling their clubs into a hayfield.

That's how young Lee Trevino got hooked in the first place. He found an iron which, unfortunately, had been owned by a bad-tempered southpaw. That meant Lee had to strike with the back of the blade when he used it.

Things have been better since 1967, when his wife, Claudia, gave him a few bucks and sent him to the US Open. She handles the money. Lee finished fifth that year, and picked up $6,000 — which he had to mail, right away, to Claudia.

When he arrived at the next stop — the Cleveland Open — his total liquid assets were $20. The entry fee there was $50. Lee got in on the cuff and paid off from his winnings.

The worst thing that could happen, of course, would be for Lee to start thinking of the golf tour as a bore but a profitable business. There are enough of that kind already.

Knock, knock — who's here?

Loud-mouth high-jumper Dwight Stones could manage only a bronze, with Canadian Greg Joy scooping the silver and Poland's Jacek Wszola grabbing the gold. For months before this, Milt had been writing about the bungling of politicians and Olympic officials when it came to mismanaging money and construction schedules. But on 29 July 1976 Milt took Stones to task for ignorantly blaming French Canadians as a whole for the problems.

MONTREAL — It's beginning to sound like 1960 all over again. That was the year the Olympics were held in Rome. Everyone who knew a discus from a dinner plate chalked in the name of John Thomas, out of Boston, as the winner of the high jump. It was the easiest guess of the Games.

Selecting a Yank to pick off this plum never was too difficult. From 1896, when the Olympics made their comeback in Athens, to the supposed John Thomas lock-up, only two athletes who were not members of the US team had ever won this event.

One was Dunc McNaughton in 1932 at Los Angeles. The other was John Winter of Australia. He won in 1948, when the Olympics were held in London. McNaughton must have put some kind of hex on his fellow Canadians. Not a single gold medal in track and field has come this way since.

This is supposed to be another can't-miss year in the high jump. A skinny, brash 23-year-old shoe salesman with a shock of honey-colored hair and a high opinion of his own talents, has nominated himself to stand up there on the top step of the ceremonial podium.

His name is Dwight Stones and, if he wins, he is going to put the knock on a lot of things. He probably will win. So you may as well get used to it. Among the knocks you are going to hear is that the conduct of the Games has been so bad, the opening ceremonies didn't have to be more than mediocre to seem inspiring.

When the word gets out — as it probably will — that Stones has put the blast on the Olympic Village, the food, the practice field, the US Olympic Committee and the French Canadians, you may not be able to hear the Star Spangled Banner for the booing.

His complaint against the French Canadians is that they did not get the stadium completed in time for the Games. Since Montreal's mayor, Jean Drapeau, is a French Canadian, high hopper Stones is correct, up to a point. It was Drapeau's bungling that delayed construction to such an extent that they were thinking of painting the lanes for the 100 meters down St. Catherine Street.

On the other hand, there are several million French-speaking Canadians, who didn't want the stadium but will be paying for it, long after Dwight Stones has cashed in on his gold medal — presuming he gets it.

There always is the possibility, of course, although it is remote, in Stones' opinion, that he may not win that gold medal. John

Thomas, the shoo-in of Rome, settled for bronze.

The gold went to Robert Shavlakadze of the Soviet Union. Only Robert's dearest friends at the putty knife factory remember that Valeriy Brumel, who finished second, took over immediately as the world's premier high hopper.

"I really am upset with the French-Canadian people," Stones said, after returning from California, where he had gone to correct some flaws in his Olympic training.

"They had six years to build this stadium. It's rude that the stadium was not finished in time for the Olympics. This is the first time there has not been a pre-Olympic meet in the stadium, a year before the Games."

If there had been a track meet in the stadium, one year prior to these Games, one of the leapers might have been picked up in error by a crane operator who was eating his lunch on the job.

Stones spent $430 on the trip to Long Beach, California, where he normally trains. He describes it as the best value he ever received for his money, although he admits he doesn't earn much.

"The last job I had, on which I paid taxes, was three years ago," he recalls. "I really didn't pay much tax because I earned less than $6,000. Before I left the Village for California, I couldn't make 6.10 (6 feet, 10 inches). Out there, I jumped 7.4 in the rain.

"I had grooved into a bad habit — taking a sidestep on my approach. The grass here (at the training center) is the most dangerous I ever saw in my life. You either get shin splints or you sprain your ankle. I can sprain an ankle just looking at it.

"I was here in March. At that time, I visited the Village and the Olympic sites. That was when I made the reservations to go back to the west coast during the Games.

"The environment here is intimidating. In Munich, I had several tracks on which to train — and a single room. Here, there is one track — and twelve to a room — with one bathroom."

A guy from Atlanta jokingly said he wanted to introduce Stones to pitcher Mike Marshall some day. Stones got the point. He retorted: "That guy's a trouble-maker. I'm glad the Dodgers got rid of him."

Crazy like foxes Canadian skiers press in practice

The Crazy Canucks set new standards for downhill racers, broke the European stranglehold on the sport and enthralled fans on both sides of the Atlantic. Their secret? Team work, as revealed here on 12 December 1978. Sadly, Dave Murray died in 1990 at age 37 to cancer. "Every race I try my hardest," he once said. "I pretend it's my last race because it could be."

TORONTO — Crazy Canucks? Best downhill ski squad competing in Europe? Does that mean the inmates have taken over the nuthouse on the slopes?

Dave Murray, veteran of Canada's overseas Hell Drivers on skids (he's 25) fielded the double-barreled question over at Schladming, nestled in the Austrian Alps.

In Sunday's first downhill race of the World Cup season, Murray finished six one-hundredths of a second behind teammate Ken Read of Calgary, who was first. Two other Canadians, Dave Irwin of Thunder Bay and Steve Podborski of Toronto, were seventh and ninth, respectively.

Asking four members of the same team to be one-two-seven-nine is like betting Les Leafs to wipe out Montreal Canadiens in a four-game set, without allowing a goal.

"Crazy?" Murray feinted for a little time. (Maybe half a dollar's worth at Ma Bell's rates.) "No, not crazy. I think it's merely a matter of the approach which we take to the practice runs.

"The Europeans are inclined to be more conservative when it's a practice run. Our attitude is that we should get the most out of the course. We realize there are only five training runs. So we don't hold anything back. Skiing is a sport of incredible variables. We feel you can't know too much about the course.

"As for our team being the best over here: on Sunday, we were the best. Next Sunday, in Val Gardena (Italy), who knows? There will be at least twenty guys in that race who could win. Four of them will be members of our team."

Murray was relaxed enough to stand a little kidding about being so far behind Read. Six one-hundredths of a second. He must have blinked an eye on one of the bends.

"In maintaining balance, you try to keep your arms out in front of you," Murray replied seriously. "At 70 miles per hour, an arm gets pushed back by the wind. Merely adjusting it costs you six one-hundredths of a second, right there."

Two hours before the race, Murray was barreling, upside down, through a clump of trees alongside a warm-up hill near the official course. The binding on his right ski had come loose. Reports from the scene blamed a class of ski students for jaywalking on the hill.

Murray said no one was to blame except himself. After his ski came off, he headed for the bush, out of control. Fortunately, he escaped fractures — or worse — and a doctor patched up a gouge in his head. It wasn't exactly the warm-up he would recommend for an official World Cup race.

While every member of the team is out to win, as an individual, the team's success is the No. 1 concern. So Read, who was the first Canadian to cover the course, was on the phone to his mates the moment he had completed his run.

"In training, the course had been icy," Murray recalled. "Then, there was a warm wind. When we went up in the morning, the course had turned mushy. It had been treated with chemicals before the race.

"Ken (Read) was able to tell us the conditions had changed again. Now, the course was more or less as it had been in training. Hey, Ken just came in. You should talk to him."

Read, whom the European ski writers have called "the world champion of training" because of his fast practice times, confessed to having said, a few days ago, that he didn't expect to see Canadians finish one-two in a World Cup event again — as he and Murray did last year in a late-season race at Chamonix, France.

"To have four Canadians in the top nine was really amazing," he agreed. "I think the real surprise was Dave Irwin's finishing seventh. He hadn't been doing exceptionally well in training (after an absence of almost two years, due to injuries). He did a remarkable job."

Far from feeling superior, because of the outcome of Sunday's opening event, Read predicted the Canadian success would make events still to come just that much tougher.

"Everybody will be out to knock us off," he reasoned. "Our philosophy is that we're over here, in their backyard. To be successful, we have to work together.

"Sure, we'll compete with each other — about two or three minutes per week."

Nations of world find love in Calgary

At the 1988 Winter Olympics, there were stars like ski jumper Matti Nykanen and ice queen Katarina Witt, and delightful side attractions like the Jamaican bobsled team and Britain's Eddie the Eagle Edwards. Yet, it was the city of Calgary and the people of Alberta who stole the show, as Milt reported on 29 February 1988. The reference to King Arthur's treacherous nephew Modred and the laundry is a poke at the news people who complained about missing laundry throughout the Games.

Calgary: *Wir lieben Dich.*
Calgary: *Nous t'aimons.*
Calgary: *Ti amo.*
CALGARY — What they are saying, Calgary, is that they love you. They are saying it in German, French, Italian and a babble of tongues from the 56 nations which have been your neighbors of the world, out here in the balmy foothills. They also are saying: "Calgary, the next time you hold a party, make sure we are on the guest list because the warmth of your friendship has been like that chinook which gave Miami a chill."

What you have done, Pardners, if you can excuse such familiarity from the East, is that you have turned Cowtown into Camelot — just as you took the Grey Cup medicine show off Bloor Street and turned it into a national bash. That was back there in 1948, when Les Lear could wither a striped shirt — or a fullback who missed a block — with a scowl because Les Lear was not a Chamber of Commerce type. Les Lear was, though, one helluva football coach.

The best part of your Camelot, Pardners (apologies again), was that Lancelot didn't hide his chivalry behind one of those silly tin suits, with a visor that made him look like an ancient version of Jacques Plante. Your Lancelot came roaring down a chute on skies and he made the richest gold strike since Swede Andersen turned that legendary shovelful of gravel, much farther north. They called your Lancelot the Flying Finn. It is the almost unanimous opinion, too, that your Guinevere was a lot more attractive, in her brevities that enhanced her triple spins and double toe loops, than she was in her original flounces and frills. No wonder the natives lined up, before dawn's early light, in the faint hope of getting a ticket that would permit them a look.

And incidentally, Calgary, you brought more people to these Games — an estimated 1.5 million spectators, who saw the events live — along with countless millions who watched on the tube, around the world. Just as important, you took the athletes to the people. The idea of having those evening clambakes in Olympic Plaza, where visiting folks from Snake Bite, Nebraska, could say "howdy" to a speed skater from Trondheim, is one of the best turns these previously frosty festivals have taken since the good Baron de Coubertin was forced to accept Olympians on ice.

Historians of such things have recorded how the function of the ancient Olympics was to bring the rival and highly competitive factions of the Greek world together for a sip of the grape or whatever Greeks sipped in those days. At other dates on their digital watches, when a Greek from Syracuse met a Greek from Olympia they were less liable to exchange felicitations than they were to exchange left hooks. During the Olympics, the bottom line was friendship. Those Olympic Plaza parties would have astounded the Greeks. They would have been as unbelievable to the Greeks as a story in the local gazettes that the great god Zeus was getting in early at night.

Instead of Greek greeting Greek at the Olympic Plaza, you

had the world greeting Greek and Greek greeting the world. Soviet skaters were tossing their ceremonial bouquets to Yanks who might have been fresh off Wall Street, as far as anyone knew or cared. You can't stretch the horizons of international friendship much farther than that. The good citizens up at Okotoks wouldn't be surprised, of course. They wept when the kids of the Soviet figure skating team, who had been training at their rink, had to wind up their training and move down here for their events. The kids wept, too.

After they had won their medals, back they went to Okotoks — gold medalists Ekaterina Gordeeva and Sergei Grinkov; and silver medalists Elena Valova and Oleg Vasiliev — to put on a show, the proceeds to be used for improvements in the rink. Out here in the foothills, friendliness seems to be a contagious thing. The United Nations should hold one of its sessions in Okotoks.

Just as there were warts in Camelot, there were warts here. Nit-pickers may record how Calgary was the first to add a touch of sand to the luge or that the sacred flame from Olympia was used to roast weenies in the hills. Those nit-pickers were not at Innsbruck in 1964, when many of the US journals ran daily boxes to record how many cameras had been smashed by the security goons and how many media people were showing scars or were in the clink. Modred was the traitor of Camelot and he was reincarnated here. They put him in charge of the laundry out at the media village, where it was presumed he could do minimal harm. Actually, he created a legacy for at least one generation of Albertans who will be using that refrigerated bobsled run. By mismatching Polish socks, matching up American jockey shorts with Chinese undershirts, and shrinking British longjohns until they looked like a traffic cop's white gloves, the Modred of the laundry built up a whole mountain of rub cloths for those beautiful sleds, whose bottoms must be polished for their runs down the hills. The wretches who abandoned the gear do so in the knowledge it will be used in a good cause. And for many years to come. You're welcome, bobsledders still unborn.

A sad $500,000 tale could fit on shirt cuff

The Ben Johnson steroid scandal and ensuing Dubin inquiry were sensational, but awfully complicated. Milt unraveled much of the complexities with this clear, concise piece on 12 March 1989.

TORONTO — Charlie Francis, the Oliver North of track and field, says he was offered $500,000 for the story he told the Dubin inquiry here during countless thousands of words in testimony and examination. Mr. Justice Charles Dubin could have written it on his starched white cuff, part of the logo of the bench.

Single spaced, it would have come out like this: "You were satisfied your steroids programs enhanced performance. Your theory was they were necessary to get what you call a level field. Clean athletes in Canada never had a chance to get top-carded. Athletes who cheat did."

Beneath the banner of the five interlocking Olympic rings, millions of people who have been following this inquiry, which was born of scandal at Seoul, may have been detoured from the real purpose of the probe. It is not to determine whether Ben Johnson was wrongfully stripped of a gold medal for finishing first in the 100 meters, nor to establish that maybe some mythical character identified merely as Kermit really spiked Ben's post-race beer.

As Dubin frequently reminded various counsel for the sundry principals involved, his mandate is to establish the extent and effect of drug use in so-called amateur sports for which the Canadian taxpayer antes a big buck. Francis has provided him with what almost certainly will become the meat and potatoes of the eventual Dubin report.

It undoubtedly was provided at the expense of the Francis career as a coach. He indicated that himself at various times when he insisted Johnson knew he had been on steroids that made him ineligible for Olympic competition and that Ben had been warned repeatedly of clearance times for avoiding detection in a test. Francis said bluntly, "My career was at stake."

To make sure there could be no misunderstanding of what Francis was telling him, Dubin had asked: "The fact of the matter is that Mr. Johnson and others in your group (Mazda Club) were disqualified from competing?" Francis agreed that was so. On another occasion, Dubin commented that, if evidence of the drug stanozolol had not shown up unexpectedly in Johnson's test following the 100 meters, he would have come home with the gold medal despite the fact he had been on banned steroids for most of this athletic career. Francis agreed that was correct.

The fact that Dubin, in quickly summing up the evidence Francis had given during a whole week of sensational testimony, was able to rattle off the timetables of drugs and mixtures with which Francis said his athletes had been prepared for competition was a reminder that Dubin didn't come into this inquiry on a rain check. He has a background in sport. True, it was professional sport. He is hearing here about what is called amateur sport, where an athlete can drive up in his Ferrari to collect his $650 monthly government grant.

When Dubin's friend John Bassett owned the Toronto Argonauts, Dubin, before his appointment to the bench, was a director of the football club. In the ebb and flow of football immigration, some weird characters arrived and departed. Some of them were partial to partners known as "bennies" that were not available in a candy store. They were responsible for

*Ben Johnson and Milt were both honored at an
Ontario Sports Awards dinner in 1986, two years before
Johnson was caught cheating and stripped of his
gold medal at the Seoul Olympics.*
(PHOTO BY MIKE SLAUGHTER, COURTESY THE TORONTO STAR)

some of the best tackles. There were programs to eliminate
them but no one ever believed they succeeded.

Angella Issajenko, whom Francis has described as the pioneer
of his group in the use of steroids, takes the stand tomorrow.
Her evidence will be critical. She could either corroborate or
deny much of what Francis has told the commissioner. According
to evidence by Francis, she not only did the steroid injec-
tions but also injected at least one other member of the group.
She also kept the main supply of bottles.

Ed Futerman, counsel for Ben Johnson, undoubtedly will
continue his exhaustive probing for evidence that Big Ben did
not know the substances with which he was injected, or which

came in pill form, were banned. ("What was the color of this substance?") Francis has said Ben did know and that he called in a panic, after setting a world record in Tokyo, to ask whether his clearance time was sufficient because he was about to be tested.

Among the badge wearers of the Canadian Track and Field Association, the tension will continue to build. Francis has told the world that some of the top people not only knew his group was on steroids but that they conspired to prevent the cheaters from being caught.

Dubin thanked Francis for his frankness and the coach who had confessed his athletic sins left with the ironic statement, "I love the sport." And he undoubtedly does. Like Oliver North, he had a good many people applauding. A little examination will reveal he practically killed what he loved because he thought it was ill.

HORSERACING

This Star is becoming Hayward's Comet

The great Native Dancer lost only one race in his entire career — that race was perhaps the most stunning Kentucky Derby upset in history. As Milt noted on 4 May 1953, there was a Canadian connection, as in so many other cases, with the Derby winner. This was Milt's third Derby — he has been going back to Louisville on the first Saturday in May ever since — 42 years in a row now to 1993.

LOUISVILLE, Ky. — Ontario-born Eddie Hayward has saddled Dark Star five times. Three times the brown son of the Australian-bred sire, Royal Gem II, has come home on the front end. Two of the three winning efforts happened to be the Kentucky Derby and the Derby Trial. So you can excuse Eddie for thinking Dark Star is a useful kind of bangtail to have in his barn. It surprised him somewhat there were not more among the 100,000 or so self-acknowledged experts at Churchill Downs Saturday who were of the same mind.

"I hardly could believe my eyes when I saw our horse quoted at 24 to one," Hayward exclaimed. "If I had been able to get to a betting window, you can guess I'd have had a piece of that."

Eddie didn't have a nickel on Dark Star. He doesn't bet because he's been a race-tracker long enough to know he can't beat his own game. His boss, Harry Guggenheim, is a non-bettor, too. Mr. Guggenheim has an academic explanation. He says an owner who bets on his horse is likely to get the wrong perspective on the race, on the jockey, on the trainer. What Mr. G. is trying to say is that some betting owners are prone to make the rider or the trainer the whipping boy because the owner lost his money.

In Mr. Guggenheim's case, you can't think of anything that should disturb him less than losing a bet. More likely, he's worried because he might win and he wouldn't know what to do with the stuff. In case you wondered about the alias which Mr. Guggenheim uses on the turf: the "Cain-Hoy Stable" is named for his plantation in South Carolina.

Mr. Guggenheim missed a lot of fun by not being at barn twelve Saturday afternoon, when Dark Star came back with the blanket of roses. Naturally, the owner was caught up in the official round of social festivities. Hayward must have broken away early, because he came striding through the stabling area to the barn which had been by-passed all week by the throngs en route to the stalls of Correspondent and Native Dancer. Now, a television crew had its gear set up. A catering firm had delivered a galvanized bucket filled with ice, out of which rose the graceful spire of the biggest champagne bottle ever blown in a glass factory.

The television crew was forced to interrupt its chore and plead for silence in the background. Exclamations of joy and loud smacking sounds were coming from the tack room. The dusky stable boys were dipping into the giggle water which had been delivered in the bucket. Hayward had no time for the grape. He crossed to where Dark Star was being grazed.

"Could we have a shot of the horse looking up, so we'd get his head against the background of the blue sky?" a photographer asked.

"No. I don't want my horse bothered," Eddie protested. "You had your chances to take shots. Now, it's his turn to eat. I think you'll agree he's earned it."

Hayward has been with Cain-Hoy stable only since last fall. Although he didn't say so himself, race-trackers say he was out

Milt interviews jockey Eddie Arcaro on the go at old Woodbine (now Greenwood) in Toronto after "old banana nose" won the 1953 Queen's Plate with the filly Canadiana. Ever an adapter to his surroundings, Milt jots comments down on his racing program, not a notebook.
(COURTESY MILT DUNNELL PHOTO COLLECTION)

of a job at the time, having parted company with the Mrs. Payson-Adams establishment. If that's true, Eddie is racing's most fortunate victim of unemployment. Jockey Hank Moreno, who rode Dark Star, would run Eddie a close second. Moreno had been getting mounts on the Calumet stock a year ago. Last winter, Eddie Arcaro got first pick from Calumet, so Moreno switched to Hayward.

Hayward was born at Broadhagen, Ontario, and learned most of his horsemanship on Canadian tracks — both as a rider and a trainer. He was trainer for the late Ruppert Bain of Toronto when the Bain silks were prominent in Ontario racing. As far as Hayward was concerned, Saturday's Derby was a truly-run race. They all had a shot at his horse. None of them caught him.

Over at barn sixteen, there was a gray colt that followed his hot-walker as if he sensed the sudden decline in his social standing. A few minutes before, he'd been the three-to-five shot, the unbeaten champ. Now, in twelve starts, he'd lost once — by the length of a man's arm. But his admiring audience was gone, the flash bulbs were gone. The big gray looked hurt and puzzled. Les Murray, the old Negro groom, gave him an affectionate slap. "Mah baby could go right out an' run that race again," he said proudly.

If they ran the Derby in heats — the way they do the Hambletonian — old Les probably was right. Native Dancer was in so much trouble and still came so close you'd have to concede him a great chance to reverse the decision. But that will have to come in another race. As far as the Derby is concerned, it wasn't Dark Star's fault if Native Dancer paused to sing Sweet Adeline with the boys at that first corner.

Only Iron Liege going for them

The great Willie Shoemaker blew the 1957 Derby by misjudging the finish line on Gallant Man. But, as fate would have it, none of it should have mattered. This column ran 6 May 1957.

LOUISVILLE, Ky. — Calumet is like the Yankees. It can beat you with its best or it can beat you with its bench. It was a so-called second-stringer named Iron Liege who strolled from his stall into football weather at Churchill Downs Saturday. He was subbing for General Duke, still suffering from a stone bruise received while earning $97,000 one sunny afternoon a few weeks ago in Florida.

Absence of the Duke from the Derby was supposed to represent a calamity for Calumet. Tears had been shed for the Jones boys — Plain Ben and Jim — and for their wealthy employer, Mrs. Gene Markey. All they had going for them was Iron Liege. So the odds on the tote board showed nine to one against Calumet when the money brokers opened their windows.

The tears and the tote showed an utter disregard for hard facts and cold history. Any time the Jones boys send a steed to the starting gate, it's plain philanthropy to quote nine or ten to one against them. If the horse were an honest nine or ten to one shot, he wouldn't be on the track in the devil's red and blue colors. That's how the Jones boys operate.

And the punters must have ignored the general knowledge that a second-stringer in the Calumet corral would be a first-stringer on almost any other range between Nantucket and Nanaimo. Take Saturday's field as an example. Outside of Bold Ruler and possibly Gallant Man, what other horse on the track would a trainer have claimed ahead of the Calumet charger?

Federal Hill? Iron Liege had beaten him, going away at a mile and an eighth in the Florida Derby. So how did Federal Hill figure to beat Iron Liege at a mile and a quarter? Round Table? Iron Liege had whipped him to a standstill — by eleven lengths — over a mile and a sixteenth at Hialeah. General Duke was behind him in the same race — which no one seemed to remember.

So if Iron Liege hung his head in the post parade at Churchill Downs it must have been that he was pondering the unpredictability of a man with a buck to bet. It couldn't have been he was suffering an inferiority complex in his role of pinch-hitter for the world's most powerful racing stable.

And as for history . . . pinch-hitters have done OK in the grueling run for the roses. This wasn't the first time Calumet had called the reserves to rake in the pieces. In '49, Ben Jones had a colt by the name of Deluxe which was fancied by the

On 6 June 1958, Milt chats with Alberta's Johnny Longden,
the winningest jockey in history, that is until a fellow named
Willie Shoemaker sat atop a thoroughbred and shattered
virtually every equine record. Longden is still the only man
to both ride and train Kentucky Derby winners.
(PHOTO BY MICHAEL BURNS, COURTESY THE TORONTO STAR)

faithful. Deluxe couldn't go to the post — but Ponder did go. He paid $34 on a two-dollar ducat. It took the newspaper guys a long time to forgive Ben. They complained he cold-watered them on his Derby chances.

And the Exterminator story is almost too familiar to bear repeating. Here was a poor country boy who had been engaged to act as a shill for the fashionable Sun Briar. Exterminator wasn't fancy at all. His old man had been sold in England for $125. On the morning of the Derby, Sun Briar was indisposed. He had a mild attack of bowed tendon. So the bag of bones named Exterminator went to the post — just so the popular Kilmer colors would be seen in the Derby. Exterminator laughed his way home. The payoff: $61.20.

Whether Iron Liege could have won without the help of the mirage which caused Wee Willie Shoemaker on Gallant Man to see the finish line at the sixteenth pole is a question that goes down in sports lore, along with the Fred Merkle mistake and the assistance which Jack Dempsey got from the ringside scribes the night Luis Firpo belted Jack from the ring, in among their typewriters.

The only thing sure is what the scoreboard shows. It says Iron Liege won. And so did Dempsey. There's another thing reasonably sure: if Shoemaker hadn't adorned himself with the goat horns, by his confession to the stewards, they might have been tacked on Willie Hartack, the tiny horsebacker whose take-home pay is bigger than Ike Eisenhower's.

Coming out of the backstretch, Hartack drove for a hole along the rail where Federal Hill had been. The gap closed as suddenly as it had opened. Hartack found himself steering Iron Liege right onto Federal Hill's back veranda. He took up and went around — losing possibly two lengths in the process. If it hadn't been for that delay, the frozen fans wouldn't have seen the tightest fit in 24 years at the finish line. Gallant Man never would have got close enough to make it a contest.

The legend of Shoemaker's bloomer will grow with the years. Dozens of authors already are describing it with authority. The cold truth is that very few of the millions who watched in person or on TV even noticed it.

Reporters who quizzed Silent Shoe in the jockey room after the race didn't ask about the incident. The Shoe didn't mention it. Sometime later, the stewards revealed in a message to the press box that they had quizzed Shoemaker who admitted his error. The writers raced back to the riders' retreat — but Willie had departed for the airport. He wasn't lingering at the scene of his crime. Nor was he remaining to brood over its consequences.

It's the horse that wants publicity

Puss N' Boots is legendary around backstretches. He once got so far ahead in one race he jumped into the centerfield lake for a swim. His antics were splashed all over newspapers across North America. As Milt reported on 9 February 1962, the horse was just plain nuts.

TORONTO — Fame is something which Frankie Merrill needs like goldfish in his water buckets. Merrill has been Canada's leading trainer of thoroughbreds many times, North America's top banana several times, not to mention regional honors in places such as Old Woodbine and Etobicoke.

In addition, he probably is the only conditioner in the world who set a new record for running the 440, dived into a lake and broke the existing Canadian mark for the dog-paddle — all whilst rescuing one of his beetles from drowning in a horse race. These feats — and others — naturally got recorded in the journals. Mr. Merrill's likeness has appeared on just about every kind of paper produced from pulp. That includes labels on horse liniment bottles.

So the publicity he has been getting in Florida of late, because of a colt called Puss N' Boots, actually itches like woollen underwear at Hialeah. Frankie is attempting to convince Puss N' Boots they don't need any more ink, unless it's on a check from the racing association.

"The horse is a publicity hound," Merrill lamented, by telephone from Miami yesterday. "But who wants it? I'd sooner get my 10 per cent of a purse. Yesterday, when it was announced over the PA system that Puss N' Boots had been scratched, a big groan went up from the crowd. Seemed like about half the people had come out to see what he'd do next. He's had a bad play in all the papers."

There was immediate speculation that Merrill had been induced to scratch the colt because several owners of other steeds in the race had indicated they would prefer to turn their own gallopers loose in a herd of Texas longhorns. They regarded Puss N' Boots as unpredictable, eccentric and a roughneck. Since this was the Bahamas Stakes, a warm-up for $100,000 romps still to come, some highly prized horseflesh had been entered.

Included were Ridan, last year's top two-year-old, Crimson Satan, winner of the Garden State Stakes, the world's richest horse race, Sir Gaylord, which may be the best of the lot, and several others. Folks who owned charges of that caliber naturally were reluctant to expose them to injury in incidents caused by irresponsible characters.

"Everybody's guessing and nearly everybody is guessing wrong," Merrill reported wearily. "Only yesterday, I talked to the stewards, and they told me to run the horse if I wanted to run him. I scratched because Puss N' Boots had trouble with his teeth. He's losing his baby teeth. This horse has been losing them later than most horses do. Why not? He does everything else different."

For those who may have missed some copies of *The Racing Form*, these are a few of the things which Puss N' Boots has done differently.

In a race over the turf course at Fort Erie, Puss N' Boots got so far in front, he decided to take a dip while the rest of the field got back into contention. So he dumped his rider, hurdled a hedge and dived into the lake. That's when Merrill set his own personal mark for early foot. Frankie sprinted from the clubhouse, did a double gainer into the drink and effected the rescue.

At Tropical Park recently, a somewhat similar situation developed. Puss N' Boots was fifteen to one on the board. This

*Trainer Frankie Merrill swims out to save his horse
Puss N' Boots after it jumped into the infield lake at Fort Erie
racetrack in September 1961. Puss N' Boots was leading the
race in the stretch and decided to dump his jockey and go for
a dip. It was one of many crazy exploits of the nutty horse.*
(TUROFSKY PHOTO, COURTESY THE TORONTO STAR)

annoyed him greatly. After getting three lengths in front at the
top of the stretch, he wandered over to the outside rail and
started staring at the palm trees.

At Hialeah, the other day, he was about to make his move at
the three-eighths pole. Instead of mowing down those bums
which he knew he could beat, Puss N' Boots feigned a fall and
tossed jockey Chris Rogers into the dirt. Rogers asked to be
excused from the mount in the Bahamas Stakes. As it turned
out, Puss N' Boots didn't run anyway.

"Hartack (Bill — don't call me Willie) has offered to ride
him," Merrill revealed. "Only thing he asks is that he be given

a chance to work him a few times. I don't know whether he will learn much about him. This horse doesn't do the same things in the afternoon he does in the mornings.

"My wife, Sally, broke him to the saddle. She works him. He's nice as pie with her. This sonofagun sees everything, hears everything. He can do everything but talk. He can run all day. The owner (Roxie Glen of Buffalo) has refused $100,000 for him. That's legitimate. We got him for $9,000. If I had my say, maybe I'd take the money. But what's 100 G's to Roxie?"

He could have danced all night

Northern Dancer's victory 2 May 1964 over favorite Hill Rise was one of the most exciting Kentucky Derbies ever. The little Canadian horse smashed the Derby record with a two-minute-flat race and thrilled an entire nation. (Only the great Secretariat has since run faster in the classic.) The Dancer went on to win the Preakness, but missed the third jewel of the Triple Crown, the Belmont. Of course, Dancer's immortality would come later, in the stables, where he would become the greatest sire the thoroughbred racing world has ever seen.

LOUISVILLE, Ky. — It takes two to tango — and Northern Dancer, a noted cake-walker from Canada, had a willing partner. The name was Hill Rise — a better-than-average hoofer from California. They put together the hottest routine since Fred Astaire teamed up with Ginger Rogers. As the Dancer warmed up with a solo number en route to the paddock, one of three gaudily garbed bands began blowing horns in his ear as he minced his way through the biggest mob ever assembled for the Kentucky Derby. There have been 90 of these Derbies — and the attendance always has been 100,000.

This time it must have been 100,001 because even Brownie Leach, who is one of the few men on earth entrusted with the true nose-count, admitted it was the largest Derby crowd ever.

You could add it was a fairly well-heeled group, too, since the handle for the day hit $5,173,018. That's approximately the national budget for the sovereign state of Windfields Farm, which Northern Dancer represents at these jam sessions.

When the horns blew in his ear, the Dancer did a buck and wing before breaking into a fox trot. His immaculately dressed trainer, Señor Horatio Luro, broke into nothing but a cold sweat. With $156,800 up for grabs, the Señor had no craving for culture. There's a time and a place for everything.

Once the horses left the gate, the Dancer began looking for his partner. He appeared to do a hesitation step, compared to his act in such classics as the Flamingo, for example. In that one, he was away third and quickly moved up to be second.

Vinegar Bill Hartack, who was in the irons Saturday, explained this. William's revelations came after a considerable delay. He stopped to sign autographs en route to the jockeys' room — which he knew was packed with newspapermen. Feeling as he does about members of that lodge, William was in no rush. When he got weary of signing his name while standing up, he had a chair sent out for his greater comfort.

Even after he arrived in the riders' powder room there were further preliminaries while he sorted out those who were acceptable. Jimmy Cannon, Willie Ratner and one or two others — and their proxies — were blackballed immediately. Another seemingly inoffensive scribbler was excused from the room because: "I don't like your attitude."

Once the purge had been completed, however, William gave one of the most complete and detailed runbacks of a race ever heard in a riders' room. It was total recall — well worth the wait through the autograph session.

The Dancer's leisurely departure from the gate was planned — just as everything is planned when Hartack is in the pilot house. Señor Luro advised an unhurried getaway.

He was seventh when they had gone a quarter of a mile, but he knew where his dancing partner, Hill Rise, was — just in front of him. The only surprise to this point was that The Scoundrel, another Californian, had shown some unexpected early foot.

The race really was won at the five-eighths pole. That's where Hartack had to make the decision that meant the big piece of the pot — or pennies from heaven. There were four or five horses in front of him along the rail. He could wait and see whether they sorted themselves out and left room to get through — or he could go to the outside of them.

For Hartack, the answer was easy. If he remained on the rail, luck would have to be with him. He felt he knew his horse, even though he had ridden it only once. That was the Blue Grass Stakes at Keeneland — the Dancer's last race before the Derby.

Ironically, it was the Blue Grass which chilled the Dancer's less dedicated supporters. The time was slow and the Dancer defeated something called Allen Adair by half a length. Even Allen Adair's own family regarded that as no great accomplishment.

"I could have opened up a lead of four or five lengths in the Blue Grass," Hartack revealed. "But what would that have proved? Beating an inferior field by four or five lengths meant nothing. By riding him as I did, I learned all the things I wanted to know about Northern Dancer. Consequently, I had perfect confidence in him. I had more confidence in him than I had in any horse I ever rode in the Derby."

It was a frenzied fire dance all through the stretch. Nothing quite so sizzling has been seen down the long lane which has featured many ticket-stoppers — such as the head-hunting of Don Meade and Herb Fisher in 1933 and Native Dancer's hopeless pursuit of Dark Star in 1953.

There also was Whirlaway's breathless rush in 1941. Mr.

Longtail ran the final quarter in 24 seconds that day — the fastest it ever had been run. The partners of the Dancer did it in 24 or less. Northern Dancer was caught in 24 flat. Hill Rise had to do better because he was coming from behind. At the wire, he was only a neck away from a snoutful of roses.

The Dancer disproved one canard in that sashay down to the mint. It had been said he resented a caning. Hartack warmed his bottom for a quarter of a mile. He responded with the fastest ten furlongs in 90 years of this Louisville extravaganza.

He also repaid the snub which Bill Shoemaker inflicted when he bailed out and defected to Hill Rise — after winning two rich pots with the Dancer in Florida. Shoemaker should have been the man operating the Windfields' money-printing machine Saturday.

"I knew Northern Dancer was a good horse," Shoemaker said. "I just thought I was going to a better one. It didn't turn out that way — not today anyway. Hartack had a handful of horse as he turned for the money. I was punching at my guy a bit."

The Shoe pulled a boner and he accepted the cost. If the same situation arose again, he probably would switch — just as he did after the Florida Derby. At least, he said he would. It likely will be claimed Hartack outrode The Shoe. But, any time a jockey gets beaten by a neck in track record time, he couldn't have been guilty of too many boo-boos.

It just could be, as Manny Ycaza, who was on The Scoundrel, said: "The best horse, he win and God bless him."

Baylor Hickman, a tall, courtly Kentuckian, put it another way. Emerging from the tack room at the Dancer's barn, Mr. Hickman stuck a rose from the Derby blanket in the buttonhole of his coat lapel. He hoisted high a glass of amber-colored gargle and solemnly intoned: "The Maple Leaf forever."

Seventy-two
seconds of agony

Unknown at the time, the Queen's Plate was Northern Dancer's final race. This column ran on 22 June 1964. The Dancer went on to bigger and better things in the breeding stall, becoming the greatest thoroughbred sire. Two decades later, Windfields turned down an offer of $40 million for Northern Dancer. His yearlings fetched millions of dollars at auctions, one for a record 10.2 million.

TORONTO — Bill (never Willie) Hartack, who solemnly tells you: "It's years since I made a mistake in my profession," held his hands a few feet apart and said: "We went through a hole about that wide."

This happened almost midway of the backstretch in the Queen's Plate and it marked the approximate moment at which several million Canadians resumed breathing. For something like 72 agonizing seconds, they had watched in stunned disbelief as Northern Dancer, an international idol, ran second-last — then last — in a field of eight homebrews that were contesting the 105th ramble for the Queen's Guineas.

The word "contesting" is used loosely because seven of the eight native sons were believed to be seeking second money. First prize of $49,075 had been conceded to the Dancer. Any colt which can win the Kentucky Derby and the Preakness Stakes is entitled to that concession.

Yet, the Dancer had only one horse — the filly, Later Mel —

beaten when the field hit the clubhouse turn. Even the filly passed him before they straightened away for the run down the backstretch. This shaped up as the greatest calamity since Casey struck out at Mudville.

Canadians, right across the country, poised a toe to kick the screens out of their television sets. At Woodbine, there were 30,000 prospective cardiac cases. It's safe to say no horse ever went to the post at a Canadian track with the near-unanimous support the Dancer had in his first appearance before the home folks as a three-year-old.

Even in the walking ring, spectators who lined the rails applauded him and called out: "We're all with you, Dancer" and "Good luck to you, Mr. (trainer Horatio) Luro." When the horses came on the track, Northern Dancer got a standing ovation — even from the few people who had placed just-in-case bets against him.

Now, with almost half of the race run, the Dancer hadn't done a thing to make anyone suspect he's the best three-year-old in North America. And, if you're ashamed of your fears, in light of what happened later, don't blush, because you had knowledgeable company. Jackie Price, the Florida horseman who touted the Dancer prior to the Derby — and kept right on calling him in every race thereafter — admitted after the Plate: "I was scared stiff for a few seconds."

Bill Hartack maintained he never had the slightest misgiving at any time. As the man at the throttle, he could feel the power which the little Dancer was striving to unleash the instant he got the signal.

"I was going at maybe three-quarters speed, with a field that was all out, and yet I was catching them," Hartack explained. "So why would I be worried? I wasn't going to be taking to the outside of horses on those turns. Mr. Luro and I had talked it over. We agreed the important thing was to keep out of jams on that first turn. After that, he wanted me to win with the least necessary effort."

As the field drove down the backstretch, the Dancer's position improved slightly. Now there was one horse behind him.

*Northern Dancer attracts applause and great attention
as he makes his way to the track for the Queen's Plate in
June 1964. The Kentucky Derby and Preakness winner was
dead last at one point in the Plate but then stormed through
for victory in his final race. The Canadian horse became
the most influential thoroughbred sire of the past
one hundred years, Milt writes.*

(PHOTO BY FRANK LENNON, COURTESY THE TORONTO STAR)

There was a horse (Return Trip) on the inside and slightly ahead of him, with big leaguer Hank Moreno in the irons. On the outside of the Dancer and slightly ahead was veteran Nick Shuk, aboard Later Mel.

That was where Hartack spotted the gap which he measured by holding his hands apart. Instead of using up his horse by going to the outside of Shuk, Hartack shot through like a hockey puck which Frank Mahovlich has rifled beneath a goalie's armpit.

There was a gasp and a roar from the stands: "There goes the Dancer." Avelino Gomez, aboard Pierlou, the second choice, was watching for the Dancer to make this move. Gomez was about fourth. Now that it had happened, these wasn't a thing Gomez could do about it.

"I'm waitin' for Northern Dancer, but Northern Dancer, he no wait for me," the Cuban lamented. Hank Moreno, a handsome and friendly fellow dressed silently after the race. He sighed and said: "Northern Dancer went by me like I was standing still. I been seeing a lot of the Dancer this year — finished second to him twice with The Scoundrel."

Going around the far turn, it was Northern Dancer, Grand Garcon and Langcrest, head and head — but very briefly. Jim Fitzsimmons, on Grand Garcon, had no illusions. He laughed as he recalled: "When the Dancer come alongside me at the three-eighths pole, I yelled: 'Take it easy, Willie.' Even at that stage, I could see he hadn't let his horse run yet."

Sam McComb, on Langcrest, wasn't fooled, either. He didn't put the whip to Langcrest. His explanation: "I knew this horse was giving his best. He's a credit to trainer Ted Mann. I was happy with second money, so I wasn't going to abuse him."

Stomping around the jockeys' room, Señor Gomez yelled at Hartack: "You not gonna leave town without pay me 80 bucks I win shootin' pool, eh. I beat you pretty good last night." Hartack retorted: "And I beat you pretty good today — for more money."

"When you theenk you got it (the Plate) win?" the Señor mocked, resorting to a stock question that usually comes from somebody in the press contingent.

"Right at the start — when I saw a burrhead like you was on the second choice," Hartack shot back — thereby winning heat, race and money.

It's a big man's world

Avelino Gomez was one of a kind. He was colorful, dramatic and a bit crazy. But he sure could ride and his competitive fire was good for racing, as Milt points out on 15 September 1965. Gomez died in 1980 after a spill at Woodbine.

TORONTO — Avelino Gomez, the Havana hot-shot, did more fist fighting between races at Woodbine the other day than Sonny Liston did in a world championship match at Lewiston.

Gomez at least has proof he was hit — a mild shiner. Whereas Liston collected three-quarters of a million for his fainting spell, Señor Gomez must shell out $100 of his life savings. In addition, he's grounded for ten days because he allegedly attempted to ram 1,100 pounds of horseflesh into the ample ear of Hugo Dittfach, a rival rider.

In the ball park this would have been called a brush-back pitch. That's the terminology which a hurler uses when he aims at the batter's eyelashes. There's no intent to injure. It merely loosens up the hitter. Stewards at a horse park take a dim view of it. They have seen jockeys launched into orbit after being nudged by a speeding thoroughbred.

When Gomez attacked Dittfach at the scale house after the race — and again in the jockeys' powder room, the stewards couldn't detect anything healthy about it. This is called conduct prejudicial to racing.

Actually, it's a wonderful tribute to the trade of horsebacking. Jockeys have been slandered for centuries as humans who pack more larceny per capita than the Dalton boys. The cynics

MRS.M.JAMES BOYLEN-OWNER
A.IRWIN TAYLOR-TRAINER **MILT DUNNELL**
7 FURLONGS 1:29
            BOWIE   FEB.10,1965

JOHN LeBLANC   - UP
HOLLYHEAD   2ND
FANCIULLA   3RD

Sports fans Mr. and Mrs. James Boylen honor Milt by naming a race horse after him. This was one of three races in a row won by Milt Dunnell the horse at Maryland's old Bowie racetrack. Milt the writer was touted to bet the horse at 21 to 1 odds in its maiden, but forgot to get his money down while in New York on assignment. The Boylens also named horses for Eddie Shack and King Clancy, but neither nag won a race. "Shack's horse ran like he skated, knocking horses down as he went along," Milt says.

(COURTESY MILT DUNNELL PHOTO COLLECTION)

always suspect more races are won over a quiet beer than are decided in the bottom stretch. This is especially true of a cynic who has blown his two dollar show bet.

Unfortunately, there have been incidents which provided the scoffers with ammunition. About fourteen years ago, the bookmakers took their phones off the hook so they wouldn't be suckered into accepting any more bets on the shoo-ins at Fort Erie.

Ten riders got the boot for life when the Racing Commission finally broke up the syndicate. The general public remembers that much longer than it's going to recall how Gomez attempted to put the slug on Dittfach in a fit of frustration over defeat in a horse race.

Hockey players have built a reputation as the world's fiercest competitors because the people who run their game accept fisticuffs as spice for the show. A five-minute penalty is a sign of respectability, without discouraging the action.

Football is somewhat less tolerant. A 265-pound tackle who throws a punch at another 265-pound tackle — wearing so much gear you couldn't hurt him with a sledgehammer — gets tossed out of the game. He may be fined fifty as well, if Commissioner Syd Halter is getting low on stamp money.

The skinny little jockey is guilty of a federal offence if he takes a poke at the boy who shut him off at the quarter pole. He's fined a C-note — maybe even suspended — when he shows the same emotions as the shinny player or the footballer.

Thus, racing, in a way, encourages the cynicism of the customer. The horse player who has blown a bet sees hockey players mauling each other. When jockeys don't do it, he concludes it's because they're all lodge brothers.

It takes a Gomez-Dittfach brawl or a Gomez-Coy altercation to remind the public that jockeys are fierce competitors, too. The Gomez-Coy collision also had hilarious overtones. It happened at Montreal, a year or so ago.

Coy's horse bumped the Señor's steed and Gomez was unseated. He lay on the track, still as death, until Coy, having finished the race, ran back to see whether he indeed had killed the Señor. Gomez jumped up and flattened him.

As Bill Risewick, the Marshal Dillon of racing in Ontario,

says: "There are officials to determine whether there has been an infraction of the rules. We can't permit jockeys to take the law into their own hands."

Well spoken, too. But who does he think those men in the striped shirts are at Maple Leaf Gardens and the CNE Stadium? In spite of them — maybe even because of them — man-to-man feuds develop.

There should be one day of the year when jockeys are permitted one punch free. Gomez would be killed, of course. Every human in the jocks' room would take a belt at him. It still would be a great public relations pitch for racing.

Albatross story: Cadillac to cart

The story of Albatross, one of history's best harness horses, is incredible. This 7 July 1971 column tells us that somewhere out there is a person who lost one million dollars by being afraid to risk another $500. At the time this column appeared, Milt was in Goshen for the induction of Prince Edward Island's Joe O'Brien into the Harness Racing Hall of Fame. Canadian drivers like O'Brien, Herve Fillion, John Campbell, Bill O'Donnell, Ron Waples and Mike Lachance have dominated the sport for years.

GOSHEN, N.Y. — Around the harness horse tracks, Bert James, an Upper Canada College old boy from Brantford, ranks with legendary characters, such as William Wright, Harry Oakes and other prospectors who struck it rich in the Ontario gold fields.

Bert, they tell you, was a car dealer in Windsor. In order to make a trade with a diversified customer, he took in three horses as part-payment on a new Cadillac. One of them turned out to be Albatross, the million-dollar three-year-old, who could be the greatest pacer of all time.

It didn't happen that way but it's an intriguing story nevertheless. Bert did accept three standardbreds as part of a deal. They took him out of Cadillacs and put him on carts — but Albatross was not one of the three steeds.

"This transaction involving the Cadillac took place about 1965," Bert recalls. "A Windsorite, whose name I prefer not to use, offered an old Cadillac, some money, two geldings and a stud for a new car.

"I was known as a swinging Caddy dealer, in those days, and I said: 'Sure, why not?' Believe me, I didn't even see the horses. To me, it was strictly a matter of dollars and cents. I figured it this way: for three horses, I could get X-number of dollars and I was out."

Proceeding on that basis, one gelding was sold quickly for $500. Complications set in when the other gelding started to win. It was trained and driven by an Ohio horseman, Joe Marsh. The gelding finally was claimed for $2,500 — after acquiring a bankroll of $13,000 at Windsor, Detroit and The Meadows in Pennsylvania. Even the stud turned out to be a bargain. He was taken for $1,000 in a claiming race.

For the three harness horses which he had acquired in the trade for one car, Bert was able to show revenue of $17,000 — not counting a lot of fun. It created a doubt in his mind as to whether the automobile was here to stay.

"By 1967, my mind was made up," he agrees. "I was out of the car business and into the horse business. Several other horses which I bought turned out very well. One of them was a trotter, Angelo Pick, which cost me $16,500. He won $65,000. Pedro Wilson was another — won about $85,000. I believe he cost me $13,500.

"Even Hope Time, who was five when I got him for $40,000, won himself out in the first year. He had earnings of $100,000 when I let him go for $20,000. It was about this time that I decided to get into the breeding game. I was looking for mares and for some yearlings that I might market. Actually, that's when I heard about the Albatross package."

The Albatross package consisted of a mare called Voodoo Hanover, her son, Albatross, and a full sister to Albatross, who was a suckling at the time. They were owned by a group of five Kentucky horsemen, who called themselves "The Voodoo Hanover Syndicate." Their spokesman was Charlie Kenney, a prominent farm manager in the blue grass.

"I paid $11,000 for the package," Bert reveals, "and my original plan was to sell Albatross, in an effort to get most of my money back. That would leave me with the mare and the suckling for free."

The plan misfired. Otherwise, Bert would be known as the man who tossed in a royal flush. He wanted $7,000 for the colt at the Harrisburg, Pennsylvania, sales. A friend, who was planted at ringside, would better any bid below seven Gs and turn Albatross back to Bert, who had purchased a big breeding farm in Pennsylvania.

The final unfriendly bid on Albatross was $6,500. Somewhere, there's a man who can say he blew a million dollars because he wouldn't gamble an extra $500. If he had gone to $7,000, he would have had the horse. Bert's shill offered $6,700 and Albatross went back to his old barn.

"Now that I had Albatross back, he had to be trained and raced," Bert says, "so I turned him over to Harry Harvey, a former farm manager for Del Miller. He lives at Washington, Pennsylvania. When Albatross won his first race, during the Grand Circuit meeting at Hazel Park (Detroit), we knew we had something extra."

Just how "extra" this colt really was became obvious to even casual bystanders at the end of 1970. Albatross had won $183,000, which was a world record for a two-year-old pacer. He was elected Canadian harness horse of the year.

It was sensational and the computer gears commenced whirring again in the former car trader's head. Albatross was staked in races worth $1,100,000 for his three-year-old campaign. That meant he could rake in $500,000 if he won all those events. Remembering that no machine is more fragile than a race horse, Bert asked himself whether one man should run all that risk. The answer was "no."

That's why Albatross was syndicated. He was divided into ten shares at $125,000 each. Bert retained 25 per cent for the James family. The Armstrongs of Brampton are in for 10 per cent.

So far, as a three-year-old, Albatross has won $183,000, which, of course, is distributed to the syndicate, of which Bert is manager as long as the horse remains on the track. Present plans are to keep Albatross in racing for at least his four-year-old term. Then, he could be retired to stud.

One of the few unhappy notes in the saga of Albatross is that Harry Harvey, who took him to the races in the first place, lost the horse to Stanley Dancer, one of the top drivers in the world.

"I think even Harvey understands why this happened," Bert James suggests. "Five of the eight members of our syndicate were clients of Stanley Dancer. One of the conditions of syndication was that he should train and drive the horse. I can tell you that Harvey received compensation, although I'm sure he would have preferred to retain the colt."

Like Harvey, in the colt's two-year-old season, Dancer thinks he has something extra. Such as: "I already have said he's the greatest pacer I ever drove. If he stays healthy he certainly will break Bret Hanover's time trial record of 1:53.3."

Bret Hanover is the one (now retired) whom harness men call "the world's fastest horse."

Only one man had a chance

Secretariat was not only the first Triple Crown winner in 25 years but also a media star whose power and personality thrilled a continent, as indicated by this 11 June 1973 column. His 31-length Belmont win entrenched him as one of the greatest race horses. More than two decades later, no horse has bettered his time in either the Derby or the Belmont. His last race was later that year on October 28 at Woodbine.

NEW YORK — Angel Cordero, Jr., a hard-riding Puerto Rican who got set down a few days before the Kentucky Derby, finally got his chance in the Belmont Stakes.

He had as much chance, that is, as any other jock except Ron Turcotte, the former bushwacker from New Brunswick. In other words, Angel had no more chance than a snowball in Belmont's betting temples, which were much hotter than hell.

"Would you say *sometheeng* for one of my countrymen?" Angel asked, dropping by Turcotte's locker in the riders' room beneath the cavernous sands. He introduced a radio man from San Juan.

"Well," said Turcotte briskly, putting in a plug for the native son, "Angel had me outrun when we're goin' down to the club-house turn."

Turcotte talked while he knotted the same horseshoe-dotted

tie he had worn to the Kentucky Derby, to the Preakness and to the Belmont Stakes — to the first Triple Crown of thoroughbred racing in 25 years.

The radio man wondered whether there had been any exchange of words when the two little rivals finally were riding head to head for a few seconds, after Turcotte got his $6,060,000 flying machine, called Secretariat, into second gear.

"I looked over and said: 'Hi Angel,'" Turcotte cracked, "but instead of saying hello, Angel said goodbye." Cordero enjoyed the joke. He thought it would go over big with the fans back in San Juan.

"When your horse hook up with Sham, so early in the race, I *theenk* to myself, maybe I got a shot (with My Gallant) because maybe you two ride each other into the ground," Cordero admitted. "Then Secretariat run Sham into the ground and go away by *heemself*. I see you look back."

"Yeah, I took a look," Turcotte agreed, "and I thought you guys must be in the post parade. You know what impressed me? He (Secretariat) ran the three-quarters faster than Spanish Riddle, who was only goin' a mile. Spanish Riddle is a fast horse. We were goin' a mile and a half. I'll bet that was the fastest three-quarters of the day."

Ron may not have realized it but there was an even more impressive fraction. Secretariat covered the mile and a quarter in 1:59 flat. That was two-fifths of a second faster than his Derby record — the fastest Derby in 99 years. Having done that, he ticked off the final quarter-mile of the Belmont in 25 seconds — all by himself.

Turcotte's decision to go for a time record was his own, according to trainer Lucien Laurin. There had been no mention of Gallant Man's old (1957) mark of 2:26.3 in the pre-race discussions.

"I told Ron to use his own judgment — as always," Lucien reported. "It didn't bother me none when I seen they went that first quarter in 23.3 seconds. When I saw the three-quarters in 1:09.4 I got a little bit worried. Maybe they were goin' too fast.

*The great Secretariat prepares for his final race,
the Canadian International, at Woodbine racetrack in
Etobicoke, Ontario, October 1973. Many of the Triple
Crown winner's records still stand, including his 1:59.2
Kentucky Derby and 2:24 Belmont Stakes marks.*
(PHOTO BY DOUG GRIFFIN, COURTESY THE TORONTO STAR)

Next thing I know, we're twenty lengths in front and I say to myself we should win this one."

The circumstances justified Turcotte's action in going against the clock when there was no competition left on the track. There will be no more racing for Secretariat after November 15 when he retires to stud under the terms of an agreement with the syndicate which anted an unprecedented $6,060,000 for him as a sire.

By riding out the colt in the last quarter-mile — when he could have cantered the last sixteenth — Turcotte added a world record to Secretariat's credentials as a prospective parent. No horse ever bettered 2:24 for a mile and one-half on dirt. There is a North American record of 2:23 for Fiddle Isle on grass. It was created on a slightly tilted Santa Anita course.

For Mrs. Penny Tweedy and others who have been urging less emphasis on earnings and mutual handles — more attention to the steeds — the most significant events of this historic matinee started at the seven-eighths pole.

Acting on instructions from trainer Frank (Pancho) Martin, Sham's rider, Laffit Pincay, had gone for the early lead. It was like the Charge of the Light Brigade — gallant but suicide.

Sham is a game animal but, in the three biggest races of his career, all within five weeks, he has been outclassed. At the seven-eighths pole, he had given all there was. He had nothing left. He collapsed.

By this time, practically every human of Belmont's perspiring 70,000 was on its feet. The roar was what you hear when the heavyweight championship of the world is about to change hands.

Money was the last thing in the mind of that multitude. Secretariat was one to nine. Nobody gets rich at those odds. What the crowd sensed was a Triple Crown for a super-colt. It also realized that Turcotte had accepted the challenge of the clock.

At the end, Secretariat was practically mobbed by admirers. It was a wonder somebody didn't find a Victory racing plate in his ear. What had happened was the rediscovery of the horse.

Another question for a philosopher

Affirmed and Alydar were hooked in a classic Triple Crown duel in 1978 with each race more exciting than the previous, culminating with a show-stopping Belmont. While Affirmed won each race, Alydar's revenge came later in the breeding barns, where he has far out-stripped Affirmed in the quality of his progeny. The last paragraph of this 13 June 1978 column refers to the colorful Laz Barrera's insistence after the Derby that Affirmed's 18-year-old jockey, Steve Cauthen, was a reincarnation of a master horseman returning to reap his just rewards.

NEW YORK — Laz Barrera, the loquacious Cuban philosopher, always has some theory to explain the mysteries of his trade. In case your subscription to *The Daily Racing Form* has elapsed, Barrera's trade is training thoroughbreds to run, all the way from the starting gate to the teller's counter at the bank.

Some time back — it could have been a few minutes after the Kentucky Derby — Laz said Affirmed, newest inductee to the Triple Crown shrine of racing, could run from here to China with the Calumet colt, Alydar, but Affirmed would be in front for the winner's bowl of rice in Peking.

It's pretty tough to argue with Laz about that. In the three Triple Crown classics — Derby, Preakness and Belmont Stakes, having a combined distance of three and fifteen-sixteenths of a mile (apologies to the metric bureaucrats) — the total difference between the two horses has been approximately the yardage a groom could throw a forkful of manure into the wind.

Someone is almost sure to ask. So the margins were a length and a half in the Derby, a neck in the Preakness and a nose here, in Saturday afternoon's Belmont Stakes, after the two steeds had battled each other, head to head, for the last half-mile.

Another of Barrera's alleged beliefs is that Steve Cauthen, the 18-year-old hardboot, actually is 81 and that Steve is the reincarnation of somebody who performed a feat of riding which astounded the world.

It could even have been in the misty past — before the evolution of the Darley Arabian, the Godolphin Arabian and the Byerley Turk, to whom both Affirmed, Alydar and all other thoroughbreds eating hay today owe their heritage.

Cauthen (The Kid) has done nothing to discredit Laz on that profundity, either. In fact, the way Cauthen engineered Saturday's Belmont, he could even have been Genghis Khan on his way to the Great Wall of China.

Between them, Laz and Cauthen have managed to outmaneuver John Veitch, trainer of Alydar, and Señor Jorge Velasquez, regarded by his peers as one of the top riders in the world.

In the Kentucky Derby, there was reason to suspect Velasquez either over-estimated Alydar or under-estimated Affirmed. He got twelve lengths back, closed a lot of ground in the stretch, but still arrived late. The guessing then was that he might have won if there had been another quarter mile to go.

On Saturday, when there was an extra quarter mile to go, Veitch's strategy was to put pressure on Affirmed early. Barrera and Cauthen practically dared them to do it.

Velasquez lamented, after the race, that he wished there had been a quicker early pace. Mr. Cauthen took care of that. He went the first quarter at a leisurely 25-second clip — which is about the speed your grandpa generates when he thinks he's going to miss his bus. In last year's Belmont, Seattle Slew covered the first quarter in 24.3. And he was running in mud. Saturday's track was fast.

"I knew," Cauthen said quietly, "that, if I had the pace slowed down, he would have to come to me if he wanted to beat me."

The result was that, at no stage of the mile and a half, was Alydar more than two and a half lengths back of Affirmed.

*Horseracing czar E.P. Taylor (*far left*); Frank Selke, former Montreal Canadien and Toronto Maple Leaf executive; Conn Smythe, the man who built Maple Leaf Gardens; and NHL president Clarence Campbell toast Milt in 1971 when he retires as* Star *sports editor. His retirement as editor did not stop Milt from writing his column.*
(PHOTO BY BOB OLSEN, COURTESY THE TORONTO STAR)

That was after they had gone only a quarter of a mile. At that stage, Affirmed was in front, with Judge Advocate, ridden by Hamilton's Jeff Fell, a length back, and Alydar a length and a half behind him.

Velasquez obviously sensed the slow pace and quickly took Judge Advocate out of the picture. After they had gone half a mile, Velasquez had driven up to within a length of Affirmed. After a mile, he was within half a length — at a mile and a quarter, it was a head. There never was a bigger margin for the final quarter.

The real question for Cauthen and Affirmed came at the three-sixteenths pole, when Alydar stuck his nose in front. By this time, Velasquez had moved Cauthen into such close quarters that The Kid no longer could whip with his right hand. He switched and whipped left-handed to the wire. That probably meant the difference between winning and losing.

So the thoughts of Laz Barrera must get the same kind of acceptance which has been tendered to the musings of other great thinkers down through the years.

Thus, a question which Laz might ponder between now and Saratoga. He vows that Affirmed will not run again before Saratoga. Affirmed will not run against older horses. He will not run on grass.

All of which is subject to Louis Wolfson, breeder and owner of Affirmed, listening to what Laz says. A year ago, Billy Turner, trainer of Seattle Slew, made certain stipulations concerning his colt. A few weeks later, Seattle Slew was in California — against Turner's advice. He got whipped. Soon, Turner was out of a job.

But that question for Laz: What kind of creature must that horse, Secretariat, have been in an earlier existence?

Maybe this is no time to be talking about Secretariat. This is Affirmed's year. But Affirmed helps to bring it into focus. Here was undoubtedly the most competitive Belmont in its 110-year history. The time was 2:26.4 — third fastest of all time.

Secretariat's time was 2:24 — almost three seconds faster — with absolutely nothing pushing him for the last mile. For the final quarter, jockey Ron Turcotte was looking over his shoulder, asking himself: "Where's everybody gone?"

In Barrera's philosophy, Secretariat must have been the reincarnation of something quick. What was it, Laz?

One Lady is gone and remaining two share their tears

This enchanting story about one tough filly and her owners appeared on 13 January 1981.

TORONTO — There were three happy ladies. Now, there are two. And they are not happy, although they did make a lot of money and the memories are bright. The bottom line, though, is tears.

It all started in 1976, when Myra and Bill Masterson, who live at Pelham, a few miles west of St. Catharines, decided to put their little filly, Happy Lady, in the yearling sale of standardbreds at the CNE grounds. Bill was upgrading the Masterson stable. Although Happy Lady was a daughter of the great sire Most Happy Fella, she just didn't seem to fit into Bill's plans.

Their good friends and neighbors, Linda and Wayne Lockey, viewed the impending departure of Happy Lady with misgivings. Wayne would wander down and watch the filly romping in the Masterson paddock. When he returned, Linda would notice his obvious distress.

The day of the sale came and they had a plan. They were at the sale, with their trainer, Jim Rankin. He was instructed to bid on Happy Lady. But the price had to be right — only one bid above $10,000. Unknown to the Mastersons, Rankin was the bidder when the hammer dropped at $11,000.

"After the sale, we encountered the Mastersons," Linda recalls now. "Myra was in tears because Happy Lady was gone. She had no idea who the buyer was.

"When I told her, she was overjoyed. She said she would be able to see Happy Lady and watch her develop. We had a better idea. She should buy back a half-interest. We'd call ourselves Three Happy Ladies. She accepted at once."

In the spring of the filly's two-year-old year, Jim Rankin kept reporting: "She sure does everything right." When it was time for her first start, at Buffalo, he announced: "I plan to go in 2:10. If Somebody wants to go in 2:08, I get beat."

Happy Lady went in 2:10 — and won. Next time out, it was 2:08. She won again. In sixteen starts as a two-year-old, she won fifteen times.

With earnings of $101,000 — a handsome return on that $11,000 sale tag — she went to California, where she won $426,838 as a three-year-old and was voted Canada's standardbred of the year.

As a four-year-old, Jim Rankin never was happy with her racing condition until late in the season. He decided she was ready to go. It rained and the track was a mess. He scratched.

"The following week, Happy Lady was supposed to start again," Linda Lockey remembers. "It snowed and the track was closed. Jim Rankin said: 'It simply isn't to be. The time has come. She's a champion. We'll let her bow out as a champion.' We did."

Happy Lady was sent to Castleton Farm in Kentucky, where Niatross, the world's greatest standardbred, recently opened his court. She was bred to Bret Hanover, one of the best sires.

Her foal was due on January 18. Her next romance was to be with Niatross. It was news of a blessed event the two happy ladies expected when the phone call from Lexington came.

What they heard, instead, was that Happy Lady, the mother-to-be, was dead. She was one of the fourteen fashionable mares that died when a flash fire leveled the broodmare barn at Castleton.

"It's like losing a member of the family," Linda Lockey says, speaking from Pelham. "She was so much a part of our lives. Yes, there was some insurance on her but there is no way of putting a money value on something like Happy Lady.

"We have the satisfaction of knowing we went first-class with her — a top breeding farm, the best sires — but we never will know how good her progeny might have been."

As Jim Rankin put it earlier: it wasn't to be.

Derby memory: raw carrots for Christmas

Sunny's Halo is only the second Canadian-bred horse to win the Kentucky Derby. Unfortunately, an ankle injury prematurely ended his career so that he didn't run in the Queen's Plate or the Belmont. He finished sixth in the Preakness. This Derby column was published on 8 May 1983.

LOUISVILLE, Ky. — It was Christmas Day for horse trainer Dave Cross, as he and his buddy-owner, Dave (Pud) Foster, came back across the track at Churchill Downs, from the most famous floral horseshoe in racing. Inside that horseshoe, they present the Kentucky Derby trophy to an ecstatic owner, while they blanket his horse with red roses.

But don't jump to the conclusion that Dave Cross figured Santa Claus came early. What had just happened here, on a drippy afternoon, when handsome Sunny's Halo won the 109th running of the famed Kentucky Derby, was exactly what Cross expected to happen.

It was the payoff of the game plan which he set up for a sore-shinned and touchy-ankled colt early last winter, when he told owner Foster: "Go ahead. Make the nomination for the Derby."

Foster, a little owner, with one broodmare, competing against the biggest outfits of the continent, had the confidence to follow through, despite two disappointing races (Laurel Futurity and Young America) which Sunny's Halo had run in late-season ventures against tough US competition.

Cross had practically gambled his professional future and his reputation as a trainer on his program to get Sunny's Halo ready for the Derby. As he said, one day, during Derby week, while he was grazing the colt: "I figure to come out of this as a jerk or a genius."

Sunny's Halo provided the verdict. Even before Sunny's Halo came charging down to the wire in front, Cross had received vindication. *The Daily Racing Form*, the *Wall Street Journal* of the horse yards, made the horse its best bet of the day — not only of the Derby.

So Dave Cross was not thinking of Christmas coming, as he walked back toward the clubhouse and heard the roar of the crowd. He was thinking of Christmas Day at Turf Paradise, a racetrack in Arizona, back in 1957.

"I was sitting on a bale of hay, eating raw carrots," he recalls. "I had three sore horses. Why would that memory come back to me after just winning the Kentucky Derby? It did.

"That day, a Christmas dinner would have cost $1.75. You could have turned the barn upside down without finding $1.75. No, I didn't think of quitting racing then. I do remember that I asked myself what the hell I was doing there. But I was just a young punk. Racing has been good to me and I like to think I never have done anything to degrade racing."

Cross is an outspoken person and he makes it clear he is unlikely to be back in Canadian racing except for his connection with Sunny's Halo and his association with Pud Foster.

That is not, he emphasizes, a case of a guy outgrowing his britches in a single afternoon at the Kentucky Derby. He was on the verge of going back to California, where he has a home, two years ago.

"Certainly, I never will leave Mr. Foster," he assures. "He has made me a rich man but there's a definite shortage of owners in Canada who are willing to pay what it costs to operate a good stable. Two years ago, when I was ready to leave, Don Miller and Doug Snowden helped to change my mind by giving me some horses."

It's safe to say that Cross has not endeared himself to some of the owners and trainers who had two-year-olds running in Canada last season. He admits: "I stepped on some feet up there."

When he says he had to take Sunny's Halo away, in order to find suitable competition for his colt ("we were beating garbage"), he is treading on more than a few corns. He is fracturing some egos.

At the same time, he has been outspoken in his defence of the Queen's Plate in conversations with members of the US media who wonder how he possibly could consider passing up the Belmont Stakes and go for the striped trousers and gray toppers.

"The Queen's Plate is no nickels and dimes race," he tells them. "It's a prestige race and there's a good purse. We can't go in both the Belmont and the Queen's Plate. I'll do whatever Mr. Foster decides to do."

Pud Foster admits he can't make a decision until he finds out who is going to buy a piece of Sunny's Halo. He feels he can't continue to go solo. The insurance on the horse, alone, is killing him. If he sells to an American breeder, the contract almost certainly would require a bid for the Triple Crown. The difference between that and the Queen's Plate, in syndication fees, would be millions.

"So far," says Dave Cross, "the offers (for a share in the colt) that have been made in Canada are ridiculous. I don't include Windfields Farm in that. I appreciate Mr. Foster's problem."

Two things are quite clear: Sunny's Halo is worth millions — and Mr. Cross is off raw carrots for Christmas.

BOXING

Mauler and Moolah soon separated

Jack Dempsey was a great heavyweight champion and a darn good story teller, as this 1 March 1950 column indicates.

TORONTO — Jack Dempsey chuckled at the recollection of what a sucker he's been. He and his manager, Jack Kearns, once went for fifty grand when they took a flyer at coal mining in Utah. Another time one of Kearns' friends chided Dempsey for being cheap. Most of the celebrities he knew, this pal of Kearns said, had given him some kind of memento. In those days Dempsey was anxious to do as celebrities did. What would this gentleman like, he wondered. The gentleman would like a case for a watch of which he was proud.

"I'd never heard of a watch that cost more than fifty bucks," Dempsey laughed, "so I told the guy to go out and buy himself a watch case. Forgot all about it until I got a bill for $4,750. I called up the jeweller and screamed. He tells me this guy has bought himself a platinum case decorated with diamonds and rubies. I told Kearns: 'He's your friend, and you'll pay half.' I made sure he did too." This was only one of many such incidents.

"Kearns was a great fight manager, but as a business man, that's something else again. I was into everything: coal mines, oil wells, gold stocks, apartment houses, hotels and restaurants. The thing you learn quickest is that a champion and his money are soon parted.

"Kearns was a great guy for surprises — like that day at Toledo when I won the title from Jess Willard. Kearns came around and asked me: 'Do you think you can knock him out in the first round?' I said I didn't know, but I didn't think so. Jack tells me: 'You'd better, because I've just bet $10,000 at ten-to-one on a first round knockout.' Our total share of the purse was only $17,500 and our expenses were well over $7,500. So here we are, fighting for nothing, unless I can get a knockout in the first round against the world champion.

"I thought I had it, too, when they raised my hands as the first round ended. Willard was down, but the bell went at the count of nine. There was such an uproar the referee didn't hear it. I was out of the ring and on my way to the dressing room — thinking of that $100,000. Next thing I knew I'm back in the ring and get banged right on the nose. Nobody's told me yet what's happened. I fought that second round without knowing why I'm fighting."

The Old Mauler enjoys his new role as referee for the wrestlers. That's what brings him to Toronto. He's a feature of Frank Tunney's Thursday night show at Maple Leaf Gardens. Dempsey's a trouper from away back so the constant travel is no hardship. Besides, he's smart enough to assess the value of keeping himself in the public eye. There was a time when public appearances, except in the ring, constituted punishment for the world's champion.

"Right after I won the title Kearns and I went to work," Dempsey recounted, "We owed money, had none, so we grabbed a chance to make $5,000 a week in vaudeville, starting at Cincinnati. Kearns got by with his part but I was the world's worst actor. I'd get on the stage and my tongue would stick. Didn't know what do say. Which didn't matter because I couldn't say it anyway.

"We started writing down our lines on little pads which we held in the palms of our hands. One day Kearns and I got into an argument. We were playing the old Hippodrome in New York.

Milt with two former heavyweight champions,
Jack Sharkey (left) and Jack Dempsey in Toronto, 1949.

"Place was so big you had to skate out on the stage on roller skates. I generally fell two or three times before I made it. Anyway Kearns was supposed to start out by saying: 'I'm going to introduce the most popular champion of all time.' Only he always said 'poplar.' I didn't know any better myself, but one day a friend tipped me off that it should be 'popular.' So I says to Jack: 'It's popular.' Kearns says: 'The hell it is, it's poplar.' I says: 'Popular.' He finally blows up and orders me to mind my own business. Tells me that from now on I take care of the work in the ring and he'll take care of the speeches."

One of the most embarrassing incidents Dempsey ever endured stemmed from a fling at burlesque. That was before he became champion. He was beginning to earn recognition for his lethal punch and Kearns gleefully announced an offer of $100 for a Sunday afternoon appearance as an added attraction at a strip and skip joint.

When the announcement came for Jack Dempsey, in person, to appear on the stage, Kearns stepped out and took the applause that was intended for Dempsey. Kearns was a fine figure in his tailored suit, with a carnation in his lapel. Dempsey created a poor impression by comparison: baggy pants and sweater coat. The chorus girls had given him an over-generous coating of make-up, so he might have passed for one of the comedians. They had told Dempsey he wouldn't have to do anything but stand on the stage. So he stood — until the customers started to pelt him with candy boxes and other bric-a-brac. Some person eventually reached through the backdrop and hauled him in. He rushed out one exit; Kearns through another. It was two days before Dempsey returned to their hotel. Then he learned the theater had refused to pay the promised century note.

The popular belief is that no person ever hit Dempsey harder than Luis Firpo, who belted him out of the ring in that "most thrilling sports incident of the last 50 years" by the Associated Press barometer.

But Dempsey says that's not so. No person, he says, ever hit him as hard as Gunboat Smith nailed him in a fight at 'Frisco. Dempsey went on to win the match, but he didn't know it until the next day, when he read it in the paper.

Science suffers;
big night for slug

Three fights after this one, The Rock walked away 49–0 and the only undefeated heavyweight champion in history. Boxing historians often downgrade Marciano's status claiming he didn't have to fight much — but as this column of 18 June 1954 shows, Ezzard Charles was no average pug.

NEW YORK — You have to conclude that slug beats science every time — or at least 46 times. That's how many times one Rocco Francis Marchegiano has gone in the past as a pro. And that's how many times he has won. When the Rock wins, it's a resounding triumph for slug. His science consists of lowering his head and bulling his way in the fray while cranking up rights and lefts. Since the law of averages works for Rocky, the same as for anyone else, a fair percentage of his punches land. And that percentage has been enough to date. It probably will be enough for some time to come. In licking Ezzard Charles at Yankee stadium last night, the Rock rolled over the best boxer he has met so far in his career. The result was a terrific shot in the veins for the boxing game. But the manly science of fisticuffs was set back several thousand years — back to the days when men tracked down their enemies with clubs. That's how the Rock fights. And that's what sells.

From the customer's point of view this must have been the most spectacular heavyweight championship fight since Luis Firpo deposited Jack Dempsey among the typewriter keys back in 1923. Dempsey, of course, was pitched back in by his newspaper friends and clubbed Firpo cold in the second round. There was that kind of action last night. But it couldn't have been the same kind of slugging because no person got knocked out of the ring. No person was even knocked down. Which should help to answer the question: "Does Rocky Marciano carry a lethal package of sleeping pills is his right hand?" Maybe he does, but he hit Charles with everything except a fungo bat in the Yankee ball yard last night and Charles refused to go down. But when he was hurt the challenger was a moving target and Marciano couldn't tee him up. At times, he made the Rock look silly, even when the champ looked to be winning from here to Hong Kong. In the tenth round, Rocky stood on one foot to put more power into his wind-up. He missed with a right that was meant to drive Ezzard's head into the center field stand. The momentum carried Rocky across the ring and it looked as if he might slide into first base.

How Charles weathered the storm of leather that broke around his noggin in the sixth round is something that's due to be debated for many months to come. The answer must be either that Charles has a bullet-proof head or that the Rock hits with less authority than you've been led to believe. They used to go down when Joe Louis landed those solid punches. It's hard to think that pugs like Tony Galento, Billy Conn and Buddy Baer, whom Louis stiffened, were more fragile than Charles. Even the Rock seemed puzzled. Halfway through the round he had punched himself out. He had to take a breather and blinked his eyes as if he couldn't believe Charles was still on his feet. Not only did Charles remain upright but when Marciano attempted to follow up his advantage in the next round, Charles stood him off with left jabs and hooks to the head. Ezzard had taken a man-sized shellacking — the kind you might get in an alley — but he was still strong. Some reflections had been cast, in the past, on the toughness of Ezzard's fiber. He had been called a timid fighter, a shot-maker who had no stomach for his work. Charles answered those critics last night. The guy showed his heart is as big as the beer signs in the outfield. Actually it was he who gained in stature as a fist fighter last night. He was well whipped, even though one of the judges gave him six rounds, with one even. But it was expected he would be well whipped. Few expected to see him around for fifteen rounds. Even Rocky's corner must have been impressed. How else could you explain the fact they allowed the Rock to continue his wild pitching right through the fifteenth round? His chin was wide open for a lucky punch, when all he had to do was keep out of trouble and let the officials count up the rounds he already had won.

This was such a rabble-rousing brawl that the International Boxing club may be tempted to do a retake. Certainly they have nothing else on tap that would have the same appeal. Outside of the first two or three rounds, when Charles effectively tied up the short-armed Rock whenever he attempted to fight at close quarters, the bombs were falling like hailstones. The mob was in a frenzy, expecting to see one of the jousters stretched on the deck. So a rematch shouldn't be hard to sell. The odds would be against it turning up another such fight. Actually, Marciano didn't suffer much damage, even though he looked as if he had stuck his kisser into a fan. Charles drew blood along Rocky's nose in the second round, but it was only a scratch. Early in the fourth round, he planted a right sock in Rocky's left eye. When the Rock kept leaving his face open, Charles landed additional punches on the sore spot. During every interval between rounds Marciano's handlers patched up his eye. Just as deftly Charles picked off the patch. He made it a bull's eye for the remainder of the fight. It was the eighth round before Marciano was able to score with an uppercut that started the claret flowing from Charles' right eye. But with all his courage and skill, Charles didn't come close to dropping the Rock on his rompers, as Joe Walcott did in the very first round at Philadelphia, two years ago. That was the first time the Rock had been off his pins. Joe was given a second chance. And you know how that one turned out.

You can't run
and still win

One of the great middleweight fights of all time was a bruiser between Sugar Ray Robinson and Carmen Basilio. Certainly the outcome has been debated over more than any other, that is until another Sugar Ray fought Marvin Hagler. One thing is beyond debate: Robinson was one of the best ever. Often described as "pound for pound" the finest fist fighter, Robinson was five times middleweight champion who won 174 fights over a career that began in 1940 and went until 1965. This column appeared on 24 September 1957.

NEW YORK — If you locked Sugar Ray Robinson and Carmen Basilio in a telephone booth, there's not much doubt about which one would be able to walk away from the scene of the mayhem. It would be Basilio. His beak might be barked and his brow would be bleeding, but he'd get the job done because of his murderous close-in attack.

If you turned them loose on a football field and told them only one could return, it would be Sugar Ray who would waltz back. Robinson would have danced the legs off the unglamorous ex-onion digger by luring him on with a stabbing left jab to the chops.

Fortunately for both of them, fights in telephone booths are neither legal nor profitable. And there's no point to chasing each other around a football field when James Dougan Norris is willing to provide a ring for the blood-letting, along with three-quarters of a million dollars as a prize.

And so Carmen Basilio is the new middleweight champion of the world. A ring is less confining then a telephone booth, thus the craggy-faced Carmen was all-out to knock this most alluring crown off the noggin of Robinson, one of the greatest ringmen of all time. In fact, there will be legions of people — Sugar Ray among them — who will say Basilio didn't earn this new bauble at all.

Because a ring does not offer sufficient room for even a cutie of Sugar Ray's caliber to take completely successive evasive action, the former middleweight champion trudged out of Yankee stadium last night, a defeated, dejected and deflated ex-king. He's plain citizen Robinson now, with no right to call the financial shot for any fighting he may do, because he lacks a title to back up his demands. As a champion, Ray called for the limit payload and got it. His insistence on the last nickel won't be forgotten by those with whom he will have to talk business as the ex-champ.

There was bitterness in the voice of George Gainford, one of Sugar Ray's regiment of managers, as he denounced last night's decision in the madhouse that was Robinson's dressing-room. Photographers were perched on stools and chairs, aiming their cameras over the heads of perspiring reporters and imploring: "Ray, look this way, please." Ray was in no mood for looking. He sat disconsolately in front of his locker, looking like a completely exhausted man. When he was ready to dress, his handlers even helped him into his underwear and pants.

"That was the worst decision of Robinson's career," Gainford grumbled. "Robinson won nine rounds by my figuring. Basilio took five and one was even. Yet they give the fight to Basilio. Didn't they see Basilio goin' around all night with Robinson's left in his face? Don't them thirteen left jabs in succession mean nothin'? Basilio gets in for a couple of shots — bang, bang — so they give him the round. Is that the way it is? That other guy was dyin'."

Unwittingly George summed up fairly neatly just why his tiger lost. Sugar Ray plastered Basilio with dozens of left jabs. But they caused irritation, rather than injury. And they were thrown mostly as defensive missiles, rather than as instruments of attack. The left jab was Robinson's radar system to keep Basilio from getting in close. Sugar Ray used it almost from the first punch of the fight, thus capitalizing on his superior reach.

But they were nuisance shots, and the stalking challenger took as many as three or four of them to get in one of his own slams. Basilio's forehead was reddened by that darting left as early as the first round. His nose bled slightly from the second round on and a cut was opened near his left eye in the fourth. His face looked like a commercial for tomato sauce for most of the fight. Much of this superficial damage was the result of those left jabs. But any advantage which Robinson gained in scoring because of that left obviously was offset by the fact that Basilio was chasing him for most of the thirteen heats.

Robinson can thank himself and his handlers for blowing the title. He proved — too late — that he didn't have to fight Basilio from a bicycle. By this time it was the twelfth round. Robinson took the offensive and nailed the Canastota clouter twice with vicious left hooks and a right uppercut. Basilio was trapped in Robinson's corner, but he weaved and bobbed his way out. Again in the thirteenth, Basilio was rocked by a left hook that almost put him on the deck. If Sugar Ray had fought any other five rounds as he did the final five, there's no doubt he would have retained his title — maybe even by a knockout. It scarcely can be argued that strategy demanded Robinson should stay away from the crowding challenger for ten rounds and then attempt to knock him out. With seven extra years in his legs, Robinson's chances logically figured to get slimmer with each round after eight.

The real story of Robinson's present status as a fist fighter may lie in the films which will show he was trading shots with a scrapper who offers little or no defence against a left hand. Yet Robinson, whose atomic weapon is a devastating left hook, was unable to put Basilio on the deck even once. And it wasn't because Sugar Ray didn't land it. The hook caught Basilio's jaw early in the thirteenth, but Carmen stood up. It exploded again in the fourteenth — this time on the neck. Basilio was shaken but he didn't go down. If Robinson has got to the stage where there are no sleeping pills left in that hook, he's at the end of the line.

He could go out with another big pay day. Any of the half million fanatics who saw last night's thriller here at the ball park or in theaters across two nations would have to come back. And they'd bring thousands with them, for this was one of the real good fights of all time. And the verdict will cause more arguments than a joker in a poker deck.

When the referee, Al Berl, who was in the ring, saw the fight practically in reverse from what the judges, Artie Aidala and Bill Recht, witnessed, there surely is room for laymen to engage in debate. It could be, of course, the New York Athletic Commission got the wrong Berl — Milton, instead of Al.

Did Clay win or Liston quit?

Milt calls Muhammad Ali the greatest athlete, not just boxer, of all time. His two fights with Sonny Liston were both shrouded in controversy. (In the rematch, a "phantom" punch knocked Liston out in the first round.) Right from the beginning, the world sensed something special about Cassius Clay — this story appeared at the top of the front page on 26 February 1964, a highly unusual placement for a boxing story.

MIAMI BEACH — Cassius Clay had the Bear at bay with a pain in his paw.

PS: So there's no pay — and that's not hay.

Cassius Marcellus, poet-laureate of pugilism — and quite

185

incidentally the new heavyweight champion of the world — will improve on that wretched doggerel when he exhausts his present theme.

And what is his present theme? It's "I'm the greatest. Who's the greatest? I'm the greatest." This is a long-playing record which may run for several weeks — or years.

Cassius Marcellus turned it on last night, within seconds of finding himself the world champion of fist-fighting because Sonny Liston, whom Cassius had vilified as The Big Ugly Bear, elected to default at the start of the seventh round.

It was one of the most bizarre endings in the history of heavy-weight championships — an ending that will stand much close scrutiny in the days ahead. Already, there is an ironic twist. The medical profession, which was asked to determine whether Clay was fit to fight Liston, now is being asked for the reason Liston didn't continue to fight.

Clay's actions at yesterday's official weigh-in raise the question of whether the 22-year-old Louisville Lip actually had flipped his lid. He ranted and babbled until even the dead-panned Liston showed concern.

It should be explained that Sonny was less worried about the state of Clay's health than he was over the possibility of a fantastic payday slipping away.

Dr. Alexander Robbins, the physician who examined Cassius, reported a pulse of 120 — against a normal beat of 54.

The doctor hinted there was evidence of extreme fright.

Clay's tirade at the weigh-in also cost him a $2,500 fine — which he probably won't pay — and there was another precautionary clocking of his pulse just before ring-time. It was found to be near normal — they said — at 64.

That cleared Cassius to win the world title as it turned out, and to explode the myth of invincibility behind which Liston had masqueraded. Today, it's Liston's turn to convince the medicos that he's entitled to the benefits of any doubts — which exist in spades.

To be perfectly blunt about it, two orthopaedic specialists have been asked whether Sonny Liston, the tough guy, the world champion of pugilism, really has the miseries in his left arm.

Or did he take a powder because he was in danger of getting licked? Just in case the answer is unsatisfactory — or unconvincing — Liston's purse is being held up.

(Robbins this morning said he would recommend that the purse be released in view of a statement by eight physicians. They agreed Liston had suffered an injury to his left shoulder that "would be sufficient to incapacitate him and prevent him from defending himself.")

World Champions have surrendered before. Jess Willard's handlers threw in the towel at Toledo, but not until Jack Dempsey had beaten their giant to a pulp. Sonny Liston had a cut under his left eye, a bump beneath the right peeper and maybe a welt or two over his ribs. It wasn't sufficient damage to justify turning in his badge as champion of the world.

So why did he default? The crowd — that's using the term loosely — was informed Sonny had dislocated his left shoulder and the doctor (unidentified) had ordered him to quit. Pure fiction, apparently.

Jack Nilon, the millionaire sandwich merchant who acts as Sonny's adviser, insisted he and trainer Willy Reddish were the ones who ran up the white flag. It wasn't a dislocated shoulder. It was bursitis. Sonny wasn't stricken suddenly. The condition had existed for some time. They simply didn't consider it serious until last night.

"The whole left arm got numb," Nilon claimed. "Sonny had complained about it from the first round. So we decided he couldn't continue. Re-match? How can we consider a re-match? This kid (Clay) will be in the army for the next two years. He's stretching an army call right now."

Nilon's admission that he and trainer Reddish stopped the fight without even consulting the commission doctor puts Liston in an extremely bad light. There was no evidence of the numbness in Sonny's arm in the fifth round — which Clay spent on the dead run, because Cassius claimed to have been blinded temporarily by some substance on Liston's gloves.

This was another cloak and dagger bit that would have ballooned to major mystery stature if Clay had lost. As the

A young Muhammad Ali entertains Toronto's press in 1966.
(PHOTO BY ED FEENY, COURTESY THE TORONTO STAR)

fighters were leaving their corners of the fifth round, Cassius began pawing at his eyes.

His trainer, Angelo Dundee, sniffed at a towel — then at a sponge. Liston came barreling across the ring like a bull. Dundee howled at Clay — and at referee Barney Felix. Cassius went into the bicycle act — keeping out of Sonny's reach. Clay threw only one punch during the whole round. Liston was the picture of clumsy frustration in pursuit.

Dundee explained the strange happenings: "When Clay started blinking I thought there must be something on our towel or sponge. I couldn't smell anything so I decided there must be liniment on Liston's gloves. That's why I yelled at the referee to check the gloves (he didn't) and I told Clay to get in there and move. After the round he told me his eyesight had cleared."

Obviously, the fifth round belonged to Liston. Even Gus Jacobson, one of the two judges, gave Sonny that one. He gave Liston only one. It also was a Liston round (of course) which referee Felix and Barney Lovett turned in.

In the sixth round Cassius bounced back. He scored with five successive left jabs to the champion's face. As Sonny came out of the crouch, Cassius caught him with a left hook. By coincidence — you're asked to conclude — that's when Sonny's arm became so numb he couldn't fight.

There's a lot to be explained. Fighters have concealed broken hands, strains, sprains — even loss of vision in one eye — in order to continue. Here was a case in which the champion abdicated because of an ailment which his handlers admit was chronic.

Be charitable and say Nilon and Reddish are humanitarians who believe the welfare of the athlete is all that matters. No prize is worth the risk of getting his block knocked off.

In that case, you will have to look for some sign of protest from the athlete. There was none. Sonny Liston, the world champion, didn't even get up from his stool when the bell sounded.

Clay was up — and dancing. There was a split second of unbelieving surprise when he saw the champion wasn't responding. Then Cassius Marcellus, the man with the jackrabbit pulse beat, threw his arms into the air. In a matter of seconds, he was howling: "I'm the greatest." And he was.

It's going to be said that Liston knew when he was licked. If he did, he knew something that didn't appear to others. Felix had the fight dead even after six beats. Judge Lovett had Liston in front, 58 to 56. Gus Jacobson, the other judge, had it 59 to 56 for Clay.

One good round was all Liston needed to give him a healthy margin. Maybe he and his handlers figured there were no more good rounds left. Suddenly, Sonny, who claims to be 30 and is alleged to be 32, looked more like 40 — which may be closer to his true age.

Father Time seemed to tap Liston on the shoulder in the third round. That was when Clay suddenly quit pretending he was a ballet dancer. He backed the champ against the ropes and flailed him with rights and lefts to the head. Blood trickled from a cut beneath Liston's left eye — the first wound Sonny had suffered in three world championship bouts.

Sonny showed apprehension. The whites of his eyes gleamed. He charged Clay in desperation. For the first time it probably occurred to him that this youthful cocky loudmouth who had harassed and ridiculed him also could fight.

Clay's speed and footwork revealed Sonny's shortcomings, which two soft shots at Floyd Patterson had covered up. Sonny couldn't hit a target that was moving. His attempts to kill Clay in the fourth and fifth rounds when he had things his own way were pathetic.

Rocky Marciano, who was no fancy-dan but quite a fist fighter for all that, exclaimed: "Liston missed a million opportunities for the knockout."

Sonny gets one more opportunity — to convince those orthopaedic specialists he isn't one more bully who got chased off the street by the new kid who just moved into the block.

Chuvalo makes good fights

Ali came to Toronto to fight Chuvalo after being run out of Chicago and a fight with Ernie Terrell because of his famous line: "I got no quarrel with them Viet Cong." Ali was at the height of his powers and still a year away from being robbed of his crown for his anti-war stand. Yet, as this 30 March 1966 column points out, Chuvalo put up one heck of a fight.

TORONTO — They had a contest between a bull and a bumblebee at Maple Leaf Gardens last night — with the usual result. The bull came out of it with his face looking like a bucket of balls at a golf driving range.

It was Cassius Muhammad Ali Clay who copyrighted the slogan: "Float like a butterfly and sting like a bee." He demonstrated the technique for a turnout of 13,918 last night.

The fact that so many morbidly curious citizens should risk the ridicule of their neighbors by attending the rites was one of the real surprises of the fight. Most of them apparently waited until they thought the scoffers had gone to bed. Then they got down to the Gardens — and discovered the scoffers hadn't gone to bed at all. They were at the Gardens, too.

The late rush exhausted the supply of $10 tickets. Harold (Onkel Mike) Ballard, a novice patron of the pugilistic arts, revealed himself as a promising prospect to succeed such shrewd operators as Mike Jacobs and Tex Rickard in pushing fights.

"What . . . we're out of $10 tickets?" Ballard exclaimed. "Well, cut the $20 tickets in half and sell them for a sawbuck. Just don't let any suckers escape."

Those who remained true to their vows of absenteeism missed the best heavyweight hostilities since the joust between Floyd Patterson and George Chuvalo at Madison Square Garden in February of 1965. Which seems to bring up a point: the two top shows in the ranks of the heavies in more than a year have involved Chuvalo, a man who fights with his face.

Chuvalo, of course, was the bull in this hopeless test with the bee. And George, the indestructible, didn't come close to winning it. He got another hometown decision, such as caused him and his manager, Irving Ungerman, extreme grief when he fought Ernie Terrell. They all voted against George again, for the same reason they voted against him before: you don't win fights simply by proving the other guy can't knock you out.

As yet, Chuvalo, who has been called the best catcher since Bill Dickey of the Yankees hung up his decker, gave a display of doggedness and gameness and durability that earned him admiration, even from the legions who have said he didn't belong in the ring with Cassius Muhammad Ali Clay.

Maybe nobody belongs in the ring with the Mecca man, but Chuvalo showed he had a better right to be there than either Patterson or Sonny Liston, one of whom has figured in each of the last five championship fights. Now maybe that's damning Chuvalo with faint praise.

At any rate, it puts Chuvalo in a unique category. He's not much of a fist fighter — but there isn't much of a fist fight unless he's one of the principals in the ring.

Chuvalo never has been knocked off his feet. That's one of the noted truisms of sport — like saying nobody ever knocked a fair ball out of Yankee Stadium into the street. George never came close to being knocked down last night.

If it were not for that record, some probing questions would have to be asked about the potency of Clay's punch. He hit Chuvalo with just about every missile in the armory last night. All he gave Chuvalo was lumps.

It was Jackie Silvers, referee of the match, who said: "How can you fault Clay for not putting Chuvalo on the floor, when you know the man never has been knocked off his feet?" Silvers, incidentally, must come from a league in which the strike zone is from the ankle to the eye. Chuvalo must have thrown 40 low punches last night. There was no indication that Jackie warned him to change his sights.

In the third round, it appeared as if Chuvalo's low shots had infuriated Clay. He unloaded a barrage of rights and lefts to the head that made Chuvalo look like the hitching post on a merry-go-round. George was the only inanimate object in sight.

Clay took some ridiculous chances in the early part of the fight. He was so confident of winning that he hooked one glove around Chuvalo's neck and invited the Canadian champion to play Colonel Bogey's March on his ribs.

This is a Clay trick which is designed to let an opponent punch himself out. If Chuvalo is anything, he's a body puncher. In the Patterson bout, he gave Floyd such a shellacking, from the hips to the armpits, that Patterson scarcely could stagger into the showers.

Clay gave no indication that he felt the tattoo from Chuvalo's fists. The crowd loved it. Those punches sounded good in the greens and the grays, but they meant almost nothing in the outcome of the fight.

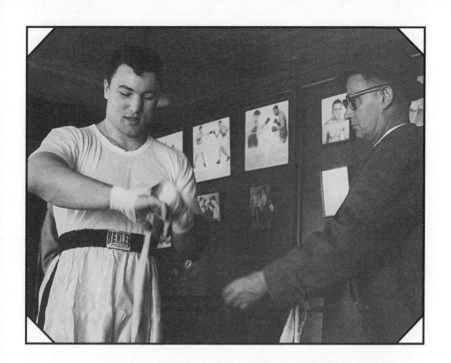

*Milt helps Canadian heavyweight George Chuvalo with his
tape while preparing for the Toronto fight with Muhammad Ali
in 1966. Chuvalo fought gamely but Ali made his face look
"like a bucket of balls at a golf driving range," Milt wrote.*
(TUROFSKY PHOTO, COURTESY THE TORONTO STAR)

Angelo Dundee, in Clay's corner, confessed he became
slightly disturbed when his fighter exposed his torso for target
practice. His greatest concern was that Clay might suffer
damage to his back. Neither he nor Clay thought of the possibility, apparently, that a butt or an elbow is not unlikely at such
close quarters.

Toward the end of the fight, Clay would maneuver himself
into a corner and create the impression that he might be a
sitting duck. When Chuvalo rushed in, Clay would slip a punch
and escape. It was a frustrating tactic for a weary pursuer like
Chuvalo, who had been plodding to the attack all night.

There's no question that Clay is the heavyweight with all the
talents. He has speed, effective jabs. Rarely does he stop a hard

punch. There wasn't a pimple or a scar on him before he went into the ring last night. There isn't one on him now.

But can he deliver a devastating punch? Last night's outing scarcely was a fair test. Hitting Chuvalo is like knocking on a hot water tank.

The second scene three years later

Before the undefeated former champion could throw his jabs, he had to cut through bureaucratic red tape. Here on 25 September 1970 Milt says Ali's leadership qualities helped change a country's view of a war, a progressive view for someone of Milt's generation who had lived through two World Wars.

NEW YORK — Cassius Muhammad Ali Clay has changed since the days when he was the unchallenged heavyweight champion of the world. But he hasn't changed nearly as much as the mood of the times.

Coming up from Miami on National's 600 miles per hour flight 92, Ali, as he wants to be known, scarcely knew what to expect. In May of 1967, the New York State Athletic Commission had been one of the first to give him the boot.

He had made it plain he would reject induction into the army. His plea that he couldn't accept military service, because of his beliefs as a Black Muslim, was rejected. Hadn't he become rich in a sport of violence? Then there was that widely quoted statement: "I got no quarrel with them Viet Cong."

Most of the things which he said then, he would say today.

Plenty of people — many of them in high places — have improved on his denunciation of the war in Viet Nam. Students at some of the top schools in the country have hoisted the Viet Cong flag, without getting more than a mention in the public prints.

None of them was the heavyweight champion of the world. Anyway, protest is accepted now. It wasn't quite that way back in the mid-sixties, when Clay commenced correcting the ills of the world.

The question of the moment was: How much had the New York State Athletic Commission been touched by change? A federal court had ruled the commission exceeded its authority in refusing Clay a license because of his stand on military service and his pacifist outbursts.

Eventually, the commission would have to abide by the court ruling — but there are ways of giving an applicant the run-around. Was that what was going to happen next?

Clay's assistant trainer, Drew (Bundini) Brown, guessed not. New York would license Ali, he speculated, so the upcoming fight with Jerry Quarry in Atlanta could be close-circuited into Madison Square Garden. Later, the Garden would be hot on the trail of a match for Ali with Joe Frazier.

"They get something: we get the license," he summed up.

"The fight with Frazier will be a mismatch," Ali proclaimed. "It'll be my solid 215 against his 200. I thought Jimmy Ellis won two rounds from Frazier. Can't help it if I do hurt the gate. All I'm tellin' is the truth."

Bundini suggested there should be two fights for Ali before he gets to Frazier. Joe has a match coming up in November, with Bob Foster, the light heavyweight champion. That would be Frazier's second big pay night in 1970. The tax bite would make further action inadvisable until next year.

"No sense in Muhammad Ali bein' idle," Bundini argued. "Remember he's got those new twin daughters to take care of."

New York weather was hot. It was obvious the reception for Ali was to be at least warm. A limousine, with driver, was waiting to shuttle him through New York's impossible traffic to the commission offices on West 47th Street.

*Milt and heavyweight champion Ingemar Johansson get
reacquainted in June 1960 before a Floyd Patterson fight.*

Dr. Edwin Campbell, the commission's physician, was on
hand with the necessary tools to assure himself that the former
unbeaten heavyweight champion was suffering from nothing
more serious than the rust of idleness.

The doctor was co-operative. He took Ali's blood pressure
for the New York photographers, the visiting photographers
and the wire service photogs. When the television crews got
their paraphernalia set up, he did it again. Each time, he
declared it to be his firm belief that Ali was OK.

Tiny Rose Lewis, the commission secretary, came in with a
request. She wanted a picture of herself standing beside the
champion whose title the commission had disclaimed. She had
promised her kids, she explained.

Pete E. Mele, the deputy commissioner, could find no
fault with the application for Ali's license, which seemed

understandable, since the form had been filled out in advance. All Ali did was sign it — for photographers from all media.

"I'm going to recommend this to the commission," Mele said — for all the media. "The commission meets Monday. You will be notified of the result."

Bookmakers are offering generous odds for any clients who wish to wager against a favorable decision on the part of the commission, which is either more tolerant or more realistic than it was in May 1967, when Ali's license was suspended.

Materialism is suspected as a factor. It's almost a foregone conclusion now that Ali and Joe Frazier will fight — somewhere — and the long range look at the loot boggles the mind.

New York, which calls itself Funtown, with a grim sense of humor, wants the fight. It would be like having the World Series and the Kentucky Derby in the same place, during the same week.

Could Madison Square Garden have used the closed circuit TV of next month's Quarry-Clay quarrel in Atlanta — without Clay being licensed in New York? The answer is cautious — but revealing. In the past, see, the commission has felt that one of its licensees should not engage in trade and commerce with a non-licensee.

Madison Square Garden promotes fights by authority of the New York State Athletic Commission. Without fights the Rangers might have to play a 90-game home season. The circus might have to stay all summer. Until Clay is reinstated, he would be a non-licensee.

For Quarry-Clay, the Garden will be in a position to offer roughly 26,000 seats, combining the facilities of the main arena and the smaller Felt Forum. No scale of price has been set yet. Until Ali-Clay gets his license, that would be presumptuous.

However, the ante was $12 for the final of World Cup soccer — and, the joint was jammed. The Atlanta fight should sell at $10. And this is only the warmup. The main event will be next February likely.

None of this is the concern of the commission — although it would be unfortunate if the biggest fight since Dempsey-Tunney went to Las Vegas or Sioux Falls.

The downfall of
a prophet

It was a record five million dollar fight between champion Joe Frazier and Muhammad Ali the first time they met. Years later, Milt would say the greatness of this fight would be exceeded only by their third encounter in Manila. This column ran on 9 March 1971.

NEW YORK — It came to pass that the greatest weakness of the prophet was his contempt for the skills of those who came to do him evil. Egotism made him oblivious to the might of the foe.

Muhammad Ali-Clay, who could foresee the future and predict, with uncanny accuracy, the course of events that were to occur, fell victim to a man whom he sought to deride.

There was no other way to explain his clowning in a fist fight for the most money and before more spectators both seen and unseen, than ever had witnessed an exchange of legalized assault and battery in the history of the art.

This was the prophet, who had predicted the fall of opponents at home and abroad, going all the way back to ancient Archie Moore. His uncanny perception failed when he trained his radar on Smokin' Joe Frazier, the slaughter-house worker who became heavyweight champion of the world.

The prophet had proclaimed that Frazier was a clod who was slow of foot and was destined to fall in six. This was the forecast which he had made for the people who paid millions of dollars for the privilege of watching on closed-circuit TV.

By coincidence it was the sixth round of this blistering

brutal contest between two superbly conditioned gladiators that Ali-Clay chose for his most absurd demonstration of disdain for Smokin' Joe.

He started his act with his old trick of holding Frazier at arm's length, by pinning his long left against Frazier's forehead. Then he backed against the ropes, covered up his face and permitted Smokin' Joe to come in and use him as a punching bag. Arriving at his corner he yelled to newsmen at ringside: "No contest."

The judges didn't see it that way. Ali lost the sixth round on two of the three cards. Only referee Arthur Mercante marked the sixth in his favor. While his trainer, Angelo Dundee, pleaded from the corner for Ali-Clay to quit the horseplay and go on with the job of earning his $2,500,000, the man who had masqueraded as a prophet did his thing as usual. He ignored the advice.

Maybe it wasn't going to make any difference. The punches which he landed on Smokin' Joe, when he did deign to get serious, had approximately the same effect as an open-handed slap at the Brooklyn Bridge.

As he did in his previous bout with Oscar Bonavena, the modern Bull of the Pampus, Ali-Clay seemingly decided last night to open up with all his artillery in the ninth.

He stood and slugged with the most devastating left hooker in the business, moving his head the necessary inches to let Frazier's smoking shots whistle harmlessly past his chin.

Although Ali-Clay drew the first blood of the fight, in this heat, when a trickle of crimson began to show from Joe's nose, there was disconcerting news from the Ali-Clay corner. Their man was hitting Frazier with hard lefts and rights — but nothing was happening. Frazier continued to bore in and showed no signs of being hurt.

The crowd of 20,455, which had paid a record $1,352,961 for the pleasure of jamming into Madison Square Garden was in a frenzy during the three-minute outburst of fireworks. It was one of the most exciting rounds seen in a prize ring here, since the night Ingemar Johansson, a longshot from Sweden, flattened Floyd Patterson seven times in one round.

When it ended, Joe was grinning as he returned to his corner. There were growing welts over his eyes and high on his left cheekbone but there was absolutely no indication he had been injured. And this, remember, was Ali-Clay's best round. Even judge Bill Recht conceded him the ninth. So it must have been impressive, because Recht's card was practically a flunk-out for Ali-Clay. Recht gave him only four of the fifteen rounds.

The days of the prophet were numbered when Smokin' Joe caught him with a devastating southpaw body smash in the eleventh.

Ali-Clay had been doing his kitty bar-the-corner routine — standing along the ropes and covering up while Frazier, who is a music buff, played pop rock up and down his ribs.

Suddenly, the blockbuster landed and Ali-Clay sagged. His mouth popped open and the whites of his eyes showed. Smokin' Joe had scored with the kind of blow that might have brought down an ox in his abattoir days.

There was no more burlesque left in Ali-Clay. He reached back for the ropes and hung on. This was when Smokin' Joe's techniques as a finisher might have been faulted. He missed with a left hook that could have stiffened the prophet for the first knockout of his career.

Instead, Frazier permitted him to weather the storm. Ali-Clay was groggy as he got back to his corner, where he was showered with water, even before reaching his stool.

If Joe had been the killer he had appeared to be in previous fights, Ali-Clay never would have returned under his own power.

It's a tribute to Ali-Clay's tremendous physical condition that he rallied from that near-knockout and foul with at least a hint of his old skill in the twelfth. While he didn't win the round, he got a split on Mercante's card.

This may disprove the argument of Ali-Clay's partisans that it was the 43 months which he spent in exile that beat him last night. Before the fight, they scoffed at the suggestion the rust and erosion of that idleness might hurt. He was, they proclaimed, in the greatest shape of his career.

After it was over, though, his assistant trainer, Bundini Brown, used those many months of inactivity as an excuse for defeat. The question arises: If Ali-Clay were suffering from that long layoff, could he have given Frazier any kind of competition in the twelfth?

And would he have been able to win the fourteenth round, in the opinion of both judges? (Yes, even Recht thought Ali-Clay had won the fourteenth.) In other words, the prophet himself sort of shot down the only alibi that was offered by his camp.

Certainly, a fighter whose mechanism had been clogged and whose reflexes had been dulled by 43 months of banishment from the ring for his refusal to accept military induction, would not have scrambled back to his feet, at the count of three, when Frazier floored him with his left hook in the fifteenth.

Almost any boxer who is active today would have remained on the deck after that smash. Oscar Bonavena wasn't hit any harder in his bout with Ali-Clay last December. And Bonavena, one of the toughest characters to ever step in resin, stayed down.

Compared to the prophet Muhammad Ali-Clay, last night's winner and still world champion, Joe Frazier is an inarticulate type. Yet, he summed up the whole story fairly well when he said: "The man underestimated me. I want him to come and apologize for the things he called me."

Frazier must be smart enough to realize that much of the prophet's oratory was sounded for the purpose of selling tickets. Even Joe's own manager, Yank Durham, recognized Ali-Clay's value at the box office, when he promised, three years ago, that any division of the pot when these two fighters met would be an even split.

However, Smokin' Joe also knows there were no tickets to be sold in the ring last night. So, when Ali-Clay snarled, "I'm gonna kill you, nigger," he was practicing his old method of downgrading his opposition. This time, it turned out to be a costly mistake.

For one of the few times in his fantastic career Ali-Clay failed to make good on a promise. At the weigh-in as late as yesterday morning, he proclaimed: "If Joe Frazier beats me, I will crawl on my hands and knees across the ring and tell him he's the greatest."

Ali-Clay didn't do that. And Frazier said he didn't expect him to do it. He wouldn't ask him to do it. Would Ali-Clay have been as generous if the roles had been reversed?

Only the prophet himself could have answered that. And, as Bundini, himself, said, in Ali-Clay's absence: "No man talks much, with his jaw all swelled up."

Science it wasn't — a sizzler it was

The boxing world couldn't have been more thrilled with the outcome of this Rumble in the Jungle. As Milt had written earlier, "Cheering against Ali is like cheering for a depression" in the fight game. This column appeared on 30 October 1974.

KINSHASA, Zaire — The greatest dance team since Ginger Rogers and Fred Astaire is back on center stage. A sizzling left hook and a swinging right to the jaw of George Foreman, the hitherto undefeated heavyweight champ of the world, put it there.

In truth, though, this dance is for special events only. Muhammad Ali, the dance specialist, scarcely broke into a two-step as he flattened Foreman at 2:58 of the eighth round in one of the freest-swinging fist-fights of recent times.

This brawl, for a record pot of ten million, was billed by

imaginative promoters as the journey from the slave ship to the championship — an appeal to black Africa, which was seeing its first title fight.

The citoyens of this crowded capital — as they like to be called — must wonder if this was a demonstration of the sweet science of which they had been hearing so much recently.

What science there was definitely was illustrated by Ali.

Most of the time, it was a pure slugging match. Foreman showed a woeful lack of polish — especially after the fifth round, in which he had Ali pinned like a butterfly to the ropes, but was unable to put him away.

When Ali finally escaped from that trap, he nailed Foreman with a left hook to the head that must have shaken George's molars. In his attempt to retaliate, Foreman took a wild left swing that missed. He finished the round leaning against the challenger.

Ali says a lot of things when he is psyching himself up for a fight. This time, though, a lot of downgrading of Foreman was borne out in the ring. Foreman was not a murderous puncher, Ali said. In this fight, it was true.

If Foreman had been the killer he appeared to be against Joe Frazier, when he won the title, he would have caved in Ali's ribs. Ali had said Foreman was a clumsy fighter.

Even George, who is a pretty honest individual, would find it tough to dispute that when he looks at the re-runs later this week. He landed left hooks to the jaw in both the second and third rounds and could have put Ali on the deck.

It didn't happen, because the champion was pawing, not punching.

In his dressing room, reclining on the rubbing board, Foreman ruled out excuses. He had not seen the referee signal the count of ten, yes, because he was following instructions of his trainer Dick Sadler in the corner.

"I saw Dick signal to stay down," he said. "Then I saw Dick signal for me to rise. I didn't realize the fight was over until I saw Ali's handlers in the ring."

At that stage, Foreman's thinking processes may not have

Joe Louis drops by to see Milt in the early 1950s
and gets a few writing tips. Milt often has written about
unscrupulous types who separated the great Louis from
his money and left the Bomber in hock to the US
government for millions in back taxes.

been quite as alert as they usually are. He had another reason
for being confused. As he mentioned, this was the first time, as
a pro, that he had been on the deck.

Foreman may have been misled by Ali's pre-fight tirade
about dancing his way to the world title — floating like a butterfly, stinging like a bee.

The last thing Ali said to the champion, before they went to
their respective corners, was: "Come on, man, we gonna dance."

When the bell rang, Ali came out flat-footed and stayed that
way practically throughout the fight.

His trainer, Angelo Dundee, scoffed at suggestions they had changed tactics because Foreman came after Ali the instant the bell sounded. Dundee wondered what would be the point of dancing when it was apparent to both him and Ali immediately that Foreman was not going to be dangerous in close.

"Hell, we could see those shots coming from left field," said Dundee. "My fighter fought just like I expected he would. I told everybody who would listen just how this fight would go."

Never, perhaps, has a knockout been so riotously received by the audience. This is Ali country — has been ever since he came down here to train. He went through with his plans to psych Foreman by stirring up the crowd of approximately 50,000 in the Kinshasa soccer park, by leading the chant: "*Ali Buma-ye, Ali Buma-ye.*"

That means "kill him, Ali," as every fight fan in this boxing-happy country seems to know. Ali, of course, stands taller today than a Watusi and is more powerful than old Mato Yambo, the one-time warrior king of the Congo.

Nobody is more popular — and certainly not more powerful — than Mobutu Sese Seko, the real bankroller of this fight. At least, nobody had better get more popular.

Ali, though, is a comfortable second on the totem pole. Even the pygmy dwellers of the Ituri Forest, where the spear still is regarded as a dangerous weapon, know now that they backed the right horse.

Ali is only the second man in history to regain the heavyweight championship. That is another item of trivia of which they are aware. The other one was Floyd Patterson.

All this stuff comes over the talking drum. That's how the tribe used to send such vital information as weather reports. But, Mboyo Bompisola, assistant general manager of the layout where both fighters trained, scoffed at such ignorance.

"You must be making joke," he suggests. "Even the forest dwellers have transistor radios these days. They have been cheering for Ali."

Okay, then, so the pygmies will agree that Foreman started looking bad in the fourth heat. The champion was the aggressor, all right, but his punches were losing some of their speed.

He looked as if he might get the job done in the fifth, but he simply didn't have the home run shot. It was a case of Foreman's deterioration from there on. When he scored with a right uppercut that should have shaken Ali's eyeballs in the seventh, Muhammad mocked him.

Ali may have known then he was about to regain the title, which he failed to take from Joe Frazier in March 1971. Who's going to take it away from him again? Ali may be the first champion in the history of the game to die of old age.

The real champion: 64-year-old Eddie

"The greatest fight I have ever witnessed" is how Milt looks back at this battle. "Neither fighter was ever the same after this one." The Thrilla in Manila column ran on 1 October 1975.

MANILA — Not since the big guns of nearby Corregidor, now rotting in the tropical sun, has there been such cannonading in this corner of the Pacific.

It ended, as big battles sometimes do, when one side accepted the inevitable decision that further resistance was futile. In this case, it was a flash of humanitarian sanity on the part of

64-year-old Eddie Futch, a man with almost 40 years of ring wars behind him.

Eddie Futch, a gentle man in a violent game, told Smokin' Joe Frazier the battle had been lost. Smokin' Joe wouldn't be going back for the fifteenth round in the Thrilla of Manila — one of those infrequent fist fights which lived up to its billing.

If you believe what you've heard of the fight racket, Eddie Futch should have been shouting in Joe Frazier's ear: "Got nothin' to worry about, man. All you gotta do is get in there. Muhammad Ali's ready for the pickin'. He's got nothin' left, champ. Go in there and git him."

It must have been a temptation to Eddie Futch, at that. There is no prize in professional sport that equals the wealth which goes with the heavyweight championship.

In these days of multi-million-dollar fights, subsidized by the tax money of countries which are hungry for promotion — and sometimes hungry for food — the monetary rewards of the heavyweight title are mind-boggling.

As manager and trainer of Joe Frazier, it would have been a windfall for Eddie Futch if Smokin' Joe had been able to regain the championship which he lost to George Foreman, after less than two years of enjoying its benefits.

"I had a duty to perform and I was determined not to shirk it," Futch said, as simply as if he had been calling balls and strikes at a Sunday school softball game.

"Joe had been getting hit hard, throughout the thirteenth and fourteenth rounds," Futch reasoned. "He was getting hit because he wasn't seeing Ali's punches.

"Ali undoubtedly realized that, too. He knew there would be only three minutes left in the fight. Ali would have been able to throw everything he had at Joe in the final round. Joe might have got hurt.

"Even though I felt Joe had a slight edge in the fight, I told him he wasn't going out for the fifteenth round. When he protested, I summoned the referee (Carlos Padilla, Jr.) and told him the fight was over.

"Have I done things such as this before? Definitely. I stopped a fight between Hedgeman Lewis and Indian Red Lopez with 30 seconds to go in the last round. In that fight, I knew we were winning. If somebody's gonna get hurt, it's no time to think of money." Eddie trained Lewis.

Eddie Futch was wrong about Smokin' Joe having an edge in the fight. If it had gone the distance, the only chance Smokin' Joe had was that he could land a knockout punch.

The cards of all three Filipino officials — Padilla, the referee, and Larry Nadayag and Colonel Alfredo Quiazon, the judges — verified that Nadayag had Joe trailing by four points after fourteen rounds. That's as close as he came on any of the score cards.

Joe lost because he was unable to follow up the only shot which seemed to put the inimitable Ali in trouble. That was a left hook, in the sixth round, which obviously shook the champ. The punch caught Ali on the jaw, following a flurry of punches, in which Ali had knocked out Frazier's mouthpiece.

"That's the same punch which put Ali on the deck in the first fight," Angelo Dundee, Ali's trainer, admitted. "This time, he didn't go down — but he was hurt when he got back to the corner."

The problem which an opponent has when he is fighting Muhammad Ali is that he never knows what to expect. When Ali announces his plan before a fight, the natural assumption is that he will do something entirely different.

This time, he did precisely what he had threatened to do: he came out flat-footed and throwing punches. Gone was the "float like a butterfly and a sting like a bee" routine.

The result was a shoot-out that had the audience of 25,000, which included President Ferdinand Marcos and his wife, in a constant uproar.

"It was the most brutal heavyweight fight I've seen since the first match between (Rocky) Marciano and (Joe) Walcott," said Murray Goodman, who probably was present for the debut of John L. Sullivan.

Eddie Futch had a more subdued appraisal: "In our times, I don't suppose we ever will see another heavyweight fight in which so many punches will be thrown."

Unfortunately for Eddie's man, too many of his punches landed on Ali's hips and elbows. Ali played his usual intelligent game. When he needed a breather, he went into his shell.

Frazier, who was the pursuer throughout most of the fourteen rounds, never did succeed in getting clean shots to the jaw through the famous Ali armor.

He did give Ali a terrific beating about the body. Some of his punches were low — bringing screams of complaint from Dundee in the champion's corner.

Ali dropped to the canvas in his corner immediately after Futch had signaled surrender. This created an impression, in some minds, that he wouldn't have finished the fight if Frazier had continued.

Nothing could be farther from fact, of course. Ali drops to the deck in order to protect himself from his friends. He can take care of his enemies. Nevertheless, he admitted he was hurt.

"I'm so tired I don't want to do nothin' but lie down," he lamented. "My hips are sore, my arms are sore, my sides are sore. Man, I gotta take a rest. This my fourth fight this year. How many months left before the end of the year? So far, I had 54 rounds of fights and the year's not over yet."

Of Frazier, whom he had derided as a "gorilla" who was overtrained and overrated, Ali said: "He's tough. He's greater than I thought he was. He's great."

As balm for his bruises, Ali will collect at least four million dollars, the amount of his guarantee, and probably much more — depending on the take from closed circuit television.

Frazier will have at least two million dollars to help heal the welts over and under his eyes. That should buy a lot of fuel for his Rolls Royce, even considering the grabbiness of the oil-exporting countries.

For Smokin' Joe, the picnic under the money tree probably is over. He is holding a "victory" party tonight.

Old age and young Spinks rob Ali of his crown

Though Muhammad Ali was to regain his crown for a record third time, clearly his glory days were past when Leon Spinks out-pointed him on 15 February 1978. Ali and Milt had a special bond of mutual respect. Several years later, Ali had begun to suffer from the onset of Parkinson's disease, Ali recognized Milt in an airport and chatted to his old friend. "The greatest athlete would have to be Muhammad Ali," Milt says. "He was the greatest heavyweight champion of all time, and he was one of the greatest salesmen and public relations personalities in the world."

LAS VEGAS — The most fantastic story in the long history of professional fist fighting ended in much the same way it started. The march of time took its toll on Muhammad Ali, 36, heavyweight champion of the universe, just as it did of Sonny Liston, the "big ugly bear" — as Ali called him — at Miami Beach in February of 1964.

There was one tremendous difference. Ali played the role of the great champion he has been, to the last ounce of energy he could summon up, in a fifteenth round desperation bid to knock out 24-year-old Leon Spinks, a rank novice as a pro who had his first professional fight only thirteen months ago.

Liston permitted his title to be taken from him while he

brooded in his corner over what he claimed to be a crippling arm injury. Sonny, who had encountered the same challenge of youth (Ali) which caught up with Ali last night, refused to answer the bell for the seventh round.

Ali went out with the cheers of the 6,000 or more fight fanatics who crammed the gaudy pavilion of the posh Hilton hotel ringing in his ear.

That was one of the ironies of an upset that stunned not only the sports world but many levels of society which never sniff the smell of resin or training camp sweat.

Muhammad Ali liked to call himself the best-known man in the world. Maybe he wasn't that — but he came mighty close. There never had been another man of his magnetism in sport.

As he left the ring in defeat last night, there were anguished cries of "*Ali, Ali*" from the bewildered audience. The new world champion Leon Spinks, a product of the ghetto in St. Louis, stood tall in the ring — as well he had the right to be. But the acclaim was for the man he beat.

As frequently happens in the boxing game, where millions of words are spilled out over the air and through the prints to describe what happened, it was another fist fighter, with no claim to articulate recognition, who said it best.

Larry Holmes, an undefeated heavyweight (26–0), who is among the candidates clamoring for the first shot at Spinks, said simply: "It was only the shell of Muhammad Ali that Leon Spinks beat tonight. I could see it coming after his fight with (Ernie) Shavers."

Ali realized the inevitable was approaching. He lost three of the most productive years of his career, from March of 1967 to 26 October 1970, while he was fighting the US government, all the way to the Supreme Court, over his refusal to join the armed forces to serve in Viet Nam. So the urge to continue, after his legs told him the game was over, may have been stronger than it otherwise would have been.

At any rate, Bob Arum, president of Top Rank, the fight promotional firm, revealed last night that Ali sought to get out of the contract for the Spinks fight, at one stage.

"Herbert (Muhammad, Ali's manager) told me I'd better get

*Muhammad Ali still roars in the ring in 1981, this time
against Canadian Trevor Berbick. But the ex-champ had
lost it and Berbick had little trouble disposing of him.
Milt has written many times that both Ali and Joe Frazier
were never the same after the pounding they inflicted on
each other during the classic Thrilla in Manila in 1975.
Ali now suffers from Parkinson's disease.*
(PHOTO BY BORIS SPREMO, COURTESY THE TORONTO STAR)

down and talk to Ali," Arum recalled. "I told Ali to think it
over for a few weeks. If he still wanted out, we would tear up
the contract.

"Well, you know what happened, Spinks had trouble with
Scott LeDoux (a draw) and Alfio Righetti (a decision in ten) so
Ali decided maybe Spinks wasn't as tough as he previously
believed he would be."

Arum, himself, takes credit for putting the knock on what
seemed to be a mismatch. Nevertheless, Bob Biron, manager of

Ken Norton, confided only yesterday afternoon, that Arum had told him he had financial backing for a Norton-Ali spectacular in Manila next May.

So Norton was a big loser last night. The fight game, as a whole, was a big loser. Arum speculated that when he said: "If the television network thinks Spinks will bring the same ratings that Ali got, Spinks will get the same kind of money. I remember when we couldn't get fights on television. Ali put the fight game on a new economic plane."

From that night in Miami Beach, the cavalcade of Muhammad Ali went to places that never had seen a heavyweight championship fight — Kuala Lumpur, Kinshasa in Zaire, Manila.

He piled up millions which the fight mob couldn't have believed in its wildest dreams. His gross from fights — excluding what he got for exhibitions and lectures — soared to $54 million last night. And just about everyone accused him of stealing last night's three million purse.

The three greatest heavyweights in history, in many rankings, prior to Ali, were Joe Louis, Jack Dempsey and Rocky Marciano. Their combined ring earnings were less than thirteen million dollars.

Ali had reason to ask whether he should have lost his title on a decision as close as the one last night. Almost any fight man would have given generous odds it couldn't happen.

The heavyweight championship traditionally changes hands with a knock-out.

Ali realized he blew the early rounds by practising the rope-a-dope which proved so effective against George Foreman in Zaire. He merely backed into the ropes and defied Spinks to break through his defence of gloves and elbows. This was planned strategy — to save his 36-year-old legs.

"I expected Spinks to tire himself out," Ali admitted. "He wouldn't tire, I got too far behind (in the scoring) to catch up."

An examination of the cards shows how costly the strategy was. Judge Harold Buck gave Ali only one (the fourth) of the first seven rounds. Ali still lost, on Buck's card, by only three points — 141 to 144. Buck's scoring cost Ali his crown.

It was going to happen anyway. Without taking a thing away

from Leon Spinks, Muhammad Ali had been only a shadow of the old Ali since 1 October 1975, when he stopped Joe Frazier at Manila, in one of the greatest fist fights of all time.

Since then, neither one of them has been worth a dime.

Hands of stone hard on Sugar in alley battle

The stench of Sugar Ray Leonard and Roberto Duran's "No Mas" rematch, when Duran simply threw up his arms and quit, has often detracted from this classic in Montreal in June 1980, when they met for the first time. Unfortunately, the hurt undercard fighter Milt mentions, Cleveland Denny, died 18 days later.

MONTREAL — Conn Smythe wasn't so far wrong, you know, when he said, long ago, that you also have to be able to beat 'em in the alley. Roberto Duran, the matured shoeshine boy from Panama, is the one you wouldn't want to meet in an alley. He also is the new welterweight champion of the world after one of the most spectacular exchanges of fisticuffs since man was equipped with knuckles.

Sugar Ray Leonard, the man he defeated here last night in the biggest money fight of all time — a possible gross of $35 million — is a student of the tap dance and a picture boxer. He has all the moves, all the finesse, the fancy footwork and the grace of a Nureyev.

But a 20-foot ring leaves little room to escape from the rush of a bull. So Sugar Ray, the pin-up boy who became a multi-millionaire overnight, lost a heart-breaking split decision.

Duran took every shot in Sugar Ray's arsenal and came looking for more. Even after the fifteen rounds ended, he taunted Leonard and invited him to engage in overtime — until one of the pair was flattened. Roberto was completely confident he was the winner.

The surprising aspect of the fight was that both fighters were able to stand up under the almost continual barrage of leather. Duran, the man with the "hands of stone," tagged Sugar Ray on the jaw in the eighth. It was the kind of shot that should have decked Sugar Ray. He scarcely blinked.

In the fourteenth, it was Leonard who cranked up an uppercut that should have removed Duran's head from his shoulders, Roberto appeared to be shaken but he retaliated by pounding Leonard in the body.

When that shot failed to drop Duran, Sugar Ray must have known the knockout which his handlers had predicted was not going to be possible. He had a right to think he had won. It was that kind of fight.

A rematch is almost a certainty, if Bob Arum and Don King, the warring promoters, can get together and arrange to cut up a few more millions. The money prospects of the next one are mind-boggling.

Duran and Sugar Ray had to stage a block-buster to prevent Trevor Berbick, the Canadian heavyweight champion from Halifax, from stealing their show. He knocked out big John Tate, who has been promoter Bob Arum's designated heavy-weight champion of the future.

The background of this match has to be known for the outcome to be appreciated. Berbick was thrown in against Tate as a sacrificial goat. But John was supposed to take him out quickly and put himself back in the heavyweight picture in the proposed match-up with Larry Holmes, because the undisputed world title had been derailed when Tate suffered a last-round knockout at the hands of Mike Weaver.

Now, the rebuilding job for big John was on. Berbick was to be his first pigeon. John Kerr, a Halifax lawyer who manages Berbick, a former member of the Jamaican Olympic team, confirmed this.

"About a month ago," Kerr says, "Bob Arum called and asked if I still managed that bum Berbick. He said he could offer me a fight but that Berbick wouldn't have a chance to win it.

"After conferring with Berbick and Lee Black (his trainer) I took the fight. We sent Berbick to Lindsay, where Clyde Gray trains. Lee Black also trains Gray."

In the opening seconds of the ninth round last night, the big John Tate bubble burst. Berbick, who had been swarming over Big John most of the way, chased him into a corner, peppering him with lefts and rights. Tate escaped and ran toward the opposite corner with Berbick in pursuit.

Just before Tate reached the ropes, Berbick caught him with a left from behind. It caught Tate on the left ear and he went down as if he had been pole-axed.

Said Berbick: "Every day is like Christmas. How I love this country."

Said Rod Kerr (John's son): "We should celebrate this by getting the gym painted."

Any pain Arum may have felt over John Tate's demise as a potential heavy weight champion will be eased by the unbelievable success of last night's battle of the welterweights.

Practically every closed circuit outlet across the country reported boom time business. The only flaws occurred here, on the actual side of the action, where the Olympic Installations Board probably wound up as the lone loser.

The OIB needed a last minute sale of $10,000 tickets, just to break even. Heavy rain, which started shortly before the time of the first bout (7:00 p.m.), washed OIB chances down the drain.

It also washed the $500 customers out of their seats. As the OIB mentioned in one of its press releases: "Unfortunately the highest priced seats are the ones that are not protected from the weather."

Instead of handing out raincoats and rubber boots — as they do for that trip beneath the cataract at Niagara Falls — the promotion here issued plastic garbage bags. So the fight made another first. Ringside fashion was garbage bags.

There also was the serious injury to Cleveland Denny in the first fight. He was taken to a hospital unconscious, after being knocked out by Gaetan Hart, who has hospitalized his two last opponents.

Then the good old World Boxing Council discovered a mistake in the scorecards. The correction gave Duran the unanimous decision. That's what he thought all along.

Sugar Ray Leonard was a loser, too, of course — but he will be able to take a lot of tap dancing lessons with his eight million dollars (estimated). That's more than the original Sugar Ray (Robinson) made in his entire career. And he was known as "pound for pound" the world's finest fist fighter.

Discord works in Tyson's favor

Outside the ring Mike Tyson has made plenty of mistakes. But inside, he was awesome, as Milt points out on 28 June 1988.

ATLANTIC CITY — Every fist-fighting champion needs an interfering wife and a designing mother-in-law whispering in his ear and tracing doodles in his bankbook. Mike Tyson used a crashing left hook and crushing right uppercut to endorse that success formula here last night, in what has been labeled the biggest one-day money event in the history of sport.

Those multi-million-dollar punches landed on the jaw of Michael Spinks, who had no such domestic distractions, at precisely 1:31 of the first round in a scheduled twelve-rounder. Fat cats who had paid as much as $1,500 for a seat were back at the baccarat and crap games before the dice had gone once around the table.

Kevin Rooney, who trains Tyson, must have been reading about the exploits of the legendary Doc Kearns, who bet Jack Dempsey's total purse on a first-round knockout when Dempsey won the title from Jess Willard, in 1919 at Toledo.

"My trainer told me in the dressing room he had bet my whole purse on the first round," Tyson explained, after the non-fight. "When I knocked him (Spinks) out and asked: 'Where's the $45 million?' he told me he was only joking."

Even without the total pot, Tyson will be able to afford whatever luxuries his wife of five months, Robin Givens, a TV actress, and her ever-present mother, Ruth Roper, have in mind. Tyson will receive an estimated $20 million. Spinks, with a guaranteed $13.5 million, qualifies as the most expensive mistake this side of the Pentagon. He earned $148,352 per second.

He had ballooned from light-heavyweight in April of 1986, when he defeated a fading Larry Holmes at Las Vegas for the International Boxing Federation's version of the world title. In his bid to upset Tyson, one of the most murderous punchers in the history of the game, Spinks was supposed to have the discord, greed and discontent in the Tyson game going for him.

Mike's wife and her mother were pictured as the disturbers. When Robin was introduced, along with a multitude of others, at ringside, the volume of boos was second only to those for George Steinbrenner, owner of the New York Yankees. Tyson was supposed to be a fighter who was neglecting his training and distrusting his handlers because of their machinations. So much for that philosophy. It evaporated as quickly as the game plan which veteran trainer Eddie Futch had developed for

Spinks — stand Iron Mike off with the jab and box him. Spinks failed to land a meaningful punch.

"Regardless of what happens in my life, there is a job to be done and I had to do it, because I'm a professional," Tyson said, in one of the few references to the pre-fight publicity concerning his wife and his mother-in-law. However, he did say later that embarrassment caused to his family by the publicity might cause him to quit fighting, but no person took the threat seriously. Like his trainer, he was only kidding.

"There's no fighter like me. I can beat any man in the world."

Spinks confessed the obvious — especially to those who paid $1,500 for a ticket — when he said, "I came up short." Sugar Ray Leonard, the retired conquerer of Marvelous Marvin Hagler, now a television commentator, made one of the more ridiculous statements of the night, when he told Spinks: "It was a good fight and we're proud of you." Sugar Ray didn't pay to get in.

Tyson's knockout was announced as the fourth quickest in heavyweight championship history. The quickest was the 55 seconds which James J. Jeffries took to dispose of Jack Finnegan, in 1900. Second was Michael Dokes over Michael Weaver, 1:03, in 1982, and Canadian champion Tommy Burns over Jem Roche, 1:28, in 1908.

This may bring a complaint from scholars of the so-called sweet science who recall the swan dive of Sonny Liston in his debacle at Lewiston in 1965. The time of that knockout was given officially as one minute. However, stop watches, which were synchronized to television films later, established the time the fight was halted as 2:12.

Tyson obviously is so superior to any fist fighter on the planet today that even the ingenious Don King may have trouble dreaming up another multi-million-dollar mismatch. Donald Trump paid a record eleven million for this one and probably got it all back. His gaming houses were wall to wall with people, and the "drop" to use a term common to the trade, at his posh gambling halls was expected to be $25 million.

This time, he had two undefeated heavyweights to be hyped into an extravaganza, which was aided by the publicity over

Tyson's wife and mother-in-law, who made the cover of at least two national magazines. There just isn't any heavyweight who can make Iron Mike turn up a sweat. And he's only 22 (on Thursday). The fight game is in the agonizing situation of having the greatest attraction since Muhammad Ali was in his prime — but actually no one who belongs in the ring with him.

Last night's result should put the chill on the sale of $1,500 seats for fights that last less than two minutes. There will be more of the same if any of the candidates on the roster of possible opponents for Tyson are paraded as logical challengers.

One of them emerged last night, in the person of Carl (The Truth) Williams, who regained the No. 1 spot among IBF contenders by winning a unanimous decision over Trevor Berbick, the former Canadian heavyweight champion. There is only one way Don King or any other promoter can make Williams a reasonable opponent for Mike Tyson. That would be to put both Williams and Berbick in the ring to tag-team Iron Mike. It might take him all of three minutes to polish off both of them.

BASEBALL

Delayed letter saved Gehrig's streak

Milt's strength has always been getting the most out of people he interviews. Here, on 7 December 1950, ex-umpire Roy Van Graflan, manager of a girls' softball team, reveals the significant role he played in two famous baseball events: Lou Gehrig's 2,130 consecutive game streak and Babe Ruth's "called shot" in the 1932 World Series.

TORONTO — Even your Aunt Agnes or your Uncle Angus could tell you that Lou Gehrig played 2,130 consecutive baseball games between 1926 and 1939. They'd remind you that's why the Columbia Clouter became labeled for diamond posterity as The Iron Horse. Sports writers have told you how Lou battled ailments over the years, grabbed taxis, defied exhausting schedules, in order to keep his amazing consecutive games string intact. It takes Roy Van Graflan, the Rochester Dutchman, to tell how the mailman saved Gehrig in 1929. The mailman saved Lou because the mailman didn't arrive.

In case you've forgotten about Van Graflan, he's an ex-umpire who worked the International and the American League. Van wears a diamond-studded miniature ball and bat for a tie pin and another big sparkler in a ring. They're both mementos from the late Judge Landis, the first high commissioner of baseball, for working the World Series in '29 and again in '32. Both were memorable series if you pause to reflect. It was in '29 that Howard Ehmke had 13 strikeouts. In the same series, the A's scored ten runs in the seventh inning to kill the Cubs. It was in '32 that Babe Ruth called his shot on a home run to center field, according to legend — a legend, by the way, which Van supports. It was Van who had called two strikes on the Babe before the ball sailed out of the park.

Van Graflan's present sports enterprises are in girls' basketball and softball. His cage club, the Filarets, claims the world's championship. Less pretentious claims are advanced for his softballers, Van's T and T's. But it's the softball team that brings him to Toronto. He's engaged in the pillage of the Sunnyside ladies' league. As of last accounting he had these lassies signed for shipment to Rochester: Theresa Jones, Peg Johnstone and Julia O'Sullivan. The Jones gal, who is 6 feet, 3 inches, is expected to double in brass by grabbing a place on the basketball squad.

Having thus established that Van Raflan's presence in our midst is motivated by larceny, we can back-track to '29. Van was working first base on this particular day, and he called Lou out on a close play. Gehrig, who had been having a rough time at the plate, protested so vigorously that Van Graflan finally ordered him out of the game. For casting what Van considered aspersions on the Van Graflan ancestry, Van wrote himself a mental memo to report Gehrig to the president of the league. He sent a telegram recommending a fine and suspension, right after the game.

The following morning, Van received a telephone call from E. S. Bernard, then president of the league. It just happened that the Yanks had shifted to Detroit to open a series. On the previous day — the day on which Van had given the heave-ho to Gehrig, three Tigers had been thrown out of a game in their own park. Instead of wiring their report, the umpires had mailed it. Bernard was still waiting for the report to arrive. In effect, Bernard explained the situation this way: "There are three Tigers who probably rate suspension as much or more than Gehrig. But I can't suspend them until I see what the umpires have to say. It wouldn't be fair to suspend Gehrig and leave them in the lineup when the two teams meet today. Therefore, I've decided to fine Gehrig but not suspend him." His decision saved Gehrig's playing streak from being broken in its third year.

"I still have my copy of the letter which Bernard sent to Lou," Van says. "Bernard told him that if he had any further reports from me of trouble with Lou, the fine would be doubled and Lou would be suspended.

"Bernard ran into Gehrig at Miller Huggins' funeral. He told Lou he was the only player I had thrown out of a ball game that year. Lou told him: 'And that one could have been prevented. I've learned since that I was out.'

"The way it came about was that Lou had asked Art Fletcher, who was coaching at first base. Art told him: 'If you want the truth, Lou, I think you were out.' "

Regarding that memorable day in Chicago, Van Graflan practically blows a gasket when he hears it said that Ruth didn't point to the spot where he'd park his homer — with one strike left.

"Who were the two men close enough to hear what Ruth said?" Van demands. "They were Gabby Harnett, who was catching for the Cubs, and myself. I was behind the plate. The Cubs, especially Grimes and Malone, were giving the Babe a terrible ride. When Ruth took a second strike and held up his finger, they howled: 'We gottcha now, lubhead.' That's when Babe called his shot. Years later, I checked with Gabby Harnett in Jersey City. He said the same as I tell you now. As Ruth rounded second, he took off his cap and started makin' mock bows toward the Cub bench. I looked out there, but most of them seemed to have ducked outta sight."

World Series can't compete with this

Bobby Thomson's "shot heard round the world" capped one of the most famous baseball games in history. "The Giants win the pennant, the Giants win the pennant..." were the famous remarks heard over and over on radio and television. Milt's column on 4 October 1951 is simply wonderful.

NEW YORK — For purely artistic reasons, they'd have been justified in calling off the World Series. After what happened out at the Polo Grounds yesterday, the series promised to be a flea circus that's run in after the lions and tigers have clawed each other to ribbons under the big top. No matter how the Giants and the Yankees try, they scarcely can help provide a pallid performance in comparison to yesterday's eye-popping banishment of the Bums by Bobby Thomson, the Staten Island Royal Scot.

Hard-bitten press box sentinels of many years' standing called this the most spectacular ball game they ever had seen. Certainly it must have been the classic of all time, excepting only a handful of World Series shows. Old Grover Alexander's strikeout of Tony Lazzeri in the seventh game of the '26 World Series, with the bases loaded, would have ranked ahead of this one. And the deciding game of the '24 series would be of greater importance as a collector's item. That's the one in which the Giants lost to Washington in the twelfth inning because a ground ball hit a pebble and hopped over Freddie Lindstrom's head.

But throw out a few World Series history-makers and you have a game that stands by itself for drama, gripping suspense and significance in both money and prestige. You'd think the script had been written in mid-August, when the Dodgers were tow-roping the field in the national league, and the Giants couldn't seem to decide whether they'd finish second or fourth. Yesterday, after 154 ball games, the Giants were out there in the ninth inning, and it looked as if they finally had run out of time and try. They were losing 4–1. And if they lost this one, all that marvelous march through late August and the month of September, in which they won 33 out of 45 ball games, meant nothing. They'd be just another club that had finished second. You've got to win the pennant to make feats like their surge to a dead heat with the Dodgers stand up.

And just to show how thin is the cushion between hero and bum, the stories you'd have been reading today, had the Dodgers gone on to the victory that seemed inevitable yesterday, would have been that the Giants couldn't expect to win the pennant with a tangle-footed outfielder playing third base. Their third-sacker, of course, is the Scottish-born Bobby Thomson, whose homer is the whole story now. Both Andy Pafko and Billy Cox hit scorchers at Thomson in the Dodger half of the eighth inning. They both drove in runs. Those smashes made Bobby look bad. That's something to remember in the coming set with the Yanks. Defensively, the Giants are weak at third.

But we were saying the Giants looked to have had the course when they came out for their half of yesterday's ninth inning. We watched Leo (the erstwhile Lip) Durocher as he attempted to generate some enthusiasm in his seemingly beaten ball club. It would be nice to report that he fired his athletes, but such didn't seem to be the case. You can say this about Durocher: the guy must have ice water for blood. He spent the last half-hour before the start of what could be the most important game of his baseball career swapping stories with baseball writers in the Giants' dugout.

When the umpires appeared to start the show, some of the

writers wished him luck. "With the barber (Sal Maglie) out there shaving, we'll be okay," Durocher said confidently.

Maglie grinned as he picked up his glove. "I still hear from the folks up around Welland," the barber observed. "They send me clippings and wires and good wishes. Tommy Morrison (Welland sports editor) sends me papers to let me know how the teams up there are getting along." Maglie managed the Welland club in the Niagara circuit while he was sitting out an exile for dumping to the outlaw Mexican league.

But as they came to bat in their half of the ninth, the barber had departed, and Durocher looked like the only Giant with any bounce left in his frame as he jogged out to the third-base coaching line. Alvin Dark's sharp single to right was a hit by a matter of inches. Gil Hodges, the Dodger first-sacker, made a great stop of the smash, but was unable to turn it into a putout. Then Don Mueller rapped a single into the same field. Durocher was at the plate, by this time, slapping Monte Irvin on the shoulder and yapping encouragement. Whitey Lockman was right behind Irvin, waving a pair of potent war clubs.

Giant fans groaned when Irvin fouled out to Hodges at first. When Lockman's single scored Dark and sent Mueller to third, there were signs of panic around the Dodger dugout. An injury to Mueller delayed the game. He finally was carted away on a stretcher, and it looked as if the interruption might cool out the Giants and give the Dodgers a chance to regain their poise. While the Giants worked over Mueller, Chuck Dressen huddled with Don Newcombe, Rube Walker and Jackie Robinson, back of the mound. They all looked stunned and hurt by the sudden change in their fortunes. Ralph Branca came slowly from the bullpen. He and Newcombe practically embraced as they met in shallow left field. It was the kind of half-hug you see among mourners.

Dressen is being second-guessed now for bringing in Branca, a notorious server of home run pitches. Carl Erskine was warming up with Branca. Dressen says he asked the bullpen coach, Clyde Sukeforth, which pitcher seemed to have the better stuff on the ball. Sukeforth named Branca, who made two pitches which must have been among the most costly in history. They cost the Brooklyn players, roughly, $7,500 per throw.

Whether Dressen should have ordered Branca to pass Bobby Thomson is something they'll argue for years to come. The Staten Island Scot is a dangerous hitter. He had two hits to his credit, including a double, when he came to the plate. He had managed to nullify one of them with a stupid bit of base-running that saw him and Lockman both trying to occupy second, at the same instant — an old Dodger trick. If the Dodgers passed Thomson, they'd get Willie Mays, one of the play-off busts.

It's supposed to be baseball elementary stuff that you don't put the winning run on the paths intentionally. That's what Dressen would have done had he walked Thomson. Branca gave him a pitch that was fairly low and over the inside corner for a called strike. The next pitch, as we saw it, from back of the plate, was slightly higher, but still in close. It found a parking space just over the left field wall.

The scene that followed beggars description. Durocher watched the ball disappear before he threw his cap in the air and turned a flip, landing flat on his back. Ushers practically mobbed the players. A drunk broke through police lines, but finally was tackled back of second base. Fans poured down from the ramparts. The Dodgers threw their windbreakers over their shoulders and started the "lonesome mile" march. Every few seconds, they looked back over their shoulders, as if they feared the Giants might not be through with them yet. New cars, television sets, payments on the mortgage had blown up in their faces. They had been practically spending their World Series money since the middle of August. One wave of a Scotch-man's hickory stick wafted it out of the park. With it, there probably went one managerial job. The predictions are that Dressen won't be back.

Baseball epitaph: He knew when to quit

Class acts like Joe DiMaggio are few and far between in baseball today. This column ran on 12 December 1951.

TORONTO — More words will be written and read about Joe DiMaggio today than about any other human on this zany old planet. Many of them will sound like sentimental nonsense a few years hence, because the sportswriting mob has a way of getting weepy over the departure of a great athlete. And DiMaggio has been great. They haven't called him the best baseball player of his time without reason.

Maybe somewhere in the flood of phrases that tell of his shining career on the diamond, some person will squeeze these seven little words: "He went while they still wanted him." Those words might help to set him aside from most of the great names we have known. Too many of them don't know when they've had the course. They're like Joe Louis, who went on and on until some states have tried to stop him by legislation. That's not for DiMag. He strides out proudly as the Yankee Clipper, a world champion.

The three greatest Yanks of all time have been Babe Ruth, Lou Gehrig and DiMaggio. Only DiMag departed in pride undiluted by pity. The Babe left his old club and went to the Braves with a contract for $25,000, a cut of the increased gate and a promise to be a manager after one season. It was the managerial prospect that got him.

A few weeks later he was out of baseball and the Braves were in the basement. A further indignity was in store for the Babe, the greatest attraction of all time in baseball. The Dodgers capitalized on his name for a year by signing him as a coach. In the following spring, they didn't offer him a contract.

Gehrig, the Old Iron Horse, was hitting .143 and crying himself to sleep at night because of his inability to control the hands and legs that had made him the idol of a nation. He was dying of an incurable disease. The baseball writers and the fans didn't know that. But they did know he was through, long before Columbia Lou finally told his manager, Joe McCarthy: "Better take me out, Joe," on a May afternoon in Detroit. That was the end of 2,130 consecutive games as a big leaguer. McCarthy didn't argue.

DiMaggio goes while they're still waving that $90,000 contract. He knows from experience that they don't love you when you've lost your punch. There were times last season when the air was chilled around the Clipper's locker.

When your own kid pleads: "Tell me a story, Dad," you could do worse than recall the Cruise of the Yankee Clipper. You'd sift out the statistical stuff, of course. The little guy wouldn't be interested in knowing that the hero of the piece hit better than .300 in eleven seasons out of thirteen as a big leaguer; that he has played in more World Series than any other player, dead or alive, and that he holds the record for hitting safely in 56 straight ball games.

You'd start out in the accredited style: "Once upon a time there was a poor boy." And this boy was poor; the eighth child in the family of a Sicilian immigrant. Then, you'd say: "This poor kid loved to play ball. He loved it so much that he'd walk two miles to get to a park, and he'd walk back after the game, because he didn't have the money for a car fare. When he earned a few shillings selling papers, he couldn't squander it on things like streetcar rides, because he knew he must turn it over to the family coffers. Eventually, this kid got to play for a professional team in San Francisco, after he had hung around the ball park watching his brother, who played for that club."

From there, you'd go on to say how this kid, just when he seemed to be going places, popped a knee and was written off by most of the big league scouts as a crippled ball player. But one big league club took a chance — and got one of the biggest bargains of all time in baseball. They acquired DiMaggio for $25,000 in cash and four players whose names you wouldn't remember.

This would be a good time to tell your kid how this boy from the coast learned the lesson of humility early. He was such a sensation in his first term in the big time that he was picked for the all-star team — an honor which escapes most players over a lifetime. By the time he got to the all-star show in Braves Field, he was thinking this big league ball was his private oyster. In five times at bat he failed to get the ball past second base and he gummed up two chances in the outfield. The papers and radio gave him a fair shellacking as a boy blunder. But the kid from the coast made them eat their words season after season.

It's a good story for your lad to know: how a really poor kid refused to be licked as a boy or as a big leaguer. In 1949, for instance, he thought he was through before the season even started. His feet were causing him torment. He missed the Yankees' first 66 games. After he finally returned to the lineup, he hit four home runs in three days against the Boston Red Sox — the team which the Yanks had to beat for the pennant. This poor boy wound up earning a million or more from baseball in salaries and extras. He was rich too, in the respect he earned from people in humble and in high places. But it wasn't always that way, because when he first went to New York, the fans tried to boo him out of the stadium. The same people have been on his bandwagon for years. It wouldn't hurt your kid to know that, either.

Win on laundry ticket, so what?

The next time Milt would see a World Series catch comparable to this one by Willie Mays would be in Game Three of the 1992 Fall Classic by Toronto's Devon White. This column ran on 30 September 1954 and the powerful Indians were beaten by the Giants.

NEW YORK — Vic Wertz pelts one that goes from here to Central Park. So it's a loud putout. Dusty Rhodes nudges one that soars a measly 280 feet. He becomes a hero. That's baseball, and it's the story of why the never-say-die Giants have the Indians backed against the door of their tepee. Wertz was entitled to extra bases, by unanimous vote of the millions who looked on TV, and the 52,757 sitting spellbound here in the Polo Grounds. But, unfortunately for Señor Al Lopez and his tribe, there was a fellow named Willie Mays who commits larceny in broad daylight. You probably saw it yourself on the magic lantern. Running at full speed with his back to the plate, the "Say Hey" kid grabbed the ball over his shoulder away out on the last frontier between the playing field and the bleachers. He was a good 450 feet from where Wertz teed off on a pitch by relief chucker Don Liddle. But for that catch of Willie's, there would have been no tenth inning. The Giants would have been licked in regulation time, and Dusty Rhodes never would have taken the Tribe to the laundry with that extra-inning Chinese homer. So that proves it wasn't cricket and the Durocher mob should refuse to accept the victory? It means simply that the Giants ambushed the Indians through superior defence and because they took advantage of opportunities. The catch by Mays and the blooper by Rhodes just happen to be the outstanding examples.

Defensively, the National Leaguers will strip the Tribe of their last piece of wampum. From where we sat, it seemed the notoriously leaky Cleveland infield blew the duke as far back as the third inning. You may recall the circumstances. Indians are leading, two to nil. Whitey Lockman launches the Giants' half of the third with a clean single. Alvin Dark follows with another single that goes through the hole to the right of second base. Maybe the Tribe had no right to expect that Dark, a right-handed swinger, would rap one to that area but we've seen shots like that gobbled up by International League infielders.

Even allowing that the Tribe's inner defence, to use the word loosely, couldn't be blamed for permitting Dark's rap to get through, you'd have to fault them for not making the double play when Don Mueller forced Dark at second. George Strickland, the Cleveland shortstop, appeared to trip over the second-base sack, thereby missing the double killing. Mueller was safe at first and scored later with the tying run. The Giants were dead in nine innings without that one.

In the "opportunities lost" column, there were plenty of indictments against the Indians. In the eighth, they had the sacks loaded, with one out. Lopez assigned the left-hand-hitting Dave Pope to bat for Strickland, a right-hand hitter, against Marv Grissom's right-handed pitching. It looked like a percentage play, especially since Pope, over the season, was a .294 hitter. Lopez had no way of knowing Pope would take a third strike. When Jim Hegan flied out, the Tribe had blown their chance to put over the haymaker.

It happened again in the tenth. With two men on and one out, Lopez lifted Hegan and sent in Bill Glynn to bat for him. This backfired, and Lopez is being second-guessed for bad brain work. Not only did Glynn strike out, but Mickey Grasso, who replaced Hegan behind the plate, made a bad throw to second base in the Giants' half of the tenth. Grasso looked like a fat man putting the shot when he attempted to head off Willie

Mays, who went down on the first pitch — as everybody in the park expected.

While Lopez is criticized, Durocher is praised for his strategy. That's the difference between success and failure. If Mays hadn't made that circus catch off Wertz in the eighth, Durocher would be on the pan for his choice of Don Liddle to replace the faltering Sal Maglie. And, whereas Indians like Pope and Glynn fanned when Lopez called, Rhodes delivered for Durocher. And you can't say Leo didn't call the shot. When he announced his starting line-up, he said: "I'm starting Irvin in left field. I want to have Rhodes on the bench — in case I get in a jam and need him."

Yanks called him disappointment

Yankee Don Larsen threw 97 pitches on the afternoon of 8 October 1956 and the journeyman pitcher gained baseball immortality for his day's work. New York won the game 2–0 over Brooklyn and later the series, gaining a measure of revenge after losing their first World Series ever to the Dodgers in 1955.

NEW YORK — The World Series sometimes is like an old-fashioned revival meeting. It brings out the best in folks who never had been too good before — and don't wind up being too good afterward. Ten thousand years from now, archeologists will dig up relics which will tell them that one Don Larsen pitched what the ancients knew as the first perfect game in the fall fiesta of baseball, a sport which was popular on the North American continent. They may even decide that Larsen was the greatest pitcher of all time. Unless they happen to uncover the ruins of the tabernacle at Cooperstown, there'll be little evidence of fellows such as Walter Johnson, Chief Bender, Christy Mathewson, Carl Hubbell, Lefty Gomez, Dizzy Dean and dozens of others who never managed to do what big Don did yesterday when he set down 27 Dodgers in succession. Johnson, who won 413 games in his big league career, needed help from an infield pebble to gain even one World Series triumph. The pebble gave a ground ball a bad hop so Walter's club, the Washington Senators, could win for him in extra innings.

Not even Don's best friends — and he has a lot of them — ever have suggested he's another Johnson — or even a Bender, although the latter word has been associated with him on occasion. The Yanks got him from Baltimore in the package that brought Bob Turley. And, of course, it was Turley they really wanted. They became so miffed at Larsen that they shipped him out to Denver. He was called back in mid-season last year and distinguished himself by allowing five earned runs in four innings of the World Series. The Yanks were still thinking of that when a hydro pole got in front of Don's car, long after the curfew hour, during spring training in Florida.

As a pitcher this year, he was described in Yankee literature as a big disappointment, because he won only eleven games, whilst losing five. What the Yanks overlooked was that eleven represented an improvement over '55, when he won nine for them.

The important thing is that when Fate gave Larsen the sign, with Yogi Berra acting as her relay man, big Don was ready. In fact he had been leading up to this momentous occasion. As Casey Stengel said in his pre-series briefing of the working press: "Larsen has to be invited to the World Series." He has lost 1–0 to Boston in eleven innings, and got licked in regulation time at home because the Yanks got only one run for him. Both these games were late in the season. He didn't look so hot in the second game of the World Series at Ebbets Field. That was the

day the Dodgers spotted the Yanks six runs in two innings —
and then whacked them bow-legged. But the cold facts are that
none of the runs off Larsen were earned. He'd have retired the
side with the Dodgers blanked in the second inning if Joe Collins
hadn't committed his first World Series error.

The point is, though, that Larsen hasn't been a big winner.
Nor was Floyd Bevens, the man who came closest to throwing
a no-hitter in series play, up to the moment Larsen did it yesterday. Bevens had a 7–13 mark with the Yanks in 1947, the
year he was within a single putout of immortality.

And Charley Robertson, the man you heard mentioned as
having tossed the previous perfect game, up to yesterday, never
had a winning season as a big leaguer. The closest he came was
in 1922, the year of his glory, when he was 14–15 for the White
Sox. So the goddess of fortune doesn't necessarily recruit her
candidates for fame from the ranks of the mighty.

There was one thing about the Larsen feat which was encour-
aging. The Dodgers didn't seem to suspect that Larsen was
throwing a spitter or had sandpaper sewn to his uniform. They
accepted the perfect game as the product of Larsen's skill. It
wasn't that way in '22 when Robertson hitched his wagon to a
star. Ty Cobb, who was playing manager of the Tigers at the
time, practically frisked Robertson before every windup. He
was sure Robertson was doctoring the ball. The Dodgers make
it look as if there's increasing faith in human honesty.

Murder trial waits for World Series

Pittsburgh had waited 33 years for vengeance over the World Series humiliation inflicted by the 1927 Yankees, the greatest team of all time. The Pirates got it. Despite being outscored 55–27 in the 1960 Series, Pittsburgh won on Bill Mazeroski's dramatic ninth-inning home run in Game Seven. Milt captures the mood of Steeltown on 4 October 1960, just before the series got under way.

PITTSBURGH — Paul Hamilton of Monroeville, Pennsylvania, is charged with the murder of his wife. Yesterday, the Mills of Justice were supposed to begin grinding out a decision to determine Hamilton's guilt or innocence. The Mills didn't grind. When court opened, Samuel Strauss, a prosecutor for the district attorney's office, addressed the judge.

"Your honor," he said, "for the first time in 33 years, the Pirates have won a pennant. It would be extremely unfair to expect a jury to deliberate at such a time on a matter of such importance, with a man's life possibly at stake, when the city is dressed in the carnival garb of a World Series and is celebrating as never before. Therefore I respectfully request a postponement."

His honor not only granted the delay — he also informed the grand jury it would adjourn at noon on Wednesday and Thursday despite the fact this was an extremely busy court with a tremendously heavy workload.

His honor didn't have to be told the Pirates, after 33 years, had come up with a pennant. If he parks his car downtown, some Pirate partisan probably has plastered a "Beat 'em, Bucs" sticker on his windshield.

This is a town with a fanatical singleness of purpose. Nothing is more important than attainment of that one goal: victory over the Yankees. Children were told by their parents this day must come, now, those children, grown to adulthood, have been telling the same thing to their children, and here, after 33 years, come the Yankees.

The names are different but the pattern is somewhat the same. The Yankees are the Yankees. In 1927, Babe Ruth had hit 60 home runs and knocked in 164 during the regular season. Lou Gehrig had driven in 175 runs and was batting .373 with 47 homers. The Yanks were known as Ruppert's Rifles then because millionaire brewer Jake Ruppert owned the ball club. There were eight Yankees batting .300 or better.

Their pitching staff was enough to make strong men shudder; they had Herb Pennock, Waite Hoyt, George Pipgras, Urban Shocker and Dutch Reuther, along with a 35-year-old bullpen wizard named Wiley Moore whom they had picked up from a class B league for the miserable sum of $4,000.

There is no comparison between the Yankees then and the Yankees now. Those Yanks of 1927 generally are described as the greatest team of all time in big league baseball. Today's Yankees merely are the best in a somewhat shabby league. That still might be good enough.

Mickey Mantle leads in home runs, even though he hit only 40. Another Yankee, Roger Maris, is a single homer behind him. The ancient wizard, Charles Dillon Stengel, won't over-awe anyone with this club. If he's going to win, it will have to be through performance — not through psychology.

One of the cherished myths of the sport is that the Yanks of 33 years ago scuttled the Pirates by scaring the pants off them in batting practice. It's a fable which Pittsburghers never have been able to live down. The story was told that Ruth, Gehrig and other Yankee sluggers rattled the foundations of Forbes

Field by whacking practice pitches into the distant bleachers. The Pirates, who were watching the display of power, never recovered from their shellshock. They surrendered in four straight heats.

Part of the legend is true. The Bucs were buried without winning a game — but they scored only ten runs in the whole series, so they were the victims of fancy Yankee pitching rather than being clubbed to death by the likes of Ruth, Gehrig and company. In the final game, the winning Yankee run was scored on a wild pitch.

However, this proud city feels there's a smudge on the Pirate's escutcheon right beneath the skull and crossbones. Civic respectability demands revenge. If it should happen that the Bucs blew four in a row again, there would be nothing left to do here except submerge the city by damming up the three rivers which meet in the downtown golden triangle. Complete obliteration would be the only out. Pittsburgh simply couldn't wait another 33 years for retribution.

There are people, of course, who are not above seeking material reward out of this community's crusade. A few tickets are being sold at prices up to $50 per copy.

Win or lose this time, the villagers at least are united. Last time that wasn't so. There was rebellion within the walls over the puzzling mystery of Kiki Cuyler. Try to picture manager Danny Murtaugh of the present Pirates benching Bill Virdon or Dick Groat and refusing to use him even as a pinch-hitter. That's what Donie Bush, who was managing the 1927 club, did to Cuyler, who had been hitting .330.

There were many versions of what happened, the one which made the best sense was that Barney Dreyfuss, a headstrong individual who owned the club, had been antagonized by Cuyler. Dreyfuss ordered that Cuyler be benched as a punitive measure. When the fans started screaming for Cuyler, they merely made Dreyfuss more determined. Cuyler sat.

The baseball writers teed off on the Pirates' owner. When Donie Bush tried to assume some of the responsibility, in order

Milt and Pittsburgh manager Danny Murtaugh
aren't impressed by a Pirates' batting practice in 1961.
Years later, with Pittsburgh trailing a critical playoff
series, Milt wrote that Murtaugh "has a face that looks
like the map of Ireland — with troubles to match."
(COURTESY THE TORONTO STAR)

to take Dreyfuss off the hook, the newspapers turned their guns on Bush. The city was torn by strife and the Pirates were ripped apart by the Yankees.

This time, the only questions on which there is any difference of opinion among the citizens concern Vernon Law's ankle and Dick Groat's wrist. Law, who was a twenty-game winner during the season, injured his ankle while the Bucs were celebrating their pennant clincher.

That's an occupational hazard on winning clubs. Last spring, when the Montreal Canadiens were congratulating each other for a fifth straight Stanley Cup, a photographer got swept into the vortex of the celebration and suffered a broken leg.

Groat's wrist was broken a few weeks back when Lew Burdette nicked him with a pitch. It doesn't seem possible he will be able to play with his usual authority at this early stage. That's one of the key questions of the games. If Law isn't ready and Groat isn't ready, the Bucs will be having a mass burial at sea.

In as a clown, out as a legend

Casey Stengel won ten pennants and seven World Series in twelve years with the Yankees. That wasn't enough. When he lost the 1960 Series he was fired. But as Milt revealed on 19 October 1960 being fired wasn't a new experience for Casey — he even once fired himself.

TORONTO — Naturally the Yankees will get their lumps for the way they sent Casey Stengel over the hill past his oil wells and back to his bank in California. They'll deserve the beating they're sure to take when the big league writers wheel up their typewriters.

The Messrs. Del Webb and Dan Topping, co-owners of the Yanks, should know from bitter experience just how devastating the assault can be. They went through it once before — in 1948 — for their calloused and frivolous firing of Bucky Harris. And the clown they hired in the popular Bucky's stead didn't help matters. The clown's name was Casey Stengel.

Bucky has just been fired again — this time by Boston. He has been on and off several payrolls in the dozen years Casey enjoyed as manager of the Yankees. Sports columnists ceased to plead for Bucky some time ago. Eventually, they'll run out of claret for Casey.

They love the grand old guy. They loved Bucky Harris. The Yanks showed they had flint where their tickers should be and ice water in their arteries when they put the pink slip in Bucky's envelope. That's what everyone said. But how many would quarrel now with that decision?

A dozen years from now, the misty eyes will be for some other manager who has been led before the firing squad. You'll know then whether the New York Yankees of 1960 goofed when they eased out the man who led them to ten pennants in twelve tries and gathered up seven world championships.

If the Yanks fall on evil days during the next decade, the verdict will be that it served them right for the shabby way in which they treated the "Ole Perfessor." If they continue to fatten on the rest of the American league — as they did under Miller Huggins, under Joe McCarthy and then under Stengel — it will be pretty well accepted that the Yankees always make the big move before it's forced upon them. Oldsters will recall how they handled people like Phil Rizzuto and Casey Stengel — sent them on their way with money in their pockets before they collapsed under the weight of their harness.

Whether the ball club was morally right or wrong in shoving Stengel out because he was 70 years of age won't even be discussed by the historians. Baseball managers live by the ax. The only way they get a job is for one of sixteen other wretches to lose his noggin. In baseball, the executions are not always justified.

Maybe it's not exactly fair to delve into the archives — where Casey is concerned — but the point is that no person ever was more familiar with the workings of the game than Charles Dillon Stengel. In 1925, Casey was president, manager and leading hitter for the Worcester club in the Eastern league. He got an offer to jump all the way to Toledo in the American association.

Naturally, his employer, the late Emil Fuchs, was anxious to retain a man who could roll three jobs into one and still bat .320. He refused to give Stengel a release from his contract. Casey got around that by writing a letter to himself saying he was fired as manager. He signed it "Charles Dillon Stengel, President." Then he wrote to Fuchs and resigned as president. Even the late Judge Landis, the first czar of baseball, couldn't find a flaw in Stengel's strategy.

Milt says legendary New York Yankee manager
Casey Stengel provided more stories than anyone in the
history of baseball. Here the two old friends chat in 1952.
Casey and the Yankees won five World Series in a row
between 1949 and 1953. Incredibly, Casey was fired in
1960 after winning ten pennants in twelve years.
(PHOTO BY LLOYD LOCKHART, COURTESY THE TORONTO STAR)

The stop-over at Worcester paid off handsomely, almost a quarter of a century later. While Casey was doing all the jobs there, he earned the admiration and respect of a fellow at New Haven whose name was George Weiss, later to become general manager of the Yankees.

It was Weiss who knew where to find a manager when the Yankees put the boots to Bucky Harris. There weren't many who shared his enthusiasm. Every person liked Casey but they couldn't picture him as a wizard of the dugout. It was a presidential election year, and Del Webb, while introducing Stengel, said: "He may not know how many states Dewey and Truman will carry but I'll tell you this much — if either Dewey or Truman ever played baseball, Casey will know how to pitch to them."

Casey can sit with his cronies now and spin baseball yarns. He probably will catch up to Kook Wilkinson, a favorite buddy. You never heard of Kook? He was a center fielder when Casey played for Kankakee. One day the batter banged a ball far over the heads of Casey and Kook. Stengel retrieved it. Kook expected Casey would throw to the infield. He turned his head to watch the flight of the ball. Casey threw to Kook instead — and knocked him colder than a mackerel. As Casey says in telling the story: "I had a good arm in them days."

When Wilkinson recovered consciousness, he ran to the center field fence and accused the kids outside the park of throwing rocks into the ball yard. After that, the players called him "Kook."

Yesterday, somebody outside the park skulled Casey.

Mountains out of Maris molehills

Roger Maris was a complicated and shy person thrust under a microscope by his powerful bat, as noted here on 20 September 1961 when he was chasing the ghost of Babe Ruth. Ten days after this column, Milt became one of the first to come out against Ford Frick's ruling that Maris' record would have an asterisk attached because he hit 61 homers during a schedule that was eight games longer than Ruth's 154-game schedule in 1927.

BALTIMORE — Fame has added some footnotes to the Roger Maris biography. In Chicago he put the blast on an umpire. Some person must have decided that was a rarity in baseball. At Detroit the Tigers' Al Kaline got the ball which Maris had socked for his 58th home run. It struck the top deck of the stand and dropped back to the outfield. Kaline tossed it into the Yankee dugout so Maris would have it for his trophy case.

Roger was asked whether he didn't think this was a generous gesture on the part of the Tiger star. His recorded reply was that anyone would have done the same thing. He also said he appreciated Kaline's act — but that part of his comment didn't get publicity.

All this is trivial and wouldn't rate mention if Maris didn't happen to be the hottest item in the world of professional sport at the moment. Everything he says and does is fodder for a hot-eyed public which has been keyed up by the Yankee outfielder's assault on Babe Ruth's old home run record.

Roger's reaction to being put on display in a goldfish bowl has brought him some poor publicity. He's sour. He's petulant. He's impatient with people who ask the same old questions.

Last night, in the Yankee clubhouse, he should have been impossible — if you accept the picture of the new Maris. He had suffered almost total defeat in the much-heralded battle of Baltimore. His final appearance at the plate had been the most humiliating of eight official trips during the two-night doubleheader. After wasting a pitch, knuckleballer Hoyt Wilhelm had struck him out with three successive throws.

Any hopes Maris still had of beating the Babe's old record of 60 home runs in a season of 154 games had evaporated into the damp air over Memorial stadium. He should have been seething.

This would have been an excellent time for Maris to tell sportswriters to buzz off and juggle their semi-colons. Instead, he received his visitors graciously. He was dressed in his undershirt and a pair of shower slippers.

The questions were ones he had heard before. Did he think he still might get the three homers he needs for a place in posterity, even though he has only one game left if he's to stay within the limit of 154 games as defined by Ford Frick, the baseball commissioner?

"I'll have four or five more times at bat," Maris estimated. "I'm not going to worry about it."

As an indication of the trouble which Wilhelm's knuckler had caused him, Maris revealed he swung on the second pitch and then wondered whether it was in the strike zone. He turned and asked the umpire and Baltimore backstop Gus Triandons. They told him it was a legitimate strike.

Skinny Brown, starting pitcher for the Birds, didn't bother him much with knuckleballs because Skinny didn't get many of them over the plate. Wilhelm, on the other hand, had three strikes in four throws — all knucklers.

While the writers crowded around the Maris locker and photographers climbed aboard dressing-room stools to focus their cameras, the rest of the Yankees created an uproar of mock protest against the attention given to Maris. There were cries for Moose Skowron, the only Yankee to hit a homer. Although they didn't wrap up the pennant last night, the Yanks know they're home and cooled out now. Their spirits were high as they sniffed that World Series boodle.

Maris dragged slowly on a bottle of pop while the questioning continued. He asked for a recess so Bob Turley, who occupies an adjoining locker, could dig out his underwear before it got trampled underfoot.

When it was over Maris had acquitted himself like a real big leaguer. There was no ranting, no complaining, no excuses. Maybe a man who has hit 58 homers in 153 games doesn't need excuses.

Over in the Baltimore room, the Birds dressed like a bunch of workmen who had done an extra shift. In a sense, that's what they did. One of last night's two games was billed originally for July 17. It was rained out, costing Maris a homer, which he failed to duplicate last night in the replay.

Hoyt Wilhelm was one of the last to get into his clothes. The baffling knuckleballer disclaimed any extra satisfaction out of striking out Maris in his final appearance at the plate.

"I didn't pitch any different to him than I did to the others," Wilhelm insisted. "Any time I'm out there, I'm bearing down. I wasn't trying extra hard just because I was pitching to Maris."

The Baltimore pitchers don't have to throw something special when they're facing Maris. Just the regular routine is pretty effective. Maris has hit only one homer off an Oriole pitcher this year — barring the one which was rained out. Chuck Estada was the victim, and the shot was fired in Yankee stadium.

While the big act here last night was something of a flop as far as the leading man was concerned, everybody in baseball should have a warm feeling for Maris and Mickey Mantle. Their run at Babe Ruth's record has been good for business — and baseball can stand something that's good for business.

There were 31,317 in the park last night. They didn't come to see the Birds, who have nothing left except a chance to finish second. Attendance here is about 150,000 below last year's figure. Disappointment with the club and resentment over Paul Richards' defection to Houston were the factors.

So those folks who booed Maris are not very consistent. If it hadn't been for Maris they wouldn't have been in the ball park.

One man's family is his fan club

Hall-of-famer Ferguson Jenkins finished his illustrious career with 284 wins, including six twenty-win seasons in a row. It was tough going at the start, though, as this 15 March 1966 column shows.

CLEARWATER, Fla. — Ferguson Jenkins has all the usual reasons for wanting to be a big league pitcher — money, recognition, the good life of the big time and the security of a baseball pension.

But the most powerful incentives are back in his hometown, Chatham, Ontario. Fergie's father — he is Ferguson, too, as were his own father and his grandfather — has clippings and trophies to prove he was quite a ball player with a semi-pro club at Hershey, Pennsylvania.

At that time Jackie Robinson and the late Branch Rickey had not been along to break down the barriers against Negro players in organized baseball. So Fergie's father never had the satisfaction of knowing for sure whether he could have made it as a big leaguer. His own hopes and ambitions are wrapped up in his son, who is getting the opportunity.

So the name of Ferguson Jenkins in a Philadelphia boxscore actually would represent the dreams of two men. Then there's Fergie's mother, who began losing her eyesight when he, her only child, was born. She listens to the stories which her husband and Fergie's wife read from *The Sporting News* and the Philadelphia papers. Then she sits down and types letters of encouragement to her son. She's a touch typist.

When Fergie was a kid in the minor baseball setup at Chatham, his father used to take him to Detroit so he could watch the Tigers and enjoy the big league atmosphere. Pops may even have pictured himself out there in a Detroit uniform.

"The thing that impressed me was the way the pitchers made the ball move around," Fergie recalls. "I knew that was something I would have to learn, too, if I intended to be a big league pitcher."

Because he's tall (6 feet, 5 inches now) and skinny, the manual which the coaches use in kids' ball seemed to dictate that Ferguson Jenkins, Jr., should be a first baseman. That's what he was until one day in a playoff game when arm trouble knocked out the team's star pitcher.

Jenkins assured the coach he could pitch a bit. He did even better than he said: he threw a two-hitter. Ever since then, it has been a steady, although sometimes frustrating climb towards the Phillies, who stage their spring tortures here at Clearwater.

Why would a boy whose baseball idols all were Tigers wind up as a modest bonus baby of the Phillies? Well, it's a matter of emphasis, as Fergie tells it.

"I attended one of two Detroit tryout schools," he explains. "As far as I know, though, the Tigers never sent anyone to see me. I had inquiries from the Orioles, the Pirates and the White Sox. They wanted to know when I would graduate from high school and they asked for clippings.

"Tony Lucadello, the Philadelphia scout, used to come

Future hall-of-fame baseball pitcher Ferguson Jenkins tries
some hoops while in Toronto, November 1967.
(PHOTO BY JEFF GOODE, COURTESY THE TORONTO STAR)

around and watch me play. He kept in touch with me and sent me instructions. If the Phils were holding a tryout school, he came and picked me up. That was the difference."

Lucadello was on hand in June of 1962, when Jenkins came out of high school. The following day, a contract was signed and Fergie invested his bonus money in a new home for his parents.

He impressed his new employers early by winning seven and losing two for Miami in the Florida State League. His earned run average was 0.95. The Philly front office must have suspected a typographical error.

Like most young pitchers, he developed arm trouble along the way. He was with Arkansas, a triple-A club, at the time, and the Phils sent him back to his former manager, Andy Seminick, at Miami.

It turned out that young Mr. Jenkins was suffering from an occupational ailment. As soon as he became a ball player, he decided he would have to start chewing tobacco. This had caused some minor infection in his back teeth and the poison was draining down into his shoulder.

"Under Seminick, I got rid of the teeth and I gave up the tobacco," Jenkins says. "I also got rid of the arm trouble, and I won twelve ball games."

He got his first shot with the Phils last September. They didn't exactly pick a soft spot for him. The Phils and the Cards were tied in the top of the ninth, with two on base, when he got the call in the bullpen.

Dick Groat was the batter. Jenkins struck him out with a letter-high fastball. He went on to pitch four scoreless innings and the Phils won. Jenkins got into six more games after that and finished with an impressive 2.25 earned run average.

Cal McLish is pitching coach of the Phils. He likes Fergie's chances. Says Cal: "What I like about him is that he throws strikes.

"Some scouts told me they didn't like his fastball. So I went down to Dallas one night and watched him work. He threw 52 fastballs before one was hit out of the infield.

"I decided I liked it."

Another chapter of colonization

Major league baseball came to Canada in 1969 and Milt was there to write about it on April 15 that year. Note that Montreal seems to have a tradition of problems when it comes to getting sports facilities ready for competition. (See 1976 Olympics column, page 120.) Rusty Staub would soon learn French and no longer require a translator as Milt pointed out here.

MONTREAL — Big league baseball landed on this island in the St. Lawrence yesterday. It found the natives friendly — just as Jacques Cartier did when he came ashore 434 years earlier.

Jarry Park, where the historic landing took place this time, had not been completed when Cartier called. As a matter of fact, it wasn't quite ready for the visit of the St. Louis Cardinals, either.

For an hour or more before Premier Jean-Jacques Bertrand threw out the first ball, a voice over the public address system kept urging those who had surrendered their lunch hour in order to be on time for the batting practices: "If your seat has not been installed, please be patient."

Incidentally, Jean-Jacques Bertrand won the distinction of becoming the first person to get booed in Jarry Park, the pioneer home of major league baseball in its first attempt to establish a colony beyond the US border.

The second mortal to get the old razzoo was Gary Waslewski, a relief pitcher for the Cardinals, who deliberately walked Mack

(The Knife) Jones, to load the bases in the Montreal half of the fourth inning. This was after Mack The Knife had clubbed Nelson Briles of the Cardinals for a homer and a triple in his first two appearances. Nonetheless, the good citizens of Montreal considered the walk an unsporting gesture.

It has been written that Jacques Cartier gazed in awe at the beauty of the land he had discovered. The same can be said of Red Schoendienst and his Redbirds when they beheld Jarry Park. They actually didn't say it was beautiful — just different.

Anyway, there wasn't much time for conversation. The Cardinals and the home-side Expos received such a rousing welcome they'd have felt warm inside even if they'd been floating down the St. Lawrence on an ice cube. Montrealers actually gave the two clubs a standing ovation when the introductions were completed. After that, the teams couldn't have beefed if they had been playing in a sheep pasture.

John Bateman, the Montreal catcher, probably said it for all following the game. It should be explained that John, who's a hefty guy, was down to his fetlocks in the soft earth back of the plate after about five innings.

"If I'm gonna have to work there, I gotta get myself a pair of elevator shoes," John insisted. "But I'm not complaining about the field. I wouldn't have it any other way. That's my comment."

Rusty Staub, at the next locker, proclaimed: "I'll say this for the outfield. It was better than that stuff we played on at Shea Stadium. Well, here's my first fan letter in French. Hey, what does this say?"

Like everything else at Jarry Park, the clubhouses were a rush job. The wonder is that they exist at all considering the shortage of time for construction. Thus, they never will be described as posh or commodious.

One of the Expo coaches sort of dated himself when he cracked: "If Shanty Hogan were here, I don't know whether he'd fit into this locker room." Shanty was a catcher of generous beam who completed his tour of duty in the big leagues about 1937.

As far as the fans were concerned, everything was lovely except the Cardinal half of the fourth inning. The weather was warm, the aluminum seats were bright and clean, even the temporary wooden chairs were acceptable.

But that fourth inning was a test of fan morale. The home heroes gave up seven runs — blowing a six-run lead which they had established with heavy timber — and committed five errors. Three of the errors were on the same hitter — Mike Shannon — which must be some kind of record. And baseball, as everyone knows, has records for establishing records.

This is the kind of inning it was: John Bateman, the catcher, dropped a popped foul. Bob Bailey, at first base, didn't drop one — because it didn't even touch his hands after he parked under it. Shannon smacked a ground ball through Maury Willis' legs without even ruffling his garters.

Jarry Park suddenly became quieter than Moosonee at midnight. It was only a temporary gloom, however. When Terrible Dan McGinn, a relief pitcher, drove in Coco Laboy with the winning run, the roars of approval bounced off the slopes of Mount Royal and rumbled down the river.

There was an aftermath of anxiety, speculation and suspicion, though. The umpires were measuring the height of the mound. (It's a routine maneuver). A rumor swept through the park: protest. The fans watched in gloomy silence. Finally, the joyous words over the PA system: "There's no trouble. We won."

The smudge of champions

The 1969 Amazin' Mets found that shoe polish helped them nail down a World Series and a whacky, wonderful season — unlike any other in baseball history. Known for years as loveable losers, the Mets rose quickly and unexpectedly. Only a few years earlier former Mets manager Casey Stengel had exclaimed aloud: "Can't anyone around here play the game?" Milt wrote this column on 17 October 1969.

NEW YORK — The champagne manufacturers are hailing the Mets today, in full-page advertisements. Champagne is a skin bracer, the way the Mets use it. They squirt the stuff all over each other in their clubhouse celebrations.

Automobile makers also are saluting the Mets. So are the producers of sugar which they allegedly use in their coffee. Up to now, though, there hasn't been a sign of recognition from the people who turn out shoe polish, the smudge of world champions.

That shows you how far the shoe polish people are lagging behind the rest of the industrial field in promotion and public relations. There should be big splurges in the prints today which would proclaim: "The Mets are No. 1 because they use Ruboff Shoe Polish."

The Better Business Bureau would have to accept it, too. Until the sixth inning of yesterday's unforgettable game, the Baltimore Orioles had the Mets over a barrel. There was a big zero for the Amazing Ones on the scoreboard.

Leading off the New York half of the sixth, Cleon Jones had his bunions brushed by a pitch that went lower than Dave McNally of the Birds intended. When Cleon started to limp down toward first base, however, he was called back by Lou DiMuro, the plate umpire.

"The ball hit the dirt," Lou ruled. He rejected Cleon's plea that the ball actually had bounced off his brogan. In the top half of the same inning, Lou had declined to send Frank Robinson of the Orioles to first, after Frank was struck on the left thigh by something which he believed to be a baseball. DiMuro insisted the ball had caromed off the bat before it nicked Robinson.

While Jones stood in silent protest at the plate, with 57,397 wild-eyed Met fans sounding the complaint for him, there emerged from the New York dugout the dignified figure of Gil Hodges, manager of the Amazings.

Within the brotherhood of umpires, there's a saying that when Gil Hodges comes out of a dugout, the umpire had better be sure he's right because Hodges seldom is wrong.

On this occasion, Hodges handed DiMuro a baseball — much as counsel for the defense would say: "I wish to enter this as exhibit A, your honor." DiMuro reversed his earlier decision. He waved Jones to first base. A black smudge on the ball was believed to be Cleon Jones' shoe polish.

Denn Clendenon, the next batter, hit the ball out of the park. The Mets were back in the game — and it wasn't long before the Birds were out of it.

Casey Stengel, the noted banker who has been experting the Series for a number of papers, most of which, Casey claims, are in Moscow — commented dryly that it's always wise to have a couple of baseballs in the dugout which are marred by blemishes of shoe polish.

Back in 1957, when Casey was managing Yankees, he blew an important decision to shoe polish in a similar situation. The batter, on that occasion, was Nippy Jones of the Milwaukee Braves. It's a tradition with the Jones boys that their shoes always are shined.

Hodges may have recalled the '57 incident yesterday. When

Milt and Canadian pitcher Ron Taylor chat in spring training of 1969. Little did they know what a wild and whacky season would follow for Taylor and his New York Mets. Taylor owns three World Series rings — two as a player with St. Louis and New York, and another as team doctor for the Toronto Blue Jays. (COURTESY THE TORONTO STAR)

the ball was deflected into the dugout, it was grabbed by Jerry Grote, the Mets' catcher, who tossed it over to Hodges.

"There was a definite smudge on it," Gil explained. "So I took it out and showed it to Mr. DiMuro. He agreed with me and sent Cleon down to first base."

In the Mets' crazy clubhouse, Cleon expressed his appreciation that an umpire could be broad-minded enough to change a decision. There was a somewhat different reaction down the hall, where the Birds were preparing themselves for a long winter of trying to explain what happened to their super-team.

"How could an umpire reverse himself, after the ball had been in the Mets' dugout?" several of their partisans raged. "It's unheard of — especially in the World Series."

One man who agreed with the decision was Dave McNally, the Baltimore pitcher who threw the ball. He realized, he said, that the pitch had struck Jones on the foot. Cleon was entitled to the base — with or without the shoe polish.

"But Frank (Robinson) also was struck by a pitch," McNally maintained. "We didn't ask the umpire to look at Frank's bruise. All we asked was that he check with the first base umpire (Lee Weyer) to see if he agreed with the ruling. DiMuro refused to do even that.

"If Frank had got on base, it's hard to say what would have happened. (He was called out on strikes, instead.) We'd have been in a position where we had two men on base, with one out. Despite all that, I guess you'd say they beat us fair and square."

Earl Weaver, who got few breaks in his first shot as a World Series manager, was inclined to agree. He called the Mets "a damn good ball club that had been disguised as a lucky one all season."

Meanwhile, jaded, sophisticated, frustrated New York was reacting like Mudville on the day of its first township championship. The hysteria in the park was predictable, because Shea Stadium has become the modern Ebbets Field, which once was the nut house of baseball.

More than 30 people were hurt in the park after Cleon Jones caught Dave Johnson's fly ball for the final put out. Some fell down steps. Two or three were pushed off the dugout roofs. Several had heart flutters.

It was downtown that the unpredictable took place. New Yorkers looked down their noses at Milwaukee in 1957 because Beertown flipped its lid when the Braves beat the Yanks for the big boodle.

Yesterday, old Father Knickerbocker went on a dancing, kissing, paper-throwing jag. Some streets, especially in the Times Square area, looked as if a blizzard had struck.

Two hours after the game, ticker tape, waste paper, invoices, canceled checks and confetti still swirled in the air currents between the skyscrapers.

On the pavement, there was more junk than had emerged from the windows when the three moonmen were serenaded here last summer. That was an estimate by the sanitation department.

Even President Nixon called the Mets clubhouse. Gil Hodges answered the phone in his little office. Hodges didn't seem to consider it unusual. After the season he and the Mets have had, it's pretty hard to get a surprise.

Clemente's stature in final chapter

Milt wrote only one column about hall-of-famer Roberto Clemente, but what a column on 2 January 1973.

TORONTO — This time, there can be no doubting the seriousness of Roberto Clemente's injuries. Roberto Clemente, one of the most talented baseball players of his time — and, until recent years, one of the most unappreciated of super-stars — is dead.

Clemente, who spent most of his eighteen years as a big leaguer defending himself against insinuations that he was a hypochondriac — that he was the type of athlete who would apply a cast to a hangnail — lost his life on a mission of mercy.

He could have been enjoying the festive season at his elaborate home near San Juan. Had he wished, he could have been picking up easy money in the Caribbean winter league. He could have been fishing or playing golf.

Clemente had given his name to the organization which was appealing for aid to the victims of the earthquake in Nicaragua. That would have been enough to guarantee its success in Puerto Rico, where he was a household idol.

He was anxious to do more than that. Throughout the holiday season, he participated in television and radio appeals for relief supplies and money. When the mercy flight was ready, he insisted on seeing the job through. The plane had gone only a short distance before it crashed into the sea.

Thus, fate provided a grimly fitting chapter to the career of an athlete whose aches and pains, injuries and disabilities had been ridiculed by scoffers who couldn't carry his shoelaces, practically from the day he joined the Pittsburgh Pirates in 1955. The stature of the man is clear, at last.

Clemente supplied them with ammunition by worrying out loud about his physical condition. He always was afraid that he wouldn't be able to play up to his potential.

The last time big league fans were destined to see him was that autumn day at Cincinnati when Bob Moose came out of the Pittsburgh bullpen to make a wild pitch that ended a tight five-game series and established the Reds as champions of the National League.

The Pittsburgh hitting had dried up in areas where it was supposed to be most productive and damaging — Clemente, Willie Stargell, Richie Hebner — and Clemente's head-wagging contortions became more vigorous with each appearance at the plate.

He believed the shoulder-shrugging and head-bobbing relaxed his muscles. They may have had a psychological value, too. Rival pitchers had to be aware that he was a dangerous money hitter — who batted .414 in the World Series of 1971.

There was little optimism in the Pittsburgh clubhouse after that game. The Pirates firmly believed they were a better team than the Reds — better than any other team in the world.

"There will be another time," Clemente consoled himself. "Yes, I will be back if I feel good."

Clemente seldom confessed to feeling fine. In 1956, the year after the Pirates stole him from the Dodgers for the $4,000 draft fee, Clemente was hitting .335 when he was certain that something in his elbow had popped.

The following season, he had the miseries in his back. Doctors despaired of finding the cause. They finally separated him from his tonsils. Roberto hired two chiropractors, during the off season, to work on his back.

The injury which provided the most material for cracks about Clemente's fragility occurred in December of 1964. Roberto was using a new power mower to manicure his lawn in Puerto Rico.

The mower churned up a rock which hit him on the hip. By this time he was one of baseball's top hitters. That he should be bruised by a pitch thrown by a lawnmower was good for much witty prose.

It wasn't so funny — especially for the Pirates — when he collapsed en route to first base after pinch-hitting in the Puerto Rican all-star game. Why was he playing baseball when he had a stone bruise on his hip? Well, the folks down there asked him to help them at the box office. He obliged.

The leg injury and subsequent complications were much more serious than even the Pittsburgh club had suspected. He finally had to undergo surgery to relieve pressure caused by internal bleeding.

Then he caught malarial fever. Doctors said that probably came from his hog farm. All the Pirates knew was that he had to miss the early part of training camp.

When the season was over, they had to admit it hadn't been such a calamity, after all. Clemente appeared in 152 games. He batted .329 to retain his league title. Another significant figure: he walked 43 times.

For a good hitter Clemente usually received few walks. He blamed this correctly on his impatience. When he got to the plate there was one thing on his mind — hit the ball.

Although he prided himself on being a team player, Clemente, on occasion, refuted the very principle which he proclaimed.

After the 1960 World Series, which turned Pittsburgh into a madhouse of joy, Clemente took off for San Juan. He by-passed the various clambakes at which the village heroes were applauded.

Clemente's feelings had been hurt because he felt his feat of hitting safely in every game had been withheld from public attention by the sportswriters, for whom he had something less than brotherly love.

His relationship with them was not improved when the baseball writers named Dick Groat, of his own club, as the league's most valuable player. Clemente felt it was an honor which he had earned.

Recognition, strangely enough, was something which seemed to shun him. His first contract as a ball player came because he played softball in a city league. One of the softball players tipped off the owner of a local baseball team that a prospect was in their midst.

Later, when the Dodgers had him stashed away at Montreal, where he was used sparingly, a Pittsburgh scout, Clyde Sukeforth, happened to spot him while he was on a mission to watch a pitcher — Joe Black.

The most frustrating incident occurred in the 1961 all-star game at Candlestick Park. Clemente hit a triple, a sacrifice fly and a single that drove in the winning run in the tenth. Next day, all the columnists wrote about the gale that blew pitcher Stu Miller off the mound.

Even Clemente would have to agree that the final assessments of his career have been factual. He has been described as one of the greatest ball players of all time — a statement of fact.

His strike zone is smaller now

Hammerin' Hank hit the historic home run before hometown fans. Commissioner Bowie Kuhn had drawn the wrath of Braves' fans by earlier ordering Aaron into the line up while the team was on the road. This appeared 9 April 1974.

TORONTO — For a cross-handed-hitting shortstop of the Mobile Black Bears, Bad Henry Aaron has come a long way. Early in his big league career Jolly Cholly Grimm, the old banjo player who managed the Braves at Milwaukee, used to joke that: "Henry Aaron's strike zone extends from the peak of his cap to the toecaps of his shoes."

What Charlie meant was that Hank Aaron was like Yogi Berra and many other long ball hitters. He frequently went after a bad pitch. This was something that changed with the years.

Eventually it got so pitchers said they didn't try to set up Hank Aaron for the strikeout: they attempted to keep him from putting the ball into the seats.

Al Downing of the Dodgers succeeded through six pitches — by keeping them out of the strike zone. The second time he threw a strike. Bad Henry made Downing an accessory to the home run that baseball historians insisted never would be hit.

They were saying as late as the middle of the 1970 season that Babe Ruth's career total of 714 home runs was in the record book to stay. Ruth didn't even need No. 715, which a committee of baseball statisticians awarded him temporarily — and then took away.

In case you have forgotten the details, the scoring rule used to be that a man who hit a homer which scored the winning run ahead of him got credit only for as many bases as required to put the winner across the plate.

At a game in Boston on 8 July 1918, when Ruth was pitching for the Red Sox and playing the outfield between pitching starts, Boston and Cleveland went into the tenth inning without either club having scored a run.

In the Boston half of the tenth Amos Strunk singled and Ruth hit a pitch into the bleachers. He got credit for a triple. In 1969 the special committee on baseball research upgraded that three-bagger to a home run. Later it had second thoughts. Who gave it authority to change the rules?

At the time it was agreed the matter was academic anyway. Willie Mays wasn't going to overtake Ruth. Mickey Mantle was through. Frank Robinson was too far back. Hank Aaron? Getting old. His home run production had dropped to 29 in 1968.

It wasn't exactly new for Henry Aaron to be underestimated. Even last fall when he had closed the gap between himself and the Babe Ruth legend to only four home runs, his own fans seemed reluctant to believe what was about to happen. The all-time attendance low for a Braves' home game (1,362) was set when he hit his 711th home run.

The real measure of Aaron's accomplishment is not that he finally eclipsed the most honored record in baseball — but that he got close. There were so many detours along the way.

When he attended high school he played softball. The board of education at his black school had more urgent needs for its funds than the purchase of baseball gear.

He joined the Mobile Black Bears on graduation. Apparently nobody bothered to tell him a cross-handed batter would wind up with the Indianapolis Clowns — which was exactly what happened.

Even after he got to the Braves, you could say he was mishandled — if you wanted to be blunt. They used him at shortstop, second base, the outfield and back to second. He never complained, although he did observe, somewhat wistfully, that he envied players who knew what their position was going to be.

It all came up roses and money on a 1–0 pitch last night. Even Bowie Kuhn, the commissioner of baseball, may have an explanation for staying away. Everyone else has an explanation. A touch of chicken pox.

Unlike NHL president Clarence Campbell who braved the insults — and the eggs — in the Montreal Forum after the Rocket Richard suspension, Kuhn couldn't face the wrath of the Atlanta fans.

Aside from Hank's homer, it was a bush league show. The Dodgers played like Little Leaguers. Curt Gowdy of NBC didn't know when Walt Alston gave unsettled Al Downing the hook.

Joe Garagiola didn't even have a bubble gum picture of the relief pitcher, whoever he is. It was Mike Marshall, who was in only 92 ball games for Montreal last season. Who was going to know him?

Cleo had nothing on Jays love affair

The birth of the Blue Jays on 7 April 1977 is a day that will be long remembered in Toronto.

TORONTO — George Bernard Shaw didn't know a spitter from a designated hitter but the caustic Irish dramatist took less time than a pickoff play at first base to assign baseball what he considered its proper niche.

Shaw called it America's Tragedy. He undoubtedly would have concluded that America's Tragedy had become Ontario's Insanity, had he been permitted to look in on today's challenge to pneumonia and chilblains at Exhibition Park, henceforth to be known as the Loony Bin.

After more than 75 years of ignoring Toronto as a potential outpost of the sport, big league baseball finally caught up to it today — in a snowstorm.

Anyone who doubted Toronto's long-time love affair with big league baseball had to become a believer today. This has to be the romance of the ages. It makes the Mark Anthony-Cleopatra affairs fade to the status of a flirtation in a singles' bar.

How else could anyone explain the presence of a reasonably sane human being in an area that was dusted by snow, swept by icy winds on the shore of a lake where you expected to see seals and walruses wrestling in the hope of keeping warm?

But there they were — (maybe you were one of them) — in their snowmobile suits and parkas, while the public address system spouted *Jingle Bells* and *Take Me Out To The Ball Game*.

If you want to know how cold it was, the best indicator is that Bowie Kuhn, the high priest of baseball, wore a coat.

Last October, when Bowie was trying to convince the good citizens of Cincinnati that a Sunday night World Series game in 45°F weather was good for them — and for television ratings — Bowie shunned extra clothing. He's had goose pimples ever since.

Terry Barthelmas, the Blue Jays' director of operations, qualified for the good housekeeping award as man of the year by keeping the Zamboni machine, designed primarily to mop up water from the stadium rug, operating as a vacuum cleaner to keep the infield free of snow.

This provided a pleasant pattern of green and white, with the outfield looking like an Arctic ice floe moving in toward open water of an emerald sea.

You might have thought that persons beset by logic or reason would have been chanting "We want to go home." Instead, they were shouting: "We want beer."

*Jack Brohamer, of the visiting Chicago White Sox,
finds the weather more appropriate for skiing during
the Blue Jays opening day at old Exhibition Stadium
on 7 April 1977.* (PHOTO BY BORIS SPREMO,
COURTESY THE TORONTO STAR)

They indicated their feelings about baseball in a Christmas
fairyland setting by sending up a loud cheer when the tarpaulins were moved from the infield.

Elliott Wahle, the Blue Jays' administrator of player personnel, who came here from New York Yankees, was moved to a
lyrical outburst of executive admiration for these new converts
to his favorite game.

"All they want is baseball," Elliott exclaimed. "Not a word of
complaint about their own discomfort. This has to be the greatest day in the history of sport."

Psychiatrists might have another term for it but how many of
them can hit an outside pitch? Lee MacPhail, president of the

American League, who is a pretty sharp cookie, certainly would agree with Wahle.

What was happening before his unbelieving eyes definitely vindicated the move which MacPhail and his associates made when they moved into the Toronto market ahead of the rival National League.

This was at a time when Labatt, who are big in the suds business, and Montrealer Howard Webster, who is big in bucks, and the Canadian Imperial Bank of Commerce, which could buy a whole league without missing the money, are getting the runaround in their sincere efforts to purchase the San Francisco Giants, an established club.

MacPhail took one look at their batting average in Dun and Bradstreet and said: "Labatt, Webster and Imperial-Commerce are the kind of people whose interest in baseball appeals to us."

All of which is mentioned merely for the purpose of establishing the background for the paradox that the group which may be the best-heeled in baseball wound up with the Blue Jays, an expansion team.

And who the hell are the Blue Jays? Well, they're John Scott and Hector Torres and Otto Velez and Pedro Garcia and Dave McKay. You'd know them as well as you'd know the people who wrote to Sid Handleman at Queen's Park and said it would be a terrible thing to sell beer in the ball yard — especially since the stuff is for sale in the provincially owned playground, Ontario Place, about 300 yards away.

In other words, you probably wouldn't know the Blue Jays at all. But what difference does that make? Each and every Blue Jay was given the kind of ovation you associate with Bobby Hull, Darryl Sittler, King Clancy and Gordie Howe.

And remember, these Blue Jays have been only three days in town. They still don't know whether Bloor and Yonge is a haberdasher which offers deals in camel-hair coats — or a night club act on the Sin Strip.

From the kind of reception they got here today from 40,000 frozen fans, you might have thought that Pete Rose, Catfish Hunter and Mark (The Bird) Fidrych had just parachuted from the snow clouds and suited up with the Blue Jays.

In other words, it doesn't matter where the Blue Jays haven't been and what they haven't done. They only thing that counts is that they're on our side.

Their pitchers may hang the curve ball up there where it looks like a ripe grapefruit to the man at the plate. Their infielders may heave the ball into the dugout trying for the double play.

After waiting 50 years for a team, Ontario partisans come prepared to excuse a clean-cut young chap who wears one of their suits — even if he doesn't play the game too well.

And, by the way, when you wonder who the hell are the Blue Jays, don't forget to ask the Texas Rangers whether they remember Blue Jay Doug Ault.

He's the home run king of the moment. The Rangers tossed him into the expansion pond.

A Yankee victory in Yankee style

Reggie's three-homer night in the World Series is one of the finest single performances in the Fall Classic but it still wouldn't win Jackson a popularity contest in his own clubhouse. This column appeared on 19 October 1977.

NEW YORK — This was a night when the back-slappers were slaughtered by the back-stabbers — a night when the Muggers murdered the Huggers — a night when Lou Piniella shook the ceremonial champagne out of his hair and said: "If the problems we had this year go on next season, this is going to be a nice fourth-place club."

It probably was symbolic of this year's champions of the baseball universe that the man who hit the ball out of the park three times, to equal the immortal Babe Ruth's old record, was the man who almost got into a dugout fist fight with his manager on national TV.

And the manager was the man who told the biggest media contingent in World Series history that the hero of last night's murder of the fellowship-favoring Los Angeles Dodgers can "kiss my *dago* ass."

The winning pitcher is a man who intends to peddle his talents in the free agent market and the winning catcher is one who has asked to be traded elsewhere.

What it all means, of course, is that the best ball club that George Steinbrenner's money could buy must be one helluva team. There were times, in mid-season, Lou Piniella said, when "we could have said 'what's the use' and packed our bags. We could have stopped worrying about Boston and Kansas City and Los Angeles."

(What about the Toronto Blue Jays, Lou? They were the ones who clobbered you 19–3 for the worst shellacking in more than a half a century in this hallowed ball yard.)

"This was the roughest season of my life," Piniella insisted. "If the season had lasted another two weeks, I don't know whether I could have made it. With the problems we had, all I can say is I don't need this kind of aggravation to make money."

Piniella had a unique — and, for the Yankees, revolutionary — proposal for keeping this year's world champions out of fourth place next year. "Why not let Billy Martin run the club? He's proved he's capable of doing it — if the players will just concentrate on playing baseball and pay less attention to getting their gripes into the papers or on radio and TV."

Without naming names, big Lou indicated that Reggie Jackson, the toast of Broadway today — and for the ensuing months — is not necessarily his choice as man of the century.

A gushing broadcaster asked him whether he didn't feel honored to be on the same baseball field as Reggie Jackson. Lou retorted that Jackson should feel honored to be on the same field with him.

But think of that tremendous performance, Lou — three home runs, off three different pitchers.

"He's paid to perform," said Lou, possibly thinking of Reggie's $2.9 million chunk of social security. "I feel honored to be on the same field as my teammates, but baseball is a team game."

With all due respects to Lou, it was Reggie Jackson's game last night. Not even Ruth could have done a better job of rising to the occasion.

He had been reported, a few hours earlier, in a national magazine, as having told club owner Steinbrenner he would not play for the Yankees, with Martin as manager, in 1978 — an ultimatum that he denied having given.

On the morning of this sixth and deciding game, Steinbrenner had announced that Jackson definitely would be back. Martin's fate would be in the hands of club president Gabe Paul.

Not to be kept completely out of the picture, Paul quickly announced that Martin would be getting a bonus (it's Steinbrenner's money) and that Billy would be back next year.

There was only one thing Jackson could do to demonstrate how badly Billy had erred in keeping him out of the clean-up spot in the batting order — until Steinbrenner interceded.

With possibly the greatest audience ever to watch a ballgame to marvel at his performance, he teed off on Happy Hooton, Elias Sosa and Charlie Hough in successive trips to the plate. He didn't keep any of them waiting — swung on the first pitch.

Even Yogi Berra, who has seen it all during the Casey Stengel era, admitted he was impressed. Yogi recalled that he once hit two homers in a World Series game himself, and thought that was pretty good.

"But," concluded Yogi, with rare perception, "when a guy gets hot, he's hot."

With the champagne flowing, the milk of human kindness suddenly surged in previously angry breasts. Reggie Jackson bellowed that he definitely would be back in New York next season. Who could afford his price elsewhere?

If there were one person for whom he felt happy, it was Billy Martin. Why? Because Martin, he said, had taken the same kind of guff (the word has been laundered) that Reggie, himself, took.

Reggie quoted a biblical text that a weak man is one who can't stand adversity. He obviously felt it applied to both him and Billy.

The man who caused much of the chaos, which almost beat an unbeatable team, stood aside from the shouting and the shoving in the bedlam of the clubhouse. This was George Steinbrenner, wearing his Yankee tie.

It was he who insisted on buying Reggie Jackson. It was he who tried to convert Billy Martin into an establishment type.

"We won't have the problems next year," Steinbrenner was saying quietly. "We learned a lot this year. Billy and I will get together in the morning to discuss next season."

For his part, Martin wanted no concessions made for the squabbling and the back-biting and the demands for trades that made the season so chaotic.

"It's like the ship owner says to the captain," Billy sighed. "He tells the captain, 'Don't let me know about the storms. Did you bring the ship in?'

"I brought the ship in."

Carter says it for everybody: "No apologies"

After losing out on the final weekend of both the 1979 and 1980 seasons, the blow by Rick Monday in 1981 was the *coup de grace* for the Montreal Expos, a team known at the time as the most talent-laden in baseball. This column appeared on 20 October 1981.

MONTREAL — They've been thrown out of their 8-karat carriage and they're back in their pumpkin — the Cinderella Montreal Expos, that is. But they're going to be remembered as the team that sent millions of Canadians on a baseball jag, right across the wide country.

How often do you get a loser that's being applauded coast to coast? Even the Dodgers tipped the hard hat to them after Rick Monday's ninth-inning home run made the Dodgers champions of the National League and sent them on their way to Yankee Stadium for tonight's opening round of the World Series.

"I know Tommy (Lasorda, the Dodgers' manager) has commented on this," Rick Monday said, "but I would like to add my word of appreciation and say what a pleasure it is to come into a city where the fans accept baseball as they do here. We're hopeful it might be the same in New York. But we don't expect it."

The script was simply too unbelievable for the Expos to have brought on the first World Series not played entirely within the country that invented the game — or improved on the old English game of rounders — or whatever.

You just can't have a guy (Jim Fanning) emerging from the front office, putting on the monkey suit and going all the way to the World Series. Why, Jim Fanning never had managed a big league club for a single minute until that day, 27 games removed from the end of the schedule, when club president John McHale told him: "Dick (Williams) is being fired. You're the manager."

If Fanning had gone on to the World Series, everyone would have expected him to win it. That's the kind of image he was creating — that he was Mr. Destiny himself and that he was pulling the strings for a group of puppets that would react to his manipulations.

There had to be a flaw in the performance somewhere. Otherwise, the story was too unbelievable. It came under circumstances that were in keeping with the rest of the drama.

Around Dodger Stadium, out there in Chavez Ravine, Rick Monday probably is remembered for extinguishing a blaze to an American flag than for setting a fire under the Dodgers. He was playing for the Cubs then — in April of 1976 — when flag-burning was fashionable. Monday prevented a couple of kooks from putting the match to Old Glory in the Dodger outfield.

As a Dodger though — he was traded in January of 1977 — Monday has been recalled more for his tiffs with manager Tommy Lasorda — and for his injuries — than for his contributions to the club.

Here in Montreal — and throughout much of Canada — he is going to be known henceforth as Gloomy Monday. With two out in the top of the ninth and the bases clear, the Expos had the seemingly unbeatable Steve Rogers working in relief of Ray Burris, who had been removed for a pinch-hitter.

The stage was being set for Expo heroics in their half of the same inning. There were signs that the Mighty Mex, Fernando Valenzuela, might be tiring. It was Monday who provided the heroics.

"After I hit that ball (a 3–1 pitch) I really didn't know where the hell it went," Monday admitted later. "I saw their outfielders (Dawson and White) racing back to the fence. Then, I knew it was out. I almost fell down between second and third."

Gary Carter, who had expected to catch that pitch — instead of seeing it go over the fence — called it a good pitch. It wasn't a cripple that Monday was just lucky enough to hit for the circuit.

"Monday had scared the heck out of me (he says heck, whereas Monday says hell), the way he was swinging the bat," Carter admitted. "I hated to see Steve get behind on a guy like that, but I had no misgivings when I saw the pitch coming up. I thought it was a good one."

It would be cynical to say the bridesmaid role is a familiar one to the Expos. They have that unhappy background of stubbing their toes before they get to the altar.

This time, they were just about to get the ring. They had their brightest moments in their thirteen-year history. It is supposed to be baseball's rule of thumb that good pitching wins the short series.

The rule held true in this series. The Dodgers got fine pitching — especially in yesterday's clincher — from Valenzuela, who is liable to wind up with both the rookie prize and the Cy Young Award, the Oscar of the profession.

But the Expos got outstanding pitching, too — except in Saturday's game here, when Bill Gullickson was unable to provide the kill with the Dodgers on the ropes.

So, if they got good pitching, why did they lose? For one thing, the numbers simply caught up to them. During the regular season, the Dodgers had a 5–2 edge. In the last two years, the count in games won and lost was 18–5 for the Dodgers.

In order to overcome those odds, the Expos had to have everything going to them. They didn't have everything going for them. Andre Dawson's thundering bat didn't even generate a whisper in the playoffs.

Overall, though, Carter said it for everybody when he reflected in the Expos' gloomy clubhouse: "This team is for real. I don't think we owe apologies to anyone."

And Fanning? Even if he will not win the World Series, it's still simply unbelievable.

Sure, root for Bosox, but don't bet on them

This prophetic column appeared on 25 October 1986. In Game Six, Bill Buckner would allow a Mookie Wilson grounder to dribble through his legs in the tenth inning, which allowed the Mets to come back and win the game and, later, the Series, in Game Seven. Note Milt's observation of Buckner being a risk defensively.

NEW YORK — A caution light blinks for American League partisans. This may not be the time to bet the farm — nor even the condo — on the Fenway Follies, as they return to the Big Apple.

It is important to remember an old cliché in sport. At least, if it isn't a cliché, you can create one. At Louisville they run for the roses; at Fenway, they run for the razzberries.

If Paul Revere had been wearing red hosiery, he undoubtedly would have fallen off his horse, far short of Lexington, and a cup of tea would be selling at $2.05 (US) in Boston today, with the deuce going to His Majesty in taxes.

If the man working the lamps, high up in old North Church, had been wearing a Boston batting helmet, the Red Coats might have come by way of New Brunswick.

What you're saying is that the Fenway Follies have flirted with successes that rival *Oklahoma*, *South Pacific* and other Broadway smash hits, many times, but something happens — something as in disaster.

Failure and the Fenway Follies have been as inseparable as seven and eleven, beans and Boston. One must remember that, for the past 68 years, the Red Sox have been striving mightily to prove it was no miscarriage of justice when they beat the Cubs (doesn't everybody beat the Cubs?) for the championship of the sixteen clubs that, at that time, designated themselves the world in baseball matters.

Each member of that victorious Boston club received $890 (US) as his share of the series loot. Since that historical occasion, succeeding Fenway clubs have been striving to show those pioneers were worth every nickel.

Those successful Red Sox of 1918 batted .186 in the series, but don't sniff in derision at .186. That's ten points higher than Wade Boggs was batting after four heats of the current renewal. And Boggs, as everyone knows, is the batting champion of all baseball.

He soared to .227 with a pair in the fifth game, but his bat obviously has been an embarrassment to the poultry people, as well as to the folks at Fenway. Boggs' faith in chicken as the keystone of his diet is folklore. He even offered a book of recipes on the delicacies of the hen coop.

Certainly, the Red Sox have a right to feel comfortable coming into Shea tonight. If they win one of two here, the champagne corks start popping. On second thought, can they feel close to being as comfortable as they were last Sunday? At that stage, they were 2–0 and could smell a sweep, with three games coming up at Fenway, where the Green Monster allegedly would devour the Mets, from fungo bat to shoelace.

But they discovered, to their dismay, that the aged horses-for-courses theory does not necessarily apply to baseball. It was like Lee Trevino once said about Montreal mayor Drapeau's rinky-dink course on which the Canadian Open was to be played. For that kind of money, the Merry Mex said, he would be happy to play right down the middle of St. Catherine Street. The Mets didn't even bother to work out at Fenway — just went out and won two of the three games played there.

Sure, any self-respecting bookmaker must favor the Fenway

Follies at this stage, but many nagging questions remain. In five games, Jim Rice has yet to drive in a run. Gimpy Bill Buckner has knocked in one run and has been a calculated risk defensively. Buckner and Rice accounted for 212 RBIs during the regular season.

Big Don Baylor and Dwight Evans knocked in 191 runs between them. Against Mets pitching, they have been good for only five. And now Baylor, one of the big hit men, becomes designated sitter instead of designated hitter. Those can be depressing deficits when applied to a team that's trying to win a World Series.

There's another set back for Fenway Follies that doesn't show in the statistics. Since the Red Sox are not starting a left-hander in either of the two remaining games, the Mets will not have Tim Teufel and Rafael Santana out there together as their double-play combo. The only people who seem to like that pair are the official scorers.

At the opening pitch of tonight's game, the edge in management strategy must go to kindly John McNamara over Davey Johnson and his computer. By offering up Al Nipper as a sacrificial goat, McNamara got his pitching rotation regrouped and rested. Which is great for the Fenway Follies, as long as it's the real Roger Clemens they see tonight.

The real Roger hasn't been around since the end of the regular season. At the moment, he's in a terrible sweat over the mound at Shea, which he describes as only a few centimeters lower than Hamilton Mountain. That could be a bad sign if Roger were a horse; they would be taking him for a walk to get familiar with the paddock.

It's important to remember that, should Clemens fail tonight, McNamara may not look like such a genius. That would leave him with Oil Can Boyd going for all the potatoes in the most important game the Red Sox have played in 68 years. Oil Can may have the arm for such an assignment. The question must arise: does he have the temperament?

Anyway, as American League loyalists, you howl "go, Sox, go," but when somebody mentions money, remember the Christmas shopping.

Jays stopped hitting, it's as simple as that

Perhaps the most painful memory for any Blue Jays fan is the end of the 1987 season. Take heart, allow Milt to ease (or perhaps rekindle) the pain with this 5 October 1987 column.

DETROIT — The crash may have been the greatest since the limestone walls of Troy came tumbling down. Baseball has few pratfalls to equal the seven-game slide of the boys in blue into oblivion. True, the Phils of 1964 took a ten-game tumble when they were leading the National League by six and one-half games, with only a dozen still to go.

Those '64 Phils recovered to win the last two games of the season and regain a kernel of respect. It still didn't save them from being known as the Phainting Phils for the next couple of decades. So the Blue Jays know what to expect. They are going to hear about their collapse in the home stretch for a long time.

No one can say how long their futility might have endured, since the season ended on their seventh successive loss. They managed to disprove one of baseball's oldest tenets — that pitching wins the games that count. The Blue Jays got two classic pitching performances from lefthanders Mike Flanagan and Jimmy Key here — two earned runs in two games. They still lost.

Why was Sparky Anderson able to bring his Tigers out of what looked like a trip to the scrap heap, after three losses in four games at Exhibition Stadium, to a sweep in his own backyard?

"I knew, when they lost the second of three games to Milwaukee, in their park, that we were back in the hunt," Sparky admitted, while his triumphant Tigers sprayed champagne around their clubhouse. Obviously, the clinching of the divisional title did not come as a great surprise because the clothing, the bats, the hardware had been covered with plastic, in the expectation of a bubbly shower.

"We opened our own coffin and left ourselves room to get out when we won that fourth game of the series in Toronto, a week ago today," Sparky added. "Then, when they couldn't beat Milwaukee, I knew we had them where we wanted them — back on grass. The Blue Jays are a much better team when they are on turf."

Sparky has a couple of luck charms in his office and one at an end locker in the clubhouse. Beneath the blotter on his desk is a picture of the Pope, who shook his hand during the historic visit to Hamtramck. Sparky's opponents — excluding the Baltimore Orioles — have considered him unbeatable ever since.

Then, there is Ray (Snacks) Shore's old golf sweater, rumpled and shredded with holes. Shore, a one-time Toronto pitcher with the old Leafs, threw the sweater into the locker in Sparky's office, after a losing game of golf on a rainy day. Sparky hung it up. The Tigers were in fourth place at the time. When they commenced their climb to the top, Sparky started giving the sweater a caress each day.

"I phoned Snacks," he cackles, "and told him the sweater stays while we're alive. The day we win it all or lose it all, the sweater goes into the trash can. Snacks worked with me for ten seasons. He is the best advance scout I ever knew."

The lucky charm in the end seat in the clubhouse is skinny and usually grumpy, with the scars of Toronto service on his hide. The name is Doyle Alexander. If he hadn't come to the Tigers, in a late deal with the Atlanta Braves, the celebrations almost certainly would have been in Toronto yesterday, instead of down here.

Members of the Tigers kept anointing him with champagne and thanking him for the coveted rings and fat checks which are available to champions of the baseball world.

Would he have returned to the Blue Jays if Pat Gillick had gone to his old buddy, Bob Cox, now general manager of the Braves, when Gillick was seeking reinforcements for the stretch run?

"I would have refused to go to Toronto," Durable Doyle insisted, brushing another shower of champagne from his hair. "I would have been willing to stay when I was there but they just didn't seem to think I was worth much to them."

Was he surprised to find himself with a club that gives him a chance at winning a World Series game? This is something that has eluded him, although he has been in pro baseball since 1968. He did pitch six innings for the Yankees, in the 1976 series, but was not credited with a win.

"There had been plenty of rumors in Atlanta," he recalled, "that some of the old guys were likely to be traded. I felt that, if some team was trying to win a pennant, I would be the first to go. But I hadn't been following the Tigers. Hadn't paid much attention to them. Naturally, I'm happy about the way it turned out."

His numbers, in eleven games with the Tigers, have even earned him mention in dispatches as a candidate for old Cy Young's award. If he were considered solely on what his pitching efforts have meant to the Tigers, Dour Doyle would have to win. In eleven starts, he has nine wins, no defeats and an earned run average of 1.53.

But keep tuned. When Sparky Anderson was asked about his starting pitcher for the real pennant party, with the Minnesota Twins, he didn't hesitate for a split second.

"It will be Alexander," he said. (Who else?) And, if the Tigers go snarling into the autumn test matches, look for Ole Doyle to be out there in Game One. But spare the ifs and buts about what he might have meant to the Blue Jays. It wasn't lack of pitching that killed the Blue Jays. It was the hitters, whose bats froze up.

*Former baseball commissioner Bowie Kuhn stopped
by in 1987 to see the former commissioner of*
The Star *sports department.*
(PHOTO BY JEFF GOODE, COURTESY THE TORONTO STAR)

They failed again yesterday, in their last chance. George Bell undoubtedly blew the most valuable player award, when one of his slugging performances might have saved both him and the Blue Jays. He finally got a single — his second in 24 trips. Sparky ordered him walked in the third inning, after both Nelson Liriano and Lloyd Moseby had struck out.

Why did Anderson call for the intentional walk? It was completely out of respect, he admitted. The way Bell had been swinging the bat, there was little reason to fear him.

Anderson made one other confession. He kept his lefthander, Frank Tanana, in the game when Lloyd Moseby led off the eighth with a single and the Blue Jays' righthanded power was coming up. If he went to his bullpen, the choice would have been righthander Mike Henneman. That would have brought Rance Mulliniks off the Toronto bench.

"Mulliniks," Sparky sighed, "is the one who has hurt me over the years."

It was a nice note on which Mulliniks starts what is going to be a long winter — maybe an embarrassing one, too, if he hits the rubber chicken circuit. People who read all those opinions about the Blue Jays being the best team in baseball will be asking what happened. Rance will tell them: "We stopped hitting. It's as simple as that."

Not a thing of beauty, but history

Canada's first World Series was one of the classics. Milt says the best World Series game he's ever seen was Game Three when Devon White made the great catch and there was a near triple play. We agree, but Milt's victory column of 25 October 1992 is even better than his Game Three piece.

ATLANTA — Good ole Bill Shakespeare wouldn't have known a slider from a knuckler, but he had it dead right when he wrote about the many events in the womb of time which would be delivered. The one that was delivered here last night certainly was a big one. Which is understandable, since it was fifteen years on the way.

It also was, you might say, slightly on the ugly side but it made sporting and geographical history, moving the baseball field of dreams to a brand new site, somewhere between Hudson Bay and the US border.

Typically, the Blue Jays had to win it twice. They were one strike away from the championship of the baseball world in regulation time, when the gods that determine such things deserted Tom Henke, the ole Terminator. Henke deserved better. But the gods obviously had another worthy guy in mind. You're talking about big Dave Winfield now.

As he said in the champagne-drenched clubhouse, Winfield was the oldest player on the team (41) and the happiest. His previous shot at that coveted World Series ring was in 1981 with the Yankees and, for a player of Winfield's stature, it was a disaster. He suffered the added indignity of having George Steinbrenner refer to him disparagingly as Mr. May — not Mr. October (Reggie Jackson).

So, when manager Cito Gaston asked him shortly before the eighth inning how his underpinning felt, Winfield knew what the skipper had in mind. He assured Cito he never felt better. Then he proved it by tearing up chunks of turf to reach a sinking line drive by Ron Gant. It was one of the most spectacular defensive plays of a game that provided several sparklers — most of them by the Blue Jays.

The millions of Blue Jays faithful are not likely to forget Roberto Alomar's diving stab and throw to Joe Carter, on first base, off Jeff Blauser's scorcher. And how about Candy Maldonado's leaping catch to rob the town's hero, Francisco Cabrera, in the ninth?

But Winfield was not through yet. Although he did say, when the Blue Jays signed him primarily as their designated hitter, that he intended to bring his glove, he was still thinking big hit. And the setting couldn't have been more spectacular if Hollywood had set it up.

It started with Jimmy Key going to bat — the first time as a major leaguer — and with the score tied in the World Series. Jimmy popped up. Devon White got enough of his torso into a Charlie Leibrandt pitch to earn passage to first base. Then Roberto Alomar, whose bat had come to life, singled.

The scenario was made to measure for Winfield when Joe

Carter hit a fly ball for the second out. There is no evidence that Winfield considered himself a brave Horatius, captain of the gate, as he knocked the dirt from his spikes and faced Leibrandt. All he did was what Horatius would have done in similar circumstances. He smashed a double into the left-field corner. White scored, waving frantically to Alomar, who was close behind him.

The network named Pat Borders the most valuable player of the whole show and there won't be any argument. Still, it wasn't an easy decision to make. Candy Maldonado's home run and his circus catch made him a legitimate candidate. Both Carter and Winfield came up big in this heart-stopper which cinched it.

Winfield put it well when he said: "I didn't do much, but I did it when it counted."

He also said the Blue Jays were the best team for which he had played. And, yes, he played for the Yankees.

Managers don't qualify for awards. They are there to provide ammunition for the second-guessers. If the Blue Jays had lost, Cito probably would have been criticized for not leaving Duane Ward out for the ninth inning. Cito played it the way he got here.

He went to Henke. This time, it didn't work. Cito's smartest move might have been when he went to Mike Timlin when Otis Nixon came to the plate, with the Braves making their last gasp, in the bottom of the eleventh.

Everyone in the park knew what Nixon would try to do. He would use his tremendous speed to beat out a bunt. He's a switcher but he's a better hitter against southpaws. Hence the switch from Key to Timlin. Nixon was an easy out. Another smart move that Cito made was when he brought in Boomer Wells, which forced rival manager Bobby Cox to lift Deion (Prime Time) Sanders, who had been killing the Blue Jays.

Cox is sure to hear the howl of the wolves for staying with Leibrandt while he had Jeff Reardon heating in the bullpen. Bobby would be too polite to say he had seen enough of Reardon already. It was irony that Cox had to be denied his dream by the team which he did so much to build. He reacted as you would suspect.

"The Blue Jays are a fine team. They deserve it," said Cox.